GUADALCANAL
DIARY

RICHARD TREGASKIS

GUADALCANAL

DIARY

Introduction by Mark Bowden

THE MODERN LIBRARY

NEW YORK

2000 Modern Library Paperback Edition

Copyright © 1943 by Random House, Inc.
Introduction copyright © 2000 by Mark Bowden
Afterword copyright © 2000 by Moana Tregaskis

LIBRARY OF CONGRESS CATALOGING-IN-PUBLICATION DATA
Tregaskis, Richard
Guadalcanal diary / Richard Tregaskis.—Modern library pbk. ed.
p.   cm.
ISBN 0-679-64023-1 (alk. paper)
1. Tregaskis, Richard, 1916–1973—Diaries.   2.   World War,
1939–1945—Campaigns—Solomon Islands—Guadalcanal.   3. World War,
1939–1945—Personal narratives, American.   4. United States. Marine
Corps—History—World War, 1939–1945.   5. Guadalcanal (Solomon
Islands)—History, Military.   6. United States. Marine Corps—Biography.
7. Marines—United States—Diaries.   I. Title

D767.98.T7 2000   940.54'26—dc21   99-086361

Modern Library website address:
www.modernlibrary.com

Printed in the United States of America on acid-free paper

12 14 16 18 19 17 15 13 11

CONTENTS

INTRODUCTION

by Mark Bowden

War makes for great stories. It by definition involves matters of historical importance, and it is rivaled by few events in life for drama. It sounds mercenary for a writer to say so, but it has always been true. Stories about battle have been popular and significant since before language was written. Even poor accounts of it—self-serving memoirs, bald propaganda—often make for compelling reading, because the deeds of war, the cruelty and self-sacrifice, the cowardice and heroism, are enacted at such extremes of human experience that they ultimately transcend the words that describe them. The very best stories of war tend to come from writers who understand this, who know their place, who recognize that the struggle they observe and record carries a great deal more weight than their account of it ever will. Abraham Lincoln touched on this when he spoke at Gettysburg, "The world will little note, nor long remember what we say here, but it can never forget what they did here." We have long remembered, of course, what Lincoln said, but even his immortal words carry less weight than the deeds of the men who fought and died. The great thing about words, however, is that they enable memory.

Remembrance is the least we owe those who accomplished heroic deeds. Their stories are needed not only to inspire warriors who will be called upon to fight in the future, but to inspire us all with the best kind of national pride. In the words of the dying captain at the end of *Saving Private Ryan*, we are called upon to "earn this."

During World War II, America fought a famous series of vicious battles against the Japanese on islands in the Pacific. Richard Tregaskis went along as a war correspondent for the first of those battles, on the island of Guadalcanal, and wrote an account—his bestselling *Guadalcanal Diary*—that stands today as one of the best of its genre. Downplaying his own extraordinary heroism, writing with great fairness and restraint, Tregaskis shaped America's understanding of the war, and influenced every account that came after, fiction or nonfiction, from Norman Mailer's *The Naked and the Dead* to the 1998 film version of James Jones' *The Thin Red Line*. Tregaskis described for the first time the look and feel and smell of the Pacific War, the oppressive tropical heat and humidity that caused rashes and strange fungi to appear on men's bodies, the terror of fighting in tall grass and in jungles against an often invisible enemy that burrowed deep in the earth and vowed a fight to the death, the odd transformation of paradisiacal Pacific landscapes into hell itself. Tregaskis brought to life the horror of that fighting, but also the inspiring camaraderie of men at war, the humorous details of life in a combat zone, the peculiar juxtaposition of the macabre and the mundane. He demystified this strange new ground war. His account revealed the hardened, professional Japanese suicide warriors of legend to be merely human, cunning, determined fighters—men vulnerable to American artillery and infantry. Above all, Tregaskis captured the stoic young Americans who calmly boarded landing crafts, knowing that probably one in four of them would be killed. His diary captured the inspiring determination and courage of typical young Americans in 1943, a motley racial and ethnic mix, who would prove to be more than a match for the fierce Japanese.

It is hard to imagine today how important this book was when it appeared in that year, just months after the fighting it describes. The fighting in Guadalcanal was the beginning of the land offensive against Japan. Today we know all about the island-hopping strategy that, together with even more important air and sea battles, gradually stripped away Japan's control of the Pacific Ocean and crushed its empire. Then, nothing was certain. The U.S. Navy had won a decisive battle in June in waters off Midway Island, but sea battles merely set the stage for the grim series of island invasions. As of August of that year, Americans had known only defeat on land against the Japanese—the ignominious flight of General Douglas MacArthur from the Philippines, the humiliating surrenders of Bataan and Corregidor. This book recorded a turning point. America was striking back.

But the diary records much more than a first American land victory. When it was published, no one yet knew what this new war was going to be like. The Allies had not yet landed on Normandy to begin the big push against Hitler, and although American soldiers had seen plenty of action already in Africa, and just weeks before had invaded Sicily, there was something especially daunting about invading a small island in a vast ocean, where neither side could readily abandon the field. What sort of enemy were these Japanese? What kind of weapons and strategies would they employ? Why were these dangerous islands with strange names halfway around the world suddenly so important? What had we gotten into?

From a purely military standpoint, the most important battle of Guadalcanal was not the one fought on land and described so vividly in this book. It was fought at sea, miles away from the island, in November, months after Richard Tregaskis' diary ends, when a decisive naval victory prevented the Japanese from landing reinforcements. The United States lost two cruisers and seven destroyers in that fight; the Japanese lost two battleships, one cruiser, two destroyers and, most important, ten troop transports. Preventing the arrival of those troops enabled the army and the stubborn, courageous Marines to finish mopping up Guadalcanal, securing their precious Henderson airfield, the first firm foothold on the long and bloody climb north toward Japan.

Any doubts about how young Marines would fare in this new war were erased by their swift victory and stubborn defenses. Tregaskis rode in on one of the first landing crafts, sharing the profound chill of foreboding as the invading force approached the beaches, and the enormous relief when it was discovered that the Japanese had been taken completely by surprise. With the island's defenders fleeing into the jungle, the landing itself was happily anticlimactic, but in the weeks that followed the fighting grew fierce. Tregaskis records the progress with calm daily entries in his diary, allowing the reader to experience the progress of the campaign just as the Marines did. There were so many acts of heroism, sacrifice, and survival to note that Tregaskis took to just listing them, encapsulating stories so remarkable that any one of them might have made a whole chapter. There's Lieutenant Richard R. Amerine (of Lawrence, Kansas),

> ... a Marine flyer, [who] came wandering into our lines today, thin as a ghost, to say he had been out in the jungles, dodging Japs and existing on red ants and snails for seven days.... Having once studied entomology, the science of bugs, he was able to subsist on selected ants and snails. He knew which ones were edible.

Or two young corpsmen, Pharmacist's Mate Alfred W. Cleveland (of South Dartmouth, Massachusetts) and Pharmacist's Mate Second Class Karl B. Coleman (of McAndrews, Kentucky):

> They told me how they had used a penknife to amputate the ragged stump of one Raider's arm after it had been shattered by a 75 explosion ... the medicos themselves had said that the man would have died if the two lads had not done such a good and quick job in the field.

Or Lieutenant (JG) Paul F. Kalat (of Worchester, Massachusetts),

> ... who had been the engineering officer on the *Little*. After his ship had sunk, he had spent some eight hours in the water, and the Jap warships, he said, "just missed me by a whisker—about 25 to 35 feet."

One wishes that Tregaskis had more fully developed these tales. But he was less concerned with the stories of individuals than with the fate of the entire effort, on which everyone's survival depended. Still, he refused to let these remarkable men and their deeds slip away unrecorded, and he always took care to note each man's hometown, knowing how important these small stories would be to those waiting for word of their sons, husbands, fathers, and brothers back home, and how much these particular men deserved to be remembered. Tregaskis saw his role more simply than do most war correspondents today, who feel the need to explain the sources of conflicts, critique the judgment of statesmen and generals, and who, in the process, sometimes forget to record the experience of war itself through the eyes of those living and dying in it.

Guadalcanal Diary is war reporting before the relationship between journalism and the military acquired its modern edge in Vietnam, where reporters were compelled to record the growing disparity between what they observed and what the U.S. military said was true. Tregaskis lived to report from that war, too, and by then he was regarded as little more than an apologist for the military. His was a voice from a different era, one in which the government and especially the military was held in the highest regard, even if GIs did gripe about the food and baffling wartime bureaucracy. His war, the one this book is about and the one that made him famous, had swept up the hearts and minds of an entire generation to an extent far greater than those of the generation in the sixties that protested against the Vietnam War. In 1943, young men were called upon to risk far more than their legal standing, or the threat of being tear-gassed on the Washington Mall. *Guadalcanal Diary* doesn't question the importance of the war against Japan, and it doesn't second-guess those sent to fight it. It is simply a story of war, free of artifice and irony. The Marines herein are presented uniformly as honest men doing their best in a terrible situation, which the vast majority of them were. Tregaskis' prose is understated, but can occasionally soar:

> I sat on the edge of the dugout and watched the bright flashes of light rising high in the sky, heard the haughty, metallic voices of the cannon. Sitting like this, virtually in the lap of a shelling attack, one felt as if he were at the mercy of a great, vindictive giant whose voice was the voice of thunder; the awful colossal scale of modern war had brought the old gods to life again.

Tregaskis writes admiringly of the men at war he risked his life to watch, but *Guadalcanal Diary* is no whitewash. He straightforwardly records racist banter of young Marines steeling themselves for battle against an alien, feared enemy, dehumanizing the men they will be trying to kill. He tells of the trophy hunters who sliced ears off the dead and pried gold fillings from Japanese teeth to make necklaces, and of those who walked among the dead and dying Japanese on a beach after a battle, shooting them one by one to make certain they were all dead. Yet this is not a work of warmongering. It neither glorifies nor condemns the acts it describes, the acts of men in desperate straits, whose determination to survive and whose anger over the loss of their friends rapidly eclipsed moral restraint. Tregaskis' warriors are not superhuman; they are just men, and this accords their accomplishment the stature it deserves. Likewise, the Japanese in his account are neither sub- nor superhuman. They fight with courage and determination, some with suicidal conviction. But they also flee in surprise when the Marines land in force, and spend most of the fight hiding from American guns. Even their vaunted code, death before the dishonor of surrender, was honored more in the breach:

Several of the Jap prisoners captured on the ridge, it seems, said, "Knife," when they were captured, and made hara-kiri motions in the region of the belly. But when no knife was forthcoming, they seemed relieved, and after that made no attempt to kill themselves.

Histories of war, analyses and critiques of strategy and tactics, studies of political decision-making—these all have an important role to play, but to become literature, true stories must capture human experience at ground level. They must reach across space and time to re-create for each new reader the experience of an actual event. A confident writer knows when he has a story nailed at this level, and leaves the large-scale analyses for scholars, whose writing is important, but is meant primarily for each other. So John Hersey in *Hiroshima* and Michael Herr in *Dispatches* confine their accounts to actual human experience, a narrative decision that has given their work the power to speak directly to the heart. *Guadalcanal Diary* was long ago embraced by the U.S. Marine Corps and has become an indelible part of its tradition, but it is not included on most conventional lists of great "literary" nonfiction, where it also belongs. Tregaskis hazarded his life to get the story, and wrote one rich with observation, hard reporting work, and personal memory, some of it unforgettable:

> The worst time in a bombing is the short moment when you can hear the bombs coming. Then you feel helpless, and you think very intensely of the fact that it is purely a matter of chance whether or not you will be hit.... You will also think about those who have been cruelly wounded or killed in previous bombings, and in your imagination you suffer the shock of similar wounds.... And while your mind is racing through these thoughts, your ears, without any conscious effort on your part, are straining to gauge the closeness of the bombs from the swishing and rattling of them.

It is writing that does what only literature can do: transport you to another time and place and acquaint you with emotions and sensations that you otherwise would never feel. It captures both the terrors and triumphs of war, its ugliness and also its awful beauty. *Guadalcanal Diary* deserves to be remembered more for Tregaskis' book than the classic but sentimental film adaptation by Lewis Seiler. The book is invaluable as an accurate, ground-level account of a turning point in history, as a superb example of war reporting at its best, and as a lasting contribution to American literature. The Modern Library has done an important service by restoring it to print.

GUADALCANAL

DIARY

I

APPROACH

This morning, it being Sunday, there were services on the port promenade. Benches had been arranged on the deck, facing a canvas backdrop on which a Red Cross flag was pinned. Father Francis W. Kelly of Philadelphia, a genial smiling fellow with a faculty for plain talk, gave the sermon. It was his second for the day. He had just finished the "first shift," which was for Catholics. This one was for Protestants.

It was pleasant to stand and sing on the rolling deck with the blue panel of the moving sea, on our left, to watch. There we could see two others of our fleet of transports rolling over the long swells, nosing into white surf.

The sermon dealt with duty, and was obviously pointed toward our coming landing somewhere in Japanese-held territory. Father Kelly, who had been a preacher in a Pennsylvania mining town and had a direct, simple way of speaking which was about right for the crowd of variously uniformed sailors and marines standing before him, pounded home the point.

After the services, ironically, many of the men turned to the essential job of loading machine-gun belts. Walking around the deck in the bright morning sun, I had to step around lads sitting on the former shuffleboard court, using a gadget which belted the cartridges automatically. All you had to do was feed them in.

The lads seemed quite happy at the job. One of them kept time with the clink of the belter. "One, two, three, another Jap for me," he said.

Others tried other ideas. One was reminded of the song "Chattanooga Choo Choo," by the sound of the leader. He hummed a few bars of the tune.

Another boy said, "Honorable bullet take honorable Jap honorable death. So solly."

"I've got a Jap's name written on each bullet," offered another. "There's three generals among 'em."

"Which one's for Tojo?" asked a buddy, offering to play straight man. "Oh, Hell, the first one's got his name on it," was the answer.

This conversation, while it did not hit any stratosphere of wit, indicated one thing anyhow: that the lads here at least were relaxed and in high spirits. Probably the facts of full stomachs and clear hot sunlight, with a pleasant breeze, contributed somewhat to the psychology of the situation.

I thought I might as well do a round-up on the morale situation aboard the ship, and so wandered through her splendid innards and turned all the promenades. In the luxurious, modern after lounge, preserved much as it had been in the recent days when the ship was a passenger-freight liner, I found things quiet; one officer was reading an Ellery Queen novel as he sat on a modernistic couch job done in red leather and chrome. A red-headed tank commander sat at one of the skinny black-topped tables where recently cocktails had been served to civilian passengers traveling between North and South America. He was writing an entry in his diary.

The black-and-cream dance floor, a shiny affair of congoleum, was vacant.

In the barroom at one edge of the salon, one of the leather-upholstered booths was filled with officers idly passing the time of day, content and happy, like the men, with full stomachs and pleasant weather.

The bar itself, a semi-circular slab of light wood, was vacant, with nobody to buy or sell the cigarettes, shaving cream, and "porgy bait"—naval, marine slang for candy—which sparsely occupied the shelves where once a gleaming array of bottles must have stood.

There was soft music, coming from the salon's speaker system. That, and the modern comfort and beauty of the place, brought the thought that this is a pleasant ship on which to travel to war, a sort of streamlined approach to an old adventure, even if there is no liquor behind the bar.

Leaving the pleasant lounge room to go out into the equally pleasant sunshine, I rounded another promenade and found at one corner of it a group of marines, most of them squatting on the deck, gathered around a blackboard.

A sergeant was holding forth as instructor, pointing to one after another of the interesting chalk symbols he had marked on the board. It was a course in map-reading. The sergeant pointed to a chalk representation of a wagon, with a horse-shoe alongside.

"What would you say it was?" he asked one of the men.

"It's a horse-drawn vehicle," said the marine.

"That's right," said the sergeant.

I went from there to the forward deck of the ship. Here, it seemed, most of the troops had congregated. They crowded all available standing and sitting space. They were occupied, on this day of rest, principally with "shooting the breeze." Some were leisurely turning over a hand of cards or two. A few worked among the complexity of steel cables, derricks and hatches, busy with routine jobs.

I climbed down a narrow ladder into the mouldy semi-darkness, relieved only by bilious yellow lights, of the No. 2 hold. Here I first found myself in a wide room, the center of which was entirely filled with machinery, wooden boxes and canvas duffle bags.

Around the edge of the room were four-level bunks of iron piping, with helmets, packs and other gear dangling in clusters.

But the place was deserted, except for two or three marines busy sweeping the deck and swabbing the floor of the dank shower room. The rest of the inhabitants were obviously engaged with duties and pleasures in other parts of the ship.

Most of the other holds, similarly, were occupied more by machinery and idle equipment than by people. Much more pleasant on topside. In one hold I found quite a few marines sleeping on their standee bunks, while in the center of the room, two marines in stocking feet chased each other over piles of black ammunition boxes. They were given some encouragement by the few men around the edges who happened to be awake, sitting on boxes or duffle bags.

I went back up on deck, satisfied that this was a peaceful, lazy day of rest almost everywhere on the ship. Everyone seemed relaxed, despite the fact that probably, today or tomorrow, we will know where we are headed, where, possibly, we may die or be wounded on a Japanese beachhead.

But the pleasing state of relaxation, this Sunday, is understandable. We have been so long wondering where we are to go that we have long since exhausted all possible guesses. One figures one might as well amuse himself while waiting to find out.

In the lounge again, I spotted Maj. Cornelius P. Van Ness, the graying, earnest planning officer of this group of troops, unfolding a message which had just been given to him by a young naval lieutenant.

"Something to do with our destination?" I asked.

He smiled. "No," he said, "but I wish it were. I'd like to know too." Even the colonel, said the major, doesn't yet know where we are headed.

After lunch, I had gone back to the stateroom to further digestion with a little bunk duty, and was passing the time of day with two of my roommates, Red Cross Worker Albert Campbell and Father Kelly, when the fourth roommate, Dr. Garrison, rushed in puffing with excitement (Dr. John Garrison, a Los Angeles dentist, was a Navy medical officer).

"A lot of ships just came up," he said, plunking his portly bulk onto his bed. "A whole navy. Better go look at 'em."

So we ambled out on deck to see the horizon spotted with ships, in a huge semi-circle around us. There were transports and freight ships, cruisers, destroyers, and the long, high, box-like shapes of aircraft carriers perched on the rim of the ocean.

Talking along the promenade suddenly became louder and more enthusiastic. Officers, sailors, marines were busy counting up totals, trying to identify the different types of ships. Charlie, our slow-speaking, colored room-boy, as usual, had the latest dope. He shuffled up to us and gave us a detailed account of the ships present. Among them he listed the "Pepsicola" and the "Luscious."

Identification, at that distance, was difficult, but one thing was certain. We had made a rendezvous with the other and main part of our task forces. We were conscious of the fact that this was one of the largest and strongest groups of war vessels ever gathered, certainly the largest and strongest of this war to date. The thought that we were going into our adventure with weight and power behind us was cheering. And our adventure-to-come seemed nearer than ever, as the new group of ships and ours merged and we became one huge force.

That night, there were movies in the comfortable, swanky, ultra-modern ward-room, where officers dined. It was a light thing called

Our Wife with Melvyn Douglas and Ruth Hussey. The colonel, amiable, polite John M. Arthur of Union, N.C.—called "Doggy" because of his fondness for the natty in clothes and grooming—sat next to me. Between reels I suggested to the colonel that it was amazing that his people could relax and enjoy themselves like this, when they were heading for the unpleasant reality of danger, bloodshed, etc. He said, yes, he thought so, too.

MONDAY, JULY 27

This morning there was much ado in the map-plastered office which the colonel has set up at the edge of the after lounge. A boat had come from one of the other ships, bringing dispatches—and the much-sought secret, it was whispered about, of our destination.

I got a look through the circular glass windows of the doors to the colonel's office, but there was too much activity to interrupt. The colonel and his staff were bending over the table, which was laden with maps, overlays of tissue, etc. There was an abundance of dispatches piled on the metal desk in one corner of the room. It looked as if the news might soon be out.

After lunch, Dr. French Moore, a naval medical commander from San Francisco, told me that I was invited to come to the colonel's cabin before dinner for a spot of tea. I surmised that at this impromptu function I would hear the news as to where we might be heading.

That was the case. Maj. Van Ness, Dr. Moore and Col. Fellers (Lieut. Col. William S. Fellers of Atlanta, Ga.) were present as the colonel drew his blackout blinds, switched on the light over his desk and set up to pour.

When we had our beverage in hand, he said to me, "Well, it looks as if we're not going to have as much excitement as we first thought."

His group of troops, the colonel explained, are not going to take part in the assault on Japanese-held territory. Only one group will be near the scene of action, he said, and that will be a support force. The remainder of his troops, said the colonel, are to go on a mission which is much less dramatic and will not involve contact with the enemy.

"Anyhow, it will be fine training for us, and I'm just as glad that it happened that way," he said. But I could see that it was a disappointment to him to forgo the excitement he had planned.

He shifted quickly to another subject. "So, if you want to be in the forefront when the landing takes place," he said, "it might be wiser for you to shift to another ship."

I had come out here for action. I agreed, and after dinner, in our blacked-out cabin, packed my bags. It took some resolution to do the job, for in the evening I had learned that the forces I would join are going to attack the Japanese strongholds on Guadalcanal and Tulagi, in the Solomon Islands.

TUESDAY, JULY 28

I was ready to leave this morning, but got word that I will not be able to transfer to another ship until tomorrow. Then the colonel and his staff will go to the flagship to confer with the ruling voices of this operation, and I will go along to make arrangements.

WEDNESDAY, JULY 29

The flagship was practically insane with activity, clogged with marine officers anxious to get their orders and settle their plans. But I managed to get the consent of Admiral Turner, commanding the landing operation, to move to another transport. The ship is one of the two which are to carry the assault troops landing on Guadalcanal—the marine outfit which is to land first, and seize the beach-head.

It was a shock to come close to my new ship. She was an ancient, angular horror, with a black, dirty hull and patches of rust on her flanks. When I climbed the rope ladder up her high freeboard and set foot on the deck, I could see that not all the Americans heading for the Solomons were traveling on the latest of ships. I had certainly come from the best and newest to one of the oldest and most decrepit.

The deck was black with slime and grit—for, as I was to discover later in the day, the ship had no modern apparatus for pumping water. The marines cramming the deck were just as dirty.

Inside the dingy foyer, I found interior decoration of the completely undecorative style of the early twenties. There were bare round metal pillars painted white, and squarish wooden steps. A few pieces of lop-sided, dirty furniture were scattered about.

I went down one level and came to the cabin of Col. LeRoy P. Hunt of Berkeley, Cal., commanding officer of the assault troops. Col. Hunt's small room contained an iron bed, a couple of broken-down chairs and a desk. But at least, the floor was clean. That was a relief.

I talked to the colonel about the ship and his troops. "Things are dirty here," he said. "There isn't enough water for cleaning up now.

"My men are pretty unkempt, too, for the same reason. They look like gypsies. But," he added, "I think they'll fight. They've got it here." He tapped his chest in the region of the heart.

The colonel, a good-looking man of middle age, tall and well built, was quite serious about the job that lay ahead for him. "It's going to be tough going on the beach," he said. "Somebody's going to get hurt."

Tonight I could see why he felt that way. An Australian plantation manager, who had supervised production of a copra "cocoanut" farm on Guadalcanal and knew the lay of the land, came aboard, and in the steaming-hot ward-room he gave a little talk on the terrain which the marines faced in landing on Guadalcanal and seizing a beach-head.

After crossing the beach, he said, the invaders would have to penetrate a field of grass four to six feet high, which would afford good cover for any Japanese defenders. Then there would be a river to cross.

The Australian pointed to a map, to the line marked "Ilu River." "The river is about twenty feet wide, the banks are five to six feet high and steep, and the bottom is silty," he said. "It's going to be nasty to cross."

It was evident from the map that the river will have to be crossed, for it runs parallel to the shore, and lies directly behind the beach where the landing will be made.

This, however, was not the only difficult part of the terrain which our assault troops must penetrate—"penetryte," said the Australian. Beyond the river lie old abandoned irrigation ditches, which can be used as entrenchments by the Japs. These ditches are covered with thick, tall grass and cannot be seen except at very close range, he said.

The Australian had finished. The marine officers were not pleased with the terrain which they will have to take. But instead of complaining, they turned to a discussion of methods to cross the river, to "penetryte the drayns," as the Australian said.

There was certainly a need of air conditioning or a fan or two in the ward-room. I found my clothes were soaking wet from top to toe. And a quick look about told me all the others had suffered similarly. I left the room and came to my stateroom, a small cubicle with old-fashioned upper and lower bunks of dark-stained wood. There was a bathroom, shared with the adjoining stateroom. The floor was black and gritty with dirt. I pressed the water lever in the basin. There was no water. A neighbor told me the grim fact of the matter. "The water's only on for about ten minutes at a time, about three times a day," he said. "And the times it's on are a mystery that only the Navy and God know about." I went to bed dirty.

THURSDAY, JULY 30

My roommate, I discovered this morning, is a short, stocky, bull-necked man named Capt. William Hawkins. He hails from Bridgeport, Conn., used to be a schoolteacher, and worries about a balding head. He is an amusing talker, speaks fast and well.

This morning, planes flew over us for hours. They were stubby Grumman fighters with distinctive square wing tips. The carriers must be in fairly close by this time.

There was firing practice, too. From the cruisers which lay in the distance, there were yellow flashes of gunfire. We heard the dull pom, pom, pom of their guns, the distant whoomp of anti-aircraft shells bursting, and saw the black bursts against the sky.

In one of the holds of this ship—which I found far dingier, dirtier and hotter and more odoriferous than the hold of the first transport on which I had traveled—I heard the men complaining about their food, and the lack of water. I asked a marine about the matter.

"Oh," he said, "don't think nothin' of that. Marines have to grouse about their chow. They always do."

This afternoon we lay to and several of the marines dived into the rather sharky waters. They were told by a non-com that they might be court-martialed if they were not eaten by the sharks.

"What do we care?" said one of the offenders. "We're going in the first wave on Guadalcanal, anyhow." That was certainly a tough, marine-fashion slant on the proposition.

FRIDAY, JULY 31

Today was a day of planning. Orders for everyone involved in the landing operation, from the majors and lieutenant colonels down to the buck privates, were being drawn up.

I heard the news that my roommate, Capt. Hawkins, is to be one of the first Americans to land on Guadalcanal. He commands B Co., which is taking the left half of the beach-head assigned to troops from our ship. Capt. William P. Kaempfer of Syracuse, N.Y., is to take the right half, with A Co. On the left flank of the strip of land which will be seized by A and B Companies, another outfit from another ship will take a strip about as long as that seized by A and B. Or in other words, the beach-head is to be divided into two halves; of these, A and B Companies, of our ship, will land on the right half; and a group from another ship on the left half.

Through the strip of beach seized by these units, our following troops will penetrate. That's the plan, at least.

Capt. Gordon Gale, a brilliant young executive officer, talked about these plans to the officers before lunch, in the furnace-like ward-room. There were maps on one wall of the ward-room, behind the blackboard, showing the coasts of Guadalcanal and the beach-head we are to take. There were *none* of Tulagi, the other first objective of the marines. I inquired and found that Tulagi is to be taken by Marine Raiders, with other troops in support. But the largest group of troops will concern themselves solely with Guadalcanal. For that, it seems, is believed to be the most heavily fortified, most heavily occupied of the Jap positions in the Solomons. And it contains a much-prized, excellent airfield which the Japs have just about finished building.

I had been down in one of the dark, hot forward holds in the morning, talking to such of the lads who were not sleeping in their four-tier bunks. Now I told the colonel that their morale had impressed me.

"This is a knock-down and drag-out fight," he said. "Things are going to go wrong on the beach, and people are going to get hurt. But those are good kids and I think they'll be all right."

In the afternoon, I watched a group of marines cleaning and setting up their mortars and light machine guns on the forward deck. The lads were taking almost motherly care of the weapons. And I could see that the working parts were cleaned and oiled so that they worked like the conjunctive parts of a watch.

Some of the lads were sharpening bayonets, which indeed seemed to be a universal pastime all over the ship. I saw one with a huge bolo knife, which he was carefully preparing. Others worked at cleaning and oiling their rifles and sub-machine guns. Some of the boys had fashioned home-made blackjacks, canvas sacks containing lead balls, for "infighting."

While working over their weapons, the marines passed their inevitable chatter, "shooting the breeze" about the girls they had known here or there, their adventures in this or that port, a good liberty they had made here or there. But now, a large part of the chatter deviated from the usual pattern. A lot of it was about the Japs.

"Is it true that the Japs put a gray paint on their faces, put some red stuff beside their mouths, and lie down and play dead until you pass 'em?" one fellow asked me. I said I didn't know. "Well, if they do," he said, "I'll stick 'em first."

Another marine offered: "They say the Japs have a lot of gold teeth. I'm going to make myself a necklace."

"I'm going to bring back some Jap ears," said another. "Pickled."

The marines aboard are dirty, and their quarters are mere dungeons. But their *esprit de corps* is tremendous. I heard a group of them, today, talking about an "eight ball," which is marine slang for a soldier who disgraces his fellows because he lacks their offensive spirit. This eight ball, said one lad, was going to find himself in the water some day. Somebody was going to sneak up behind him and push him overboard. Others agreed, and, looking around at them, I could see that they meant it.

Tonight at supper we talked about the projected "softening up" of Guadalcanal by Army B-17's. That bombing should be beginning tomorrow morning, it was suggested. We don't know the exact date on which we'll make our landing, but figure it should be within a week or so. And the "softening" process should last about a week.

Tonight the weather was cloudy and overcast, and the moon was shrouded with clouds, but you could hear the assorted wails of marines singing all about the decks. It seems a good many of them prefer to sleep in lifeboats, around stanchions, or simply on the deck, rather than to stay below in their quarters. It is hard to walk about the blacked-out ships without falling over some of them.

"Blues in the Night," with a chorus about how "My Mama done told me a woman was two-faced," seems to be the most popular song.

There were also older favorites like "Old Mill Stream" (with harmony) and "Massa's in de Cold, Cold Ground." I heard the song at several parts of the ship.

In the calm of the night, with only the sound of water rushing past the ship for accompaniment, there were the usual tales of this or that girl, this or that adventure, passed in the darkness. And I heard some more of the now-familiar "grousing about food," the marine tradition of complaining that the "slum" (stew) served was no good.

SATURDAY, AUGUST 1

At breakfast this morning, the conversation revolved about a favorite topic—home. We had beans for the meal, and this brought up the word Boston, which was enough to start a course of reminiscing about Boston (for the majority of those aboard are Easterners), about New York, Bay Head, N.J. Said Lieut. Ralph Cory, a former diplomatic attaché who is now our Japanese interpreter: "I'd like to be back sailing a boat on Chesapeake Bay."

Said "Doc" Stevenson, a Navy warrant-officer in the Medical Corps, "Hell, if I was back there, I wouldn't be out in any *boat*."

"That's right," said Cory. "I'd settle for the White Mountains, or Cape Cod."

Passing down a companionway to my room, I heard one marine say to another, "What's on at the Regent tonight, Jack?"

"Man, don't talk that way," said the other. "You make me feel bad."

At 11:30 the beep-beep-beep of "general quarters" call sounded, and there was a great rush along decks and up and down ladders as the speaker system barked: "Man all air defense stations." At 11:50, however, the stations were secured. The unidentified aircraft which had been spotted was identified as friendly.

I saw the colonel on the wing of the bridge. "These boys are anxious to get into the scrap," he said. "They'll fight."

"If it works out I'll have a good story," I said.

"You mustn't think of it any other way than that it's got to work out," he said.

I stopped to talk to Lieut. Snell (Evard J. Snell of Vineland, N.J.), who is in charge of much of the paper-work involved in this effort, and he estimated that probably one in three boats will reach the shore in our attack attempt, for, he said, we will probably be faced by very strong forces. Probably, he said, three out of four of us would survive the assault; that was his estimate.

When I saw the memorandum which had been prepared on the terrain which we are to take, I could understand his high estimate of casualties.

"From our landing point," said the memorandum, "our forces will have to cross a stream about twenty feet wide and 400 yards south of the beach. The name of the stream is the Ilu and it runs westward and parallel to the shore into the Tenaru River. Actually it is backwater from the Tenaru and except in the rainy season is still and stagnant. Its banks are steep, boggy and from five to six feet high. The bottom is silty. One method of crossing would be to cut down the banks and throw the excavated ground into the stream, filling it up. If necessary this crossing could be topped with trunks of cocoanut trees.

"On the south bank of the Ilu," the memorandum went on, "is high grass averaging four feet in height which affords possible positions for machine guns, riflemen, etc., with a field of fire extending across the stream toward the beach."

Another river which our forces will have to cross, said the memorandum, is the Tenaru. "The banks of the Tenaru average eight to ten feet in height and are covered with grass and thick brush affording possible positions for riflemen and machine guns. Just beyond the west bank of the Tenaru are deep holes about six feet deep and 100 feet long, which have been scooped out by the river during the floods, thus forming natural, concealed positions.

"The Tenaru follows a serpentine course with a current averaging four knots. During the rainy season and floods the water rushes at much greater speed. The river is full of deep holes well over a man's head.

"After fording the Tenaru our forces will advance across the Tenaru plantation.... This consists of cocoanut trees planted regularly in groups of four in a diamond formation. The result is that lanes of observation radiate in all directions. Most of these lanes are twenty-seven feet wide. Others are of lesser widths. Now they are beginning to be overgrown, but nevertheless afford good observations and fields of fire.

"On leaving Tenaru plantation our forces will emerge onto a grassy plain. Here the grass, if it has not been burned out by the Japs, is about four feet high. Though the ground is mostly firm, after a half mile it becomes swampy in patches and wooded at the headwaters of Alligator Creek.

"At this season these headwaters are usually dried up and easily crossed. The woods however are dense with a visibility of hardly five yards. There are no roads or paths. Between the trees are thorny vines and thick low underbrush through which it is necessary to cut passage."

That did not sound like an easy—or safe—terrain through which to advance. I suppose many others aboard shared my qualms about the approaching ordeal. However, we could not expect that it would be easy.

There was a meeting for platoon leaders in the ward-room this afternoon. For two hours, the roomful of men sweated and steamed, while orders were read. There were new, larger maps of the beach-head on the wall.

Lieut. Col. Maxwell, commanding officer of a large group of assault troops, presided. It was three o'clock when the meeting began.

"Gen. Rupertus (Brg. Gen. William H. Rupertus of Washington, D.C.) is taking the other islands," said the colonel. "We are going to capture Guadalcanal Island.

"When we land on this beach here" (the colonel's Southern background was noticeable in the way he pronounced "heah"), "the first thing we strike a few hundred yards from the beach is a creek. It's quite an obstacle. We didn't know about it until a few days ago. It's too late to change our plans, so we're going to land here."

The colonel went through the details of our landing plan, and concluded, "Now that's enough of the background to get you started. Capt. Gale will now read the orders."

Capt. Gale began, "Order No. ———. Plan of landing Annex D landing diagram ... Co. B will advance ... fire on targets of opportunity."

Everyone was waiting for the item which would name the day of landing. But we were disappointed. For, finally, when Capt. Gale reached it, he read, "Paragraph X: Day and zero hour to be announced."

Col. Maxwell read an estimate of enemy strength, which placed their numbers at an ominously large figure. He spoke of the indications that the Japs are well equipped with machine guns and artillery.

Then a lieutenant rose to read "Annex E to General Order No. 3," which ended with "Paragraph D: Burial: Graves will be suitably marked. All bodies will bear identification tags."

The order "Naval Gunfire and Air Support Annex," however, lent somewhat of a cheering note to the meeting. It told of a terrifically heavy concentration of fire and intensive dive-bombing attack to be directed against Japanese shore installations before our landing.

There was a detailed account of the intensity and location of fire each participating war vessel was to deliver. The list ran on for half an hour, and the sum total was vastly impressive.

There were other orders, and then Col. Maxwell rose to deliver the final "pep talk."

"This is going to be a difficult matter," he said, "with the rivers to cross, the grass four to five feet tall, and the drainage ditches....

"But it can be done and it must be done and we've got to lead the way.

"There's only one thing to do," cautioned the colonel. "Get out of the boat, say 'Follow me,' run like hell and take these people with you....

"It's the first time in history we've ever had a huge expedition of this kind accompanied by transports. It's of world-wide importance. You'd be surprised if you knew how many people all over the world are following this. You cannot fail them."

SUNDAY, AUGUST 2

Church services were crowded this morning, for the day of our landing is drawing close and more and more of the men aboard, "the Padre," Father Reardon, told me, want to settle themselves in some sort of spiritual self-understanding and be prepared for at least the possibility of death. The general feeling is that our landing will take place some time before next Sunday; that therefore this is the last Sunday for Communion and the straightening of souls.

I watched Father Reardon, his face pale in the flickering light of the votive candles, as he chanted the mass. He was kneeling, rising automatically as if mesmerized, with his eyes half shut and his lips moving only faintly, as in a dream.

I saw the marines filing out of services, stopping in the companionway to kneel against a bare wall which for the time being was a holy station. In another hour or two it would again become merely a wall, and the church would become the mess hall. I watched one particularly well-muscled fellow, whose broad, sinewy back and heavy arms gave the impression of tremendous physical power. His broad face was passive and dreamy as he knelt by the wall and made the sign of the crucifix.

After the Catholic ceremonies, came the Protestant, also crowded. There was a sermon, with a proper dash of science, on memory and its part in duty, delivered by a fat young man in blues. There were hymns, and, after the services, Communion.

After lunch, I went into Hold No. 3 to watch the occupant of a neighboring cabin, Lieut. Donoghue (Lieut. James V. Donoghue of Jersey City, N.J.) telling his machine-gun platoon about the plans for landing. Today was the day on which, all over the ship, platoon leaders first passed the details of our attack plan along to their men. Donoghue's session was typical; his men are going ashore in the first wave of assault troops.

Under a yellow electric light in the dingy hold, Lieut. Donoghue, a huge, beefy fellow who used to play football for Notre Dame, unfolded an already well-worn map.

"Company B will land here at zero hour," he said, pointing with a stubby finger. "You know we'll be with 'em. We're in the first wave." There was no sound from the circle of men.

"We are the assault wave guide," continued Donoghue. "See, here's where we land, to the right here." Then he went through the details of the operation.

"I recommend you take along a change of underwear," he said, and that brought a laugh.

"Well," concluded the lieutenant, "that's the dope. You want to go in there expecting the worst. I expect the naval bombardment will soften the place up a lot. I'm depending on you to take things over if I get knocked off."

At 2:30 in the afternoon the leaders of the assault companies, Capt. Kaempfer of A Co., and Capt. Hawkins of B Co., met with their platoon leaders in the ward-room. For two hours they pored over plans. And that, they told me, was only the beginning. It will take days of study and mental drilling to get the facts of the planned operation down to the last buck private.

At 3:30, general quarters was sounded, but it was only a rehearsal. There was practice firing into the bright blue sky with our anti-aircraft machine guns and small cannon. It was pleasant to watch the streaks of tracer bullets branching up into the blue, and then, as they burned out, shrinking into bright glowing spots clustering like stars for a moment, and then fading.

Up on the bridge, I found a happy group of ship's officers and men. Now at least we are on our way directly toward our objective. The watch officer told me that our base course is pointed straight at the Solomons.

In the beautiful white sunlight on the open signal bridge at the top of the ship, I found Col. Hunt and his staff officers relaxing. The colonel, seated in a canvas chair under an awning, was reading a magazine with as much contentment and calm as if he had been sitting on his front porch of a Sunday afternoon back home.

At supper tonight, it was made known that the day of our landing is to be Friday, August 7th, five days hence. The zero hour is not yet known, but it will be in the early morning.

After supper, Maj. Milton V. "Mike" O'Connell (a former New York newspaperman and public relations counsel) gave a lecture to the officers on Japanese jungle-fighting tactics. Genial, portly "Mike" drew a laugh when he warned the lads to be as silent as possible while advancing against the Japs.

"We can beat the Japs at their own game of silence," he said, "if you don't yell back and forth. You know how the marines are; some marine'll yell to his buddy: 'Hey, Bill, is that C Company over there?' " Maj. O'Connell waved his short arms wildly, mimicking the enthusiasm of his typical marine.

"Don't let your men get curious and run over to see if B Company is over there, or what kind of chow [food] they've got. If your man gets too curious, he'll be chow himself."

The major warned of the Jap sniper's trick of tying himself in a tree, waiting until you have passed by, and then shooting you. "Don't take any chances," said the major, "it's better to shoot a few cocoanuts than miss a Jap egg-head."

In our cabin tonight Capt. Hawkins and I talked over the coming offensive. He said the men were ready. All over the ship, he said, he had seen them sharpening their bayonets, oiling their knives, cleaning and sighting along their rifles. "And they do it without being told," he said, as if awed by the phenomenon.

MONDAY, AUGUST 3

After lunch today I walked out on the bow of the ship, where there were groups of marines scattered over the piled gear, boats, ropes, hatch covers, ammunition boxes and assorted machinery that filled the deck. The sunshine was bright and there was a pleasant cool breeze.

Some of the men were still whetting bayonets and knives, and others were cleaning and oiling their guns. Others were grouped around a four-handed game of cards. One little group of men lounged by the starboard rail, idly watching one of their number who was throwing half-dollars over the side. He had a big stack of them in his left hand.

"He's trying to make 'em skip on the waves," one of the group explained to me.

Now another marine, armed with a pile of half-dollars, also

began to throw the money over the side. "I won't have no use for it anyhow," he explained.

"I've seen many a guy make liberty on as much money as they're throwin' away," suggested a sailor who was watching.

"Oh, hell," said one of the marines, "money don't mean a thing out here anyhow. Even if you stay alive, you can't buy anythin'."

Brownie, the sailors' dog, began to bark. On the bow some of the men were hosing down the decks, and they had excited him.

"Did you know Brownie got his tetanus shots, just like us?" asked one of the marines. "He's got a tag marked with his name and the date of his tetanus shot; and it says on there, 'Class, Dog.'"

By this time the crowd of marines and sailors in our particular group had increased in size. Spotting my "C" arm band, they knew I was a news correspondent and had come up with the pleasingly straightforward idea of getting their names in the paper.

I asked where the majority of the marines aboard came from. "Boston and New York," said one of the boys. "We take a poll every day. Right now Boston's leadin'."

As we were talking, a short, chubby boy with a shaved head came up and stood at the edge of our circle. "There's the youngest guy on the ship," said one of the marines. The lad told me he was just seventeen, and that his name was Sam Gearhart and he came from Allentown, Pa.

"You must have joined up before you were seventeen, Sam," I said.

"I did," he answered. "But they can't throw me out now."

An even younger-looking lad ambled by on the deck. I asked him how old he was. "Eighteen," he said. He looked about fifteen at the most. He said his name was Thomas H. Pilant and his home was in Harlan, Ky.

The other marines told me a story about Pvt. Pilant. "His face is so small," said one of them, "that he can't get into a regular gas mask. They won't let him go in with the assault wave."

The other, older marines, kidded Pilant about his fate. "That's all right," they said. "You'll go on galley duty."

Col. Hunt issued a mimeographed notice to his troops this afternoon. "The coming offensive in the Guadalcanal area," he wrote, "marks the first offensive of the war against the enemy, involving ground forces of the United States. The marines have been selected to initiate this action which will prove to be the forerunner of successive offensive actions that will end in ultimate victory for our cause. Our country expects nothing but victory from us and it shall have just that. The word failure shall not even be considered as being in our vocabulary.

"We have worked hard and trained faithfully for this action and I have every confidence in our ability and desire to force our will upon the enemy. We are meeting a tough and wily opponent but he is not sufficiently tough or wily to overcome us because We Are Marines [the capitals were the colonel's].

"Our commanding general and staff are counting upon us and will give us whole-hearted support and assistance. Our contemporaries of the other Task Organizations are red-blooded marines like ourselves and are ably led. They too will be there at the final downfall of the enemy.

"Each of us has his assigned task. Let each vow to perform it to the utmost of his ability, with added effort for good measure.

"Good luck and God bless you and to hell with the Japs."

In the late afternoon, I listened while Lieut. Harold H. Babbin of New York City, a swarthy, cheerful fellow with a good Bronx accent, passed on his instructions to his platoon. Most of his talk centered around the Japanese tactics of jungle fighting. The circle of tough lads, many of them with unshaven faces, listened good-naturedly, interrupting occasionally, but not too often, with remarks.

Lieut. Babbin warned against booby-traps, such as helmets, bayonets, or other items of interest which the Japs might leave about with a rig of wiring to cause an explosion when they were picked up.

"When you see a .45 or something with beautiful pearl" (he pronounced it "poil") "on it and beautiful engraving, don't pick it up," he said. "It might blow up."

"The most beautiful poil in the woild," one of the lads mimicked. But Babbin was used to that. He smiled and went on.

"If a Jap jumped on you from a tree," he asked, "what would you do?"

"Kick him in the b————," answered a marine.

"That's right," said Babbin. "You hit the nail on the head."

"You might see a Jap sniper hanging from the top of a tree, lookin' dead," the lieutenant continued, "because they tie themselves in with ropes. He might be playin' possum. So, don't hesitate to throw another .30 up there, bounce him off the tree again. That's good stuff."

"Yeah," somebody piped up, "it might hurt him."

After the meeting was over, Babbin said to me, "They're a tough gang."

One of the sergeants told me: "That's a weapon platoon, and they've got to carry about fifty pounds of stuff each, a lot of 'em. But they'll keep up with anybody. Sometimes they get ahead of the infantry. Even with receivers, guns, and all that. They don't give a s——— for anybody. They say, F——— you, if you can do it, so can I."

TUESDAY, AUGUST 4

This day went slowly. We are still plodding toward our goal, in the open sea, and there is little to do but re-check preparations already made. Capts. Hawkins and Kaempfer, leaders of the assault companies, were in a huddle with their N.C.O.'s for three hours this afternoon. They passed out sector maps which had been prepared yesterday, drilled the details of their plans into their own minds and those of their subordinates.

On deck the lads lounged about, still shooting the breeze, still sharpening knives. "I just want to kill a Jap, that's all," said one of them to me.

Some of the men tossed empty tin cans over the stern and shot at them with .45 automatics and sub-machine guns, until the officers ordered an end to the matter.

Many lads had written the word "Fight" in black ink on the backs of their jackets. Talk of ferocious designs on the Japs reached a new high.

On the forecastle, a group of men sat around a howitzer, lovingly occupied with cleaning and greasing the parts. Next to them, a poker game went fast and furiously, with stacks of bills blowing in the wind.

"A lot of the boys are putting money in the regimental safe to be sent home," a marine told me. "One put in $450 today, and me, I cracked away 125 bucks. I thought of getting into a crap game, but then I thought if I won, I wouldn't know what to do with the money."

WEDNESDAY, AUGUST 5

This morning at breakfast, Lieut. Cory said, "Two days more to go." "Forty-eight hours," said Lieut. Manterfield. And we all remarked that amazingly there are no cases of jitters evident anywhere. Except, somebody suggested, for one doctor. He, it was said, is scared to death. [Note. I was later to see this certain doctor acting with the greatest coolness and bravery under fire.]

"Scuttlebutt"—the Navy and marine name for unfounded rumor—was rampant today. Naturally, it would be, for we are riding up to the climax of our expedition, and as yet there has been no action. We had expected some—and now busy imaginations are filling the gap.

One story was that one of our accompanying cruisers had found, and sunk, a Japanese submarine traveling on the surface. A marine told me he had seen the flashes of gunfire himself. I checked the story with the ship's executive officer. He laughed. "There was some heat lightning early this morning," he said, "behind that cruiser."

Another story told how we had discovered a lifeboat full of natives, the remnant of the crew of colored sailors from a merchant ship which had been sunk by a Jap destroyer. This story was equally easy to track down. It originated this morning, when our task force slowed for a few minutes for a motor whale-boat, carrying dispatches from one transport to another. It is not clear by what process the boat's crew became Negroes.

This morning, in the bright sunlight of the ship's upper deck, I watched Col. Hunt passing the time of day with his officers. He was in high spirits, going through the tap-dance routine he used to do, he said, when he was a student in Stanford University before the First World War. He sang his own accompaniment, a bass rendition of such tunes as "I Want a Girl Just Like the Girl That Married Dear Old Dad."

The colonel could still turn in a very passable buck and wing. He was excellent, too, at the exit with the lifted straw hat. I decided his youthful exuberance arose because now he was getting into the zone of action. He had been one of the heroes of the First World War.

At supper tonight there was a mimeographed message placed under each plate. "The ———— [name of ship] has been singularly honored to be entrusted with getting ashore the first assault wave of the first U.S. ground force offensive action in the present war," it said. "Our ship has a good name. I expect it to have an honored and revered name after this coming action." The message was signed by the captain. Another note was also printed on the sheet. "We may expect sudden attack from submarines or bombers at any time from now on."

In the cabin, I found Capt. Hawkins busily oiling his sub-machine gun and his cartridges. He did not seem nervous. In the course of conversation I asked him how he felt about being one of the leaders in the assault wave. "I don't feel funny about it," he said. "I don't feel any more nervous than if I were being sent out to do a tough job in civilian life—you know, like trying to sell a big order, when there's a lot of sales resistance." The captain had once sold groceries, wholesale, in Boston.

THURSDAY, AUGUST 6

It was easy to see that this was the day before the big event. Sailors were busy rigging big booms to the heaviest of our landing lighters, so that they could be quickly launched. At several parts of the ship, canned rations were being issued: concentrated coffee and biscuits, meat and beans, vegetable stew, chocolate bars—enough for two or three days' subsistence until field kitchens can be rigged on Guadalcanal.

In the ship's armorer's shop, working single-mindedly at the benches, giving their weapons a last-minute check of adjustment, were a crowd of officers and men.

At luncheon, one of my table-mates, Lieut. Patrick Jones of Kansas City, said that he expected to transfer to another ship to-morrow before going ashore. The ship, he said, is carrying our reserve of ammunition, and gasoline. It would be too bad if she were hit by a bomb or shell.

"As I fly over Kansas City," said Lieut. Jones, "I'll drop off a souvenir, saying 'From Pat.' "

We all wondered at the fact that our task force, now well within range of the Japs, was not attacked by submarine, plane or surface craft. But there was not even an alarm.

The weather has been greatly in our favor. All day today, there was a heavy overcast, and visibility was very short. Unless the Japs had come very close, they could not have spotted us. But still, we were amazed, and I, for one, wondered if the Japs might have prepared a trap for us to walk into.

Dr. Malcolm V. Pratt, the senior medical officer aboard, who won distinction in the First World War, told me an amusing story this afternoon.

"I went below to look around in the hold last night," he said, "expecting to find the kids praying, and instead I found 'em doing a native war dance. One of them had a towel for a loin cloth and a blacked face, and he was doing a cancan while another beat a tom-tom. In one corner of the room, there were about four or five boys wrestling around, but no one paid any attention to them."

As the afternoon wore on, I saw marines tying up their packs, with blanket rolls neatly folded over the top, and standing the finished products in tidy rows along the bulkheads. Men carrying armfuls of black-cased hand grenades hurried up and down the companionways. On deck, working parties were breaking out medium-heavy artillery ammunition.

Tonight at dinner, some of the officers betrayed signs of nerves. One was sure he heard the anti-aircraft machine guns firing on our upper deck. Another said he could hear it too. But it was merely the sound of heavy drums being moved about.

It was announced tonight that breakfast will be served at 4:30 A.M. We will reach our launching point at about 6:20. The zero hour has not yet been set, but it will be somewhere near 8:30.

After dinner, I talked to Col. Hunt, in whose assault boat I will be going ashore. He said that Col. Maxwell and some of the other officers would be going in another boat. "No use putting all your eggs in one basket," he said, and that had an uncomfortably hazardous sound.

In the men's mess hall, center of most of their activities including church, I found a close-packed crowd of marines with a sprinkling of sailors. Most of them sat on the benches—talking loudly in order to be heard against the jazzy boom of a juke box, and filling the air with cigarette smoke. A marine jitterbug, minus his shirt, his torso shiny with sweat, cut racy jive steps near the juke box, while another marine danced the part of the girl. After a few moments two sailors joined in the fun, themselves cut a rug or two.

In the officers' ward-room, three groups of officers entertained themselves with three separate, polite games of hearts.

I walked the deck in the dark, damp night. There was no trace of a moon—fortunately. At ten o'clock I came back to the men's mess hall and the officers' ward-room. The lights were out. All the life was gone from both places.

LANDING

FRIDAY, AUGUST 7

It was no trouble to get up at four o'clock this morning, without benefit of alarm clock, for my mind had been trained for this day for a long time.

Everyone was calm at breakfast. We knew we must be very near our objective by this time, probably at the moment passing directly under the Jap shore guns. And the fact that we had got this far without any action made us feel strangely secure, as if getting up at four o'clock in the morning and preparing to force a landing on the enemy shore were the perfectly normal things to do of an August morning in the South Seas. We had a heavy breakfast and passed a normally humorous conversation.

Up on the deck the situation was the same. Everyone seemed ready to jump at the first boom of a gun, but there was little excitement. The thing that was happening was so unbelievable that it seemed like a dream. We were slipping through the narrow neck of water between Guadalcanal and Savo Islands; we were practically inside Tulagi Bay, almost past the Jap shore batteries, and not a shot had been fired.

On the deck marines lined the starboard rail, and strained their eyes and pointed their field glasses toward the high, irregular dark mass that lay beyond the sheen of the water, beyond the silently moving shapes that were our accompanying ships. The land mass was Guadalcanal Island. The sky was still dark; there was yet no pre-dawn glow, but the rugged black mountains were quite distinct against the lighter sky.

There was not much talking among the usually vivacious marines. The only sounds were the swish of water around our ship, the slight noises of men moving about on the forward deck.

Up on the bridge I found the ship's officers less calm than the marines. Theirs was the worry of getting the ship to anchorage without her being sunk, and they seemed high-strung and incredulous.

"I can't believe it," one lieutenant said to me. "I wonder if the Japs can be that dumb. Either they're very dumb, or it's a trick."

But there was no sign of any tricks as we plowed on into the bay, and the sky began to throw light ahead of us, and we could see even the misty outline of Tulagi and the Florida group of islands squatting to the east and north.

Now the rugged mass of Guadalcanal Island, on our right (to the south), was growing more distinct, and the sharp shoulders of the high mountains could be seen. But there was no sign of any firing from shore, nor were any enemy planes spotted.

Suddenly, from the bridge, I saw a brilliant yellow-green flash of light coming from the gray shape of a cruiser on our starboard bow. I saw the red pencil-lines of the shells arching through the sky, saw flashes on the dark shore of Guadalcanal where they struck. A second later I heard the b-rroom-boom of the cannonading. I should have been ready for that, but was nervous enough so that I jumped at the sound.

Our naval barrage, which was to pave the way for our landing, had begun. I looked at my watch. The time was 6:14.

Two minutes later, a cruiser astern and to our starboard side began firing. There were the same greenish-yellow flashes as the salvo went off, the same red rockets arching across the sky, geysers of red fires where the shells struck shore, a terrifying rumble and boom of the explosion.

Now, fore and aft, the two cruisers were hurling salvo after salvo into the Guadalcanal shore. It was fascinating to watch the apparent slowness with which the shells, their paths marked out against the sky in red fire, curved through the air. Distance, of course, caused that apparent slowness. But the concussion of the firing shook the deck of our ship and stirred our trousers legs with sudden gusts of wind, despite the distance.

At 6:17, straight, slim lines of tracer bullets, a sheaf of them, showered from the bay in toward the shore, and simultaneously we heard the sound of plane motors. Our planes were strafing, we knew, though in the half-light we could not make out the shapes of the aircraft.

Then there were more showers and sheafs of tracers needling into the dark land-mass, and we could see the red lines forming into shallow V's, as, after they struck into their targets, they ricocheted off into the hills.

A moment later my heart skipped a beat as I saw red showers of machine-gun tracers coming from low on the shore and apparently shooting seaward at an angle toward our ships. Was this the answering fire of the Japs? Was heavier firing going to follow? Was this the beginning of the fireworks?

The answer was not clear. When the firing was repeated a few seconds later, it looked more like ricochet than it had before.

Whatever the firing was, it stopped shortly after that, and from then on, there was no visible Jap resistance.

At 6:19 another cruiser, dead ahead of us, began firing. A moment later other warships joined, and the flash of their firing, and the arcs of their flying shells, illumined the sky over a wide span ahead.

Other ships of our force—the group under Gen. Rupertus—had turned to the left toward Tulagi, and there were the heavy reports of cannonading coming from them now.

At 6:28, I noticed a brilliant white spot of fire on the water ahead, and watched fascinated, wondering what it was, while it burgeoned into a spreading sheet of red flame. Planes were moving back and forth like flies over the spot.

"It's a Jap ship," said the ship's officer standing next to me. His field glasses were leveled on the flames. "Planes did it," he said. "They were strafing."

Now the sheet of red flame was creeping out into a long, thin line, and then it was mounting higher and higher into a sort of low-slung, fiery pyramid. For long minutes we watched the flames while the din of our thundering naval guns increased and reached a climax around us.

Ahead of us, to the left of the still brightly burning Jap ship, I saw a bright, white pinpoint of light blink into existence. It was a masthead light riding atop the Australian cruiser which had led our procession into the bay. (The *Canberra*, sunk in subsequent naval action in the Solomon Islands area.)

Our ship was still moving forward, however, and the flaming ship ahead was growing nearer. In the light of the red-orange flames we could see that it was not a large ship, and that it was low in the water. Possibly it was 120 feet long. "What kind of ship is it?" I asked a deck officer.

"They say it's a torpedo boat," he said. But it was in fact a schooner which had been carrying a load of oil and gasoline—whence the flames.

Our dive-bombers were swooping low over the beach. In the growing daylight you could see the color of the explosions where bombs were landing. Some, which struck at the edge of the water, had a bluish tinge. Others, hitting farther back in the sand and earth, were darker.

As the planes dived, they were strafing. The incandescent lines of their tracers struck into the ground, then bent back ricocheting toward the sky to form the now-familiar shallow V.

Our ship and one other, the vanguard of the transport fleet, slowed and stopped. Immediately, the davits began to clank as the boats were lowered away. There were a hubbub of shouts and the sound of many men moving about the ship. On the forward deck, a donkey engine began to chuff and puff. It was time for the beginning of our landing adventure.

It was daylight, but ahead the mass of flames that was the burning Jap boat glowed as brightly as in the dark of night. There were new explosions, as we watched, within the fire—probably gasoline tanks. A burning oil slick spread across the water astern of the boat. And the thought crossed my mind that if there had been anyone alive aboard that ship, he certainly was not alive now.

Our ship and the other transports had swung bow-in toward Guadalcanal, and landing boats were in the water. More were on the way down to the tune of clinking davits. All around us, we could hear the muffled thrumming of engines; boats were cutting in and out at every angle, circling, sliding close alongside. It was cheering to see that each boat carried a small American flag at the stern.

Troops, a mass of moving green uniforms, jammed the forward deck. A sailor leaned over the rail with a signal flag, beckoning landing boats to come up beside the rope nets that served as dismounting ladders. There was something peaceful about the bustle of activity. For a moment one almost forgot about the Japs who might be waiting on shore with machine guns and artillery to blast us out of the water as we came in for a landing.

Our accompanying cruisers, which had stopped firing for a few moments, were opening up again. One, lying astern and to our starboard side, was sending salvo after salvo into a dark point of land. A column of dense black smoke was rising from the spot where the shells were landing. And as we watched, the base of the column glowed red and orange, and the boom of a distant explosion came to us.

We knew a gasoline or oil dump had been hit, because the red flames continued to soar at the base of the smoke column, and from time to time there were new explosions, so that the flames leaped momentarily higher into the sooty black smoke.

I walked among the troops gathered on the forward deck, and found them silent and nervous—a contrast to the gaiety and song which had filled the few preceding days. There did not seem to be much to say, although a few lads came up with the inevitable, "Well, this is it."

The first of our marines clambered over the rail and swung down the rope nets into the boats. The boats pulled away and more came up, and the seeping waterfall of marines continued to slide over the side.

I got word that it was time for me to debark. I took one last look around the ship. Toward Guadalcanal shore, I could see the cruisers still pasting shells into the landscape. On the point of land (Kukum) where the bombardment had set afire a fuel dump, there was a new fire now: two columns of smoke instead of one. From Tulagi-way, across the bay, one could hear the sounds of heavy cannonading. The landing must be going ahead there.

It was just eight o'clock when I hit the deck of the bobbing landing boat. Col. Hunt and his staff officers were already aboard. This was to be a "free" boat; the colonel could take it ashore at any time he pleased. He might go in after the first landing wave, and, at any rate, we would not be later than the fifth wave.

At 8:06, a covering screen of fighter planes appeared and flew low over the fleet of transports. They shuttled back and forth overhead, weaving a protective net in the sky.

For a long time our landing boat circled astern of our ship, while we sat on the bottom, keeping our heads below the gunwale in the approved fashion.

At 8:34, the Navy coxswain swung our boat around and we headed for the shore. We were moving slowly, however, throttled back.

Kneeling so that I could look over the gunwale, I saw that our warships close to Guadalcanal shore had ceased firing for the time being, though from the north, Tulagi-way, came the sound of heavy cannonading.

At 9:02 our boat was moving toward the beach at full throttle when the line of cruisers and destroyers ahead of us began a terrific bombardment of the shore. This, we knew, was the "softener" which would, we hoped, sweep the beach clean of any Japanese machine-gun or artillery emplacements, and make our landing easier.

Scores of naval guns blasted simultaneously into the shore. The din of their firing was intense. Sheets of yellow flame welled from the gun barrels up and down the line, and along the beach a line of blue and black geysers leaped up where the shells were striking.

At 9:05 the intense bombardment on the shore was ending. A haze of dirty black smoke hung over the edge of the land. And we were heading straight for it.

We followed, not too distantly, the first wave of landing boats, which we could see as an irregular line of moving white spots against the blue water, each spot dotted at the center with black. The white spots, we knew, were foam; the black, the boats themselves, making maximum speed toward shore.

We could not see the boats strike shore; but signals rose ahead of us on the beach. The colonel turned to the rest of us in the boat and smiled. The agreed signal for a successful landing. A signalman stood on our motor hatch and wig-wagged the good news back to our mother ship.

It was quickly acknowledged.

The fact of a successful landing, however, did not mean that our effort to take the beach-head would be unopposed. We ducked well below the level of the gunwales as we reached a fixed line of departure, a certain number of yards from shore, and forged ahead.

At 9:28 we passed the boats of the first wave, coming out from the beach to the ships to get another load of troops. We poked our heads up to see that they showed no signs of having been damaged by enemy fire. We gathered a little more courage now and raised our heads to see what was happening. Lieut. Cory, squatting next to me, shouted to me over the rumble of the motor that perhaps there were no Japs. Still, it seemed that this would be too good to be true. Perhaps the Japs were merely drawing us into a trap.

At 9:40 we were close enough to land to see isolated palm trees projecting above the shore—sign that we were coming close to whatever trap the enemy might have prepared.

In our boat there was no talking, despite the excitement of the moment. The motor was making too much noise, at any rate. We sat and looked at each other, and occasionally peeped over the side to glimpse other boats plunging shoreward in showers of spray around us, or to cock an eye at the strangely silent beach.

At 9:47 we were close enough to the shore to see a long line of our landing boats drawn up on the dun-colored sand, close enough to see a wallowing tank moving along the shoreline, tossing plumes of spray before and behind. We could make out throngs of our troops moving on the beach amongst a line of thatched roof huts. We then became very courageous, since it was apparent that there were no enemy troops in the vicinity.

At 9:50, with a jolt, our boat grounded on the dun-colored sand. Our debarkation was leisurely. I jumped carefully from the bow and got only one foot wet, and that slightly; hardly the hell-for-leather leap and dash through the surf, with accompaniment of rattling machine guns, which I had expected.

From down the beach, a jeep, evidently the first ashore, came past us. There was noise, and motion, everywhere, as more troops leaped from beached landing boats, and working parties struggled to unload bigger barges coming in with machinery, equipment, supplies.

A group of five fighter planes zoomed close overhead. A tractor was being hauled from a tank lighter. I saw two marines setting up a small generator between two bamboo huts which had been knocked silly by the shellfire. The generator would run a radio.

One shattered thatch hut had already been occupied as headquarters for a company of Marine Pioneers. Evidence of civilization is the oilcloth sign they have posted outside their headquarters—with the green lettering "Shore Party CP—A Co." Pioneers were busy straightening out the interior of the shack. It was a peaceful scene.

But just behind the strip of sandy beach, heading inland, I found a much less secure atmosphere. Scattered through the cocoanut grove I could see marines crouching behind trees, with their rifles at the ready. From the jungly woods to the south came the occasional crack of a rifle. Groups of marines, their faces muddied and sprigs of bushes fastened to their hats for camouflage effect, were forming up in patrols. "I want you guys to watch every tree," said a top sergeant, giving his platoon instructions.

I attempted to discover if any opposition had been encountered. "I heard machine-gun firing when I came in," said one marine, "but I don't know whether it was ours or the Japs'."

"There's a little firing in there," said another marine, motioning toward the jungle. "Looks like the Japs'll take to the hills. Another Nicaragua. They'll be in here alive next month, fighting in the jungles."

At 10:20 a procession of jeeps towing carts of shells moved through the cocoanut trees and out toward our forward positions. The procession was a reminder that deep inland our troops might at that moment be tangling with the Japs.

But there were no sounds of cannonading coming from inland. Only from the direction of Tulagi, twenty miles to the north, could we hear the boom of distant cannon fire.

Back on the beach the activity of peaceful unloading continued. The sand was now torn and rutted by constant traffic of jeeps and tractors. Our first tank was being pulled from a lighter. Anti-aircraft guns were being rolled out and set up on the beach, their barrels pointing seaward.

A medical-aid station had been set up on the sand, under a Red Cross banner. The attending medico, Dr. C. Douglas Hoyt, said that there had been no casualties so far—except for a lad who cut his palm with a machete while trying to open a cocoanut. That was cheerful news.

By this time, fast-moving Col. Hunt had evaporated from the beach, taking his staff with him. I set out to overtake him, using his command post telephone lines—which it seemed had sprung through the conquered terrain almost instantaneously—as a guide.

I passed through the coastal belt of cocoanut palms, then through a beaten path cutting through a field of shoulder-high parched grass, and then into the thick, shadowy jungle, where, fortunately, a trail had been cut.

The Ilu River, which had sounded so sinister and impassable in the memorandum passed about on board ship, was disappointing. It was a muddy, stagnant little creek, almost narrow enough to jump across.

Beyond the stream, it was easy to make one's way through the wet, smelly jungle, for the marines had cut a swath three or four feet wide—wide enough to allow passage for ammunition carts. The trail penetrated for miles into the jungle—the advance elements of marines were thousands of yards beyond that—and scarcely two hours had elapsed since our first wave hit the beach. What wonder workers these Americans are!

I found Col. Hunt's command post, as it was called, actually only an undistinguished part of the jungle, where communications men were busy installing field telephones. It was time for lunch. We squatted in the matting of soft, wet leaves and opened ration cans.

Things were quite peaceful. The colonel said that apparently no resistance had been encountered by our landing party. If there were any Japs about, they had faded into the hills. Capt. Charles V. Hodgess, one of our Australian guides and the former owner of a cocoanut plantation on Guadalcanal, joked about the ease with which we had occupied Guadalcanal thus far. "I'm exhausted by the arduousness of landing against such heavy fire," he said.

After we had eaten, I worked my way back to the beach, to find the transports lying close in, swarms of hustling lighters still rushing back and forth. Half-ton trucks had been brought in and were moving up and down the beach already hauling stacks of crates—food, medical supplies, spare parts, ammunition.

Some of the marines were still occupied with cracking cocoanuts along the beach. Others had gone in for a dip, to rest muscles wearied by four and a half hours of unloading.

I went back to the jungle, headed for the colonel's advance party—and missed the first Japanese air raid on the marines at Guadalcanal.

At 1:30 I heard the quick, basso "whoomp, whoomp, whoomp" of anti-aircraft fire, and saw the sky fill with the dark-brown smudges of shellbursts. The sky was overcast, and there were no planes visible, but the droning of motors could be heard. It was evident that the Japs were after the transports and warships in the bay, for the anti-aircraft bursts were concentrated over that area. Trees then blocked my view of the ships; but I was to learn later in the day that they had not been hit.

For a few minutes, the noise of plane motors grew louder, and then, amidst the steady drone, I heard the crescendo whine of a diving plane, followed by the unmistakable rattle of aircraft machine guns, probably one of our own fighter planes diving on the Japs.

At about 1:40, the sound of anti-aircraft firing stopped. A few moments after that, a flight of eighteen of our fighter planes swung out of the overcast sky and swept across Tulagi Bay. Evidently the air raid was over.

I caught up with the colonel's party in the woods, and plowed steadily along with them through jungle trails until just before four o'clock we reached a pleasant cocoanut grove. We had just sat down to rest our bones when a terrific concentration of anti-aircraft fire could be heard breaking, and again the bursts were visible in the sky.

The command "Take cover" was passed, and we slid for the bush, wondering if the Japs would come in and strafe our troops. But this time, as the last, their target was evidently the ships. The anti-aircraft fire this time lasted five minutes. We neither heard the bombs nor saw the planes. Then the raid was over. It had been as tame as our landing. (But I was later to find out that for the ships involved, the raid had been furious. Jap dive-bombers had attacked our warships, damaging one. Two of the attackers had been shot down by anti-aircraft fire.)

At this juncture Dr. Pratt came up with our party. He said he had been talking to an eyewitness of the first air raid (at 1:30), and that this eyewitness had said that he saw two Jap planes shot down and their pilots descending in parachutes. But the "scuttlebutt" is being passed around among the men that there were as many as six Jap planes shot down in the first raid. (False: there were three shot down, two by our fighters, one by anti-aircraft.)

We rested in the cocoanut grove for a few minutes before moving on. It was quite peaceful, despite the rifle shots that cracked in the woods about us. For it was now the general assumption amongst our group that there were no Japs in the vicinity.

Sgt. William A. Davis (of Evansville, Ind.), an engineer, came up to tell me he believed he was the first marine to be shot at in the Guadalcanal campaign. He made a wrong turn somewhere and got out ahead of the advance troop elements, shortly after the landing. Two shots were fired at him, he said, and they came within a few inches.

In the cocoanut grove, it was bizarre to see a marine pick up a telephone and hear him say "Operator" into the receiver. It seemed strange, too, to hear French horns, sounding exactly like those you might find on a fashionable roadster, tooting in the jungle. It happened they were attached to the tanks.

"I'll be right out," said a marine after one such toot; as if his girl were waiting outside with the top down.

There was an end even to this amusement. We had to get up and march again for miles through the jungle, through cocoanut groves, across boggy streams and over steep little hills.

At 4:30 we came out of the trees to an open field of tall grass. Two marines stood at the edge of the field. They had their .45 automatics in their hands, and seemed a little nervous. One of them approached the colonel.

"We found fresh chopped trees, which looked like they'd been cut about an hour ago, sir," he said. "We think it was a Japanese gun emplacement."

But half an hour later, after some more painful trudging under heavy packs, we had not seen any signs of the enemy. We halted, then, in a grove of tall, slender, white cocoanut palms—which must have been beautiful when it was well kept. Now there are piles of decaying palm fronds and aged, rotting cocoanuts on the ground; but we settled down to rest without a murmur of complaint. Anything would look like home after the day's hiking.

We had a canned ration supper, and since there was no water, many of the lads busied themselves with knocking down green cocoanuts from the trees, and cutting them open for milk. Some of the marines had already learned the art of rapid cocoanut-cracking. One such was P.F.C. Albert Tardiff (Albert C. Tardiff of Newark, N.J.), who opened one for me in two minutes flat.

Bedding down for the night under the tall palms and a panoply of soft stars would have been a beautiful experience, except for bugs, mosquitoes and thirst—which unfortunately were all too present.

With the coming of the dark, the mackaws began to squeal in the tree-tops, and rifle shots became more numerous. The sentries were jittery on this their first night on the island. I awoke from time to time to hear the call of "Halt!" followed almost immediately by volleys of gunfire.

Once, near midnight, I woke to hear a sub-machine gun cracking very near the grove. Then a rifle barked. Then another. And soon, five or six guns were firing simultaneously, and the bright white tracer bullets were zipping in several directions over the grove where we slept. Some of the slugs whined through the trees close by. And then the firing fell off, and died, and we went back to sleep again.

SATURDAY, AUGUST 8

A runner came back from our foremost elements this morning to report that the airport, prize of the Guadalcanal invasion, has been reached and that, as yet, no contact has been made with the enemy.

But one of our sentries, who had a post last night at the outskirts of our cocoanut grove, said that, at just about daybreak, a patrol of about 150 Japs passed close by our bivouac and then took off into the bush.

Col. Hunt pointed up the morale. "This is no picnic," he said, obviously concerned over the fact that we have had an easy time of the campaign thus far. "We've got to be careful."

The colonel was in exuberant good spirits this morning, proba-bly, I guessed, because he had found that he could undergo the rigors of an all-day hike and feel sturdy the next morning—as he had a quarter of a century ago in the First World War.

The colonel set his helmet on the ground, sat himself down on it, and unfolded a map, while his staff, gathered around for the day's orders, watched.

"I'll tell you what I know and then you'll know as much as I do," he said. He pointed a big finger to a spot on the map. "Here's where we are," he said. "We've got to work down there and get to the Tenaru. Probably we'll wade around the mouth of the river." He went into the details of our plans.

The colonel passed along the good news that operations on Tulagi and Gavutu, across the bay, were going well. Tulagi, assaulted by the Raiders, was "O.K." despite heavy resistance, he said. The troops, attacking the neighboring island of Gavutu, had "taken their first objective and the rest is in the bag."

The colonel folded up his map brusquely, as if he were snapping shut a book he had just finished. "Well," he concluded, "there's the set-up. Better get packed up and stand by to move on." He stood up and clapped me on the shoulder. "Well, it looks like we might run into something this morning," he said. "Are you ready for a fight? It looks as if business is picking up." It was plain to see that he was lustily looking for a scrap.

But we trudged along through the jungle for miles, reached and forded the river, passed through another cocoanut grove, scared up a herd of horses, and came out on the beach again—without seeing a single Jap.

"I wish those f— — — — — Japs would come out and fight," one sweaty, dirty marine lamented, indulging in the marines' favorite adjective for anything distasteful. "All they do is run into the jungle."

We passed through a little village of tin-roofed huts on the beach. The white-plastered walls had been holed and in some cases shattered by the naval gunfire. The roofs had been turned into sieves by flying H.E. (high explosive) fragments.

Evidently these huts had been used as barracks by the Jap troops, for there were signs bearing Japanese inscriptions hung on the walls. I took one to Lieut. Cory, the interpreter. "It says Unit No. 3," he said, "in charge of so-and-so."

Sailors are amazingly efficient souvenir hunters. I saw some of them here with our advance units; they were busy collecting the Japanese signs.

A tank rumbled past us as we plodded down the beach. On the rear of the tank, in large white letters, was painted the name "M. J. Bob." Another passed, it carried the name "Edna."

I stopped to talk with Col. Frank B. Goettge, and he told me word had come that casualties—and fighting—had been heavy on Tulagi, Gavutu and Tanambogo. There were still stubbornly resisting, isolated groups of Japs to be cleaned up on Tulagi, he said, and on Gavutu the marines had lost a lot of men. Estimates of casualties ran as high as 60 percent (later found to be much lower). The marines had had a particularly good deal of trouble in trying to get across the causeway between Gavutu and Tanambogo, he said. The causeway was only eight feet wide and seventy-five yards long, and it was swept by machine-gun fire.

Col. Goettge suggested that probably the Japs would be in today to try another attack on the transports, which still lay close off-shore, and so, when Col. Hunt's people cut from the beach back into the jungle, I stayed behind on the shore—and saw one of the most awe-inspiring spectacles I have ever witnessed.

It was just noon when the quick, paced whoomp-whoomp of anti-aircraft firing began and I could see black bursts plastering the whole dome of the sky over Tulagi. I could see the flash of gunfire coming from the gray shape of the Australian cruiser out in the bay. Then the other warships took it up, and the whomping sounds came in overlapping clusters and volleys. Overhead, the canopy of anti-aircraft bursts was spreading thicker—and farther—over the sky.

Then the thunder of the big anti-aircraft guns was augmented by the fierce rattling of smaller anti-aircraft guns, and the whole sound swelled in a quick diapason until it seemed to swarm into your ears. Suddenly I saw the first Jap, a long, flat-shaped plane moving in among the transports like some preying shark, skimming over the water below the level of the masts, and I thought "Torpedo plane!"

Now I could see other Japs, the same flat, sinister shapes, prowling low over the water, darting among the transports. And there were black spouts of water rising amidst them: the splashes of bombs, or perhaps torpedoes being launched by the enemy aircraft.

The ships were moving over the horizon now, racing for the narrow straits which led to the open sea—trying to get out before they were hit. But the splashes of bombs and torpedoes were coming more frequently, and closer.

Our fighter planes dived into the foray. I saw one of them rout a Jap plane out of the fracas and chase it fiercely, with the Jap apparently in panicky flight toward the western tip of Guadalcanal. I heard the popping and rattling of the American's machine guns, continuing for seconds on end, and suddenly the Jap began to trail smoke. Then fire came at the root of the smoke plume, and the plane, falling, traced a gorgeous, steadily brightening curve across the sky. I watched, fascinated, while the plane arched into the water, and the slow white fountain of a great splash rose behind it, and then the white turned into brilliant orange as the plane exploded and sent a sheet of flame backfiring a hundred feet into the sky.

I turned my field glasses back to the transport fleet, in time to see a huge flash of fire, as red as blood, burst along the upper deck of one of the transports. Then a clump of sooty black smoke billowed out from the blood-red roots and towered up into the sky. The transport must have been hit directly. (I found out later that one of the Japs had crashed, apparently by accident, into the ship just aft of the bridge.)

Almost simultaneously, three other columns of smoke rose just over the rim of the horizon. I surmised that other ships had been hit.

The panorama of action stretched all the way from east to west. I had seen one Japanese plane fall in flames far to the left. Now, to the right, two others were falling in clouds of smoke.

In the center of the picture the stricken transport was still burning. The red flames mounted into the smoke, spreading belches of fire high up into the cloud as an explosion evidently occurred.

But suddenly the sky was empty of Jap planes. The awful storm of firing had stopped. The raid was over. I looked at my watch. It was 12:10.

At 12:54, the transports had turned and were moving to their anchorage off our beach. But out in the middle of the bay, the badly hit ship was still burning, with her fires evidently out of control. (She was later abandoned and scuttled.)

A marine, passing by, told me he had counted six of the Jap planes falling. (I found later that there had been forty Japanese planes attacking; that sixteen of these were shot down on the spot, and the remaining twenty-four destroyed by our fighters, one by one, as they streaked for home, after the raid. The Jap torpedo bombers had not gone after the warships, contenting themselves with merely strafing the transports as they passed by.)

I started back inland, to catch up again with the marine forces making their way toward the airfield. At 1:30, I passed two marines bringing in the first Jap prisoners—the first enemy people I had seen close to.

There were three of the Japs, walking in single file, while the marines, looking huge by comparison, shooed them along like pigeons.

The Japs were a measly lot. None of them was more than five feet tall, and they were puny. Their skins were sallow. The first two in line had shaved heads and were bare from the waist downward; the marines had been diligent in their search for weapons.

The third Jap had been allowed to keep his khaki-colored trousers. He wore a scraggly beard which made him look even more wretched, and on his head he had a visored cap of cheap cloth with a cloth anchor insignia.

The Japs blinked their eyes like curious birds as they looked at me. The first in line gaped, a gold tooth very prominent in the center of his open mouth.

The interpreter, Lieut. Cory, said he had just interviewed the Japs, and that they had told him they were members of a Navy labor battalion. They had been captured in a labor camp which lay just ahead.

A few minutes later I caught up with the temporary command post in a grove of trees. Maj. (now Lieut. Col.) Bill Phipps (William I. Phipps of Omaha, Neb.) was riding a captured Jap bicycle up and down a track road which cut through the woods.

The bike was apparently brand-new, a good-looking job much like the typical English bicycle, with hand brakes and narrow tires. This was the first of a great stock of booty we were to capture.

"There are lots more like this down the road," said Maj. Phipps. "And lots of other stuff, including trucks."

Capt. Ringer (Capt. Wilfred Ringer of Brookline, Mass.) was about to lead a party to the camp. I went with them.

Down the road we passed a few more marines riding shiny Jap bicycles. One careened amongst a group of marching troops, narrowly missing several. "No brakes!" he shouted. But finally he discovered the mechanism for bringing the machine to a stop. An American was being educated in foreign ways.

To one side of the road rested three Jap trucks, with fresh gray paint and apparently in first-class condition. They looked like the latest American models, but carried a Jap trademark.

Across the road sat a Ford V8 sedan, camouflaged in green, and carrying the Jap Navy license plates with white anchor insignia—apparently an official's car.

When we entered the Japanese tent camp we knew why we had been able to sail into Tulagi Bay and under the Jap guns without being fired upon. The enemy had been caught completely unawares.

In the first of the big tents—there were scores of them—we burst in upon a breakfast table left completely *in medias res.* It looked as if the Japs had left by the back door as we came in the front.

Serving dishes, set in the middle of the table, were filled with meat stew, rice, and cooked prunes. Bowls and saucers around the edge were mostly half full of food. Chopsticks had been left propped on the edges of the dishes, or dropped in haste on the floor mat.

In other tents we found more signs that the Japs had run in panicky surprise when our assault began. Shoes, mosquito nets, toilet articles, soap and other essentials had been left behind.

Walking through the Jap tent camp, we could see the reason for their hasty withdrawal. Many of the tents had been ripped by H.E. fragments and some knocked flat; groups of cocoanut palms were shattered, their trunks rent and tops blown off by shellfire, and in one little grove we found two shell-blasted bodies, now well attended by flies. One body sat at the foot of a tree, eyes staring straight ahead. The left leg had been nipped off at the knee, and the lower part of the leg, with the shoe still on the foot, lay a few feet to one side.

In another tent which was an infirmary, and completely stocked with drugs and surgical instruments, we found one emaciated patient sitting on his bed of matting. He told Lieut. Cory that he was suffering from malaria.

As we walked on through Jap territory, that afternoon, we began to realize the huge quantities of booty we had fallen heir to. Passing by the airport, which was by now completely occupied by our troops, I saw rows of brand-new wooden barracks—so new that the Japs had not yet moved in.

I climbed aboard a tank and rode to Lunga Point, and there found the largest Jap camp, and great quantities of equipment.

We rode past a large gray frame-house which I was told contained a Jap electricity plant—ready for use; we passed through a grove where our shells had torn half the trees asunder, and came to a huge motor-transport dump, complete with repair shop. Here there were at least 100 Jap trucks, Nipponese versions of the Chevrolet.

Beyond the truck dump we came to a great camp of tents, the largest we had yet seen, and at a beautiful bend in the river, the buildings which had evidently been the Jap headquarters. Here there were shacks which contained iron beds (most of the acres of surrounding tents had only board platforms topped with mats), handsome French telephone receivers, radios, riding boots standing in corners.

The house which had evidently been occupied by the commanding officer was well stocked with luxuries such as big bottles of saki, small bottles of wine, a large radio set, and nearby stood a bathtub, crowning luxury on this hot tropical island.

Along the road passing the Jap headquarters, a long line of our own trucks and jeeps, moving personnel and supplies forward, were passing; a captured Japanese car was one of the procession. On the other side of the road, in the Jap truck dump, marines were starting up the Nip vehicles, most of which, it seemed, were ready to go except for ignition keys.

Few of our troops, evidently, had investigated one Jap house, with open sidewalls. I wandered in and found a large drafting table equipped with properly up-angled drawing boards in the center of the building, and a desk on a sort of porch at one end. Around the edge of the room were shelves filled with blueprints, drafting supplies, stocks of paper, record books. This had evidently been the headquarters office.

One of the drafting boards had half-finished plans, drawn on tissue paper, pinned to it. The drafting pen lay across the center of the drawing, evidence of a helter-skelter withdrawal. Nearby a French phone lay beside its receiver—as if a conversation had been interrupted by our arrival.

Around the headquarters buildings I saw great stores of food: stacks of crates filled with canned goods, cases of a soda pop labelled "Mitsubichampagne Cider," and two varieties of Japanese beer. There were also large tins of hardtack and boxes of sweet biscuits.

Some of the passers-by had already sampled the Jap canned goods. I saw that there were canned pears and peaches and pineapple, goulash, crabmeat, shredded fish and salmon, hardly the primitive diet on which the Japanese is traditionally supposed to subsist.

I walked on down the road, seeking Col. Hunt's command post, passed a Jap refrigeration plant, and came to a large warehouse full of food. Obligingly, the Nips had even left cooking kettles behind.

Col. Hunt told me that he had encountered no Japs all day. But as the afternoon sky grew darker and evening came closer, the feeling that we might have walked into a trap grew more pressing. To gain all this booty without a struggle seemed too good to be true.

At 4:32 in the afternoon we had our first alarm. We heard shots to our left and behind us, coming from deep in the woods. A few seconds passed in silence, and then, suddenly, I heard our men shouting loudly and violently, saw them running for cover, flopping down in the brush to face our left rear. I thought, "This is it! This is the trap! They've got us." I could see in the faces of the men around me that they thought this was the fight for their lives which they had been expecting.

But it was a false alarm. The colonel, afraid that in our nervousness we might fire on our own supporting troops coming up behind, walked boldly through our hasty skirmish lines and down into the woods whence the rifle shots had come.

I followed, to find the cause of the alarm. Three Japs had bolted from one of the tents in the camp; possibly they had been caught there by our advance as they tried to get some food, and they had been shot. Two were dead. One lay on the ground, breathing hard. There was a small bloodstain on the back of his shirt, the color of wine. A corpsman ripped off the shirt. There was a hole about the size of a dime in the man's back.

"He won't last," said the colonel, looking at the wound. "That's an internal hemmorhage."

Corpsmen came up with a stretcher and carried the wounded man away, and he was given medical treatment; but he died soon after.

It was 6:15, and we were back at the command post, when one of our officers was brought in on a stretcher. It was Lieut. Snell, the colonel's aide.

Lieut. Snell was suffering from paralysis, although he could speak. A veteran of the World War and in his middle years, accustomed to office work, he had been overcome by heat and exertion. An officer told me that Snell had lost consciousness four times earlier that day, but kept the matter quiet and attempted to stay with our moving column.

The colonel wanted to do something to cheer his aide. So he took Snell's little pocket flag—an eight inch by twelve inch star-spangled banner which the lieutenant had carried with him in China and the Philippines—and had it hoisted on the bare flagpole at the Japanese headquarters. It was touching to see the little flag, proud but pitifully small, ride up the mast, to see Snell's eyes watching it, and his mouth twisting and contorting as he tried to smile. (Later, Lieut. Snell recovered completely and rejoined the colonel.)

In the evening I heard a story which Col. Hunt had modestly not told me: that he had led the "point" of our troops crossing the Lunga River.

Usually, it is a private's or corporal's business to lead the point, the very forefront of an advance. But when the colonel reached the Lunga, and found our troops holding back there and anxiously eying the forbidding dark woods across the bridge, he had led the way. Behind him went his staff—including the chaplain, Father Reardon, who was unarmed.

When we bedded down for the night, on the ground, I shared Father Reardon's poncho. We pulled it as closely as possible around us, for the sky looked dark and rainy.

We were awakened by gunfire at about eleven o'clock. "There's something moving in the river," somebody said. People all around us were shooting, with sub-machine guns, pistols, rifles. Again the tracer bullets made dazzling patterns in the dark. After ten minutes, the shooting stopped. If there had been any Japs in the river, they were certainly dead, or had retreated, by that time.

III

CONTACT

SUNDAY, AUGUST 9

A little after midnight this morning, the rain began to pour down on Guadalcanal. I withdrew myself from Padre Reardon's poncho and sought refuge in one of the Jap tents. It was fairly well filled already with marines, but I found a place to lie down, and slept until about one o'clock, when men all round me began to stir and talk, and coming half awake, I heard the sound of a plane buzzing overhead.

It did not sound like one of our planes. The motor had a ragged, high-toned sound. We all stopped talking and listened. "It's a Jap," somebody said.

A few minutes later we had the proof. In the direction of the beach where we had landed, a greenish-white glow flickered in the sky. It was a flare. We stood in the drizzling rain, silently, and watched while the Jap cruised over Guadalcanal, dropping flares in several sectors of the sky. Was this the prelude to a Jap landing, we wondered. The plane came over us three times, and then we heard the sound of the motor growing fainter and fainter, until it had gone.

I had just dropped off to sleep again, when again I woke to find people whispering, and this time to hear the brroom-brroom-brroom of cannonading coming from the sea, evidently quite close.

It had stopped raining. We stood in a quiet group under the palms, listening and watching. The flashes of the gunfire were filling the sky, as bright and far spreading as heat lightning. And a few seconds after each flash, we could hear the booming of the guns that had caused it.

The salvos of firing came with increased intensity, so that the sky was lighted by the quick flashes for minutes on end, and the rumbling of the firing had almost a continuous sound. Then, for a few moments, the flashes and the booming stopped; the sky was quiet, and then the cannonading began again, seeming louder, brighter and closer than before.

We knew then that there was a sea fight going on. Possibly, it was the battle for Guadalcanal. Possibly, if our people out there lost the battle, the Japs would be ashore before morning, and we would have to fight for our lives. We knew the fate of all of us hung on that sea battle. In that moment I realized how much we must depend on ships even in our land operation. And in that moment I think most of us who were there watching the gunfire suddenly knew the awful feeling of being pitifully small, knew for a moment that we were only tiny particles caught up in the gigantic whirlpool of war. The terror and power and magnificence of man-made thunder and lightning made that point real. One had the feeling of being at the mercy of great accumulated forces far more powerful than anything human. We were only pawns in a battle of the gods, then, and we knew it.

The cannonading continued, booming loud and bright and stopping, then starting again, for an hour and a half. And we stood and watched, speculating as to what was happening out there.

Meanwhile a Jap plane came to buzz overhead in the dark and drop flares—over the beach where we had landed, over the airport, out over the sea to the northwest, whence the firing was coming.

At about 2:30 some of the men said they were sure the sound of cannonading was growing fainter, and that this meant the Japs were being driven back. At three o'clock the last ponderous barrage of firing came to an end.

I sought refuge this time in a Japanese sedan, probably the Jap commander's vehicle, which had been left at the side of the road. The soft cushions felt good. Except for the slight disturbance of being bitten by mosquitoes, I was quite comfortable for the rest of the night.

This morning I made a trek to the temporary command post of Gen. Vandegrift (Maj. Gen. Alexander A. Vandegrift of Washington, D.C., and Lynchburg, Va.). The general, a red-cheeked, exceedingly affable man, told me that the casualties on the other side of the bay, on Tulagi and Gavutu, have not been as heavy as at first estimated. On both islands, the Japs holed themselves up in caves and dugouts, he said, and fought to the last man. The conquest of Tanambogo was complete, he said, and today, the smaller island, Makambo, was being taken. The marines also had a secure foothold on the largest island across the bay, called Florida or Ngela. That was good news. But there was no news as yet about what happened in the sea battle to the northwest this morning.

Back at Col. Hunt's command post, in the late afternoon, I heard an amusing story:

Our forces reaching Kukum, which had been an enemy strong point but was abandoned when we arrived, found many guns ready to fire, complete with ammunition, this morning. Among the guns was a three-barreled pompom of about one-inch bore.

The marines fired a few test rounds from the pompom, today, and the shells fell into the water halfway between Kukum and Matanikau, which is the next village down the coast.

Soon after the shells hit, a white flag was raised over Matanikau, indicating 1—That there are Japs in that village and 2—That they are anxious to surrender.

Apparently, said the colonel, the Japs thought that the pompom was firing at them, and they got frightened.

But the humorous part of the situation was that the marines were so busy, checking over the captured guns at Kukum and setting up new batteries there, that going down to take the Japanese at Matanikau would have been only a nuisance. So the marines kept on about their work, ignoring the frightened Japs. And that, it seems, must have been the most awful blow of all to the Jap morale, in view of the Oriental concept of face.

MONDAY, AUG. 10

This morning I went to Kukum to join a patrol of marines going to Matanikau to investigate the Jap offer to surrender. Kukum, I found, was a group of tin-roofed shacks along the coast, with a few little piers built out into the water. The shacks had been severely damaged by our shelling; there was scarcely a wall that was not pocked by H.E. fragments.

Behind the row of houses and shacks, shells had ripped into a co-coanut grove, and struck squarely into a gasoline dump; it was here that we had seen the great fire on the morning of our landing. Evidently explosions had run through the fuel dump like wildfire, for the charred drums were puffed up like burned marshmallows, as if they had exploded from the inside outwards.

But here too, I was told, much usable material had been captured by our people, including food, an abundance of machinery, and some untouched stores of gasoline and oil, as well as the guns and ammunition.

The plan of our patrol to Matanikau today was explained to me by Capt. Kaempfer, who was leading the expedition. The pompoms were going to fire a few more rounds in the direction of the Jap-occupied village, in the hope that the white flag would be run up again. Then our patrol would be in a position to move in and investigate. That was the plan; what actually happened was far different.

As we were about to start, Capt. Gale urged us to watch carefully for snipers. One of his men was shot in the stomach by a Jap last night, before the Jap was killed, he said. And another marine was shot in the leg, this morning, without ever seeing his assailant.

"I don't want to be an alarmist," said Capt. Gale, "but there might be snipers in any of these trees. It's best to keep a sharp lookout."

We watched the trees carefully as we moved out of the bivouac area and started down the coast, keeping about a quarter of a mile inland so as to avoid being seen by the enemy during our approach to Matanikau.

But we saw no Japs for some hours, though there were several false alarms. At about 9:30 a runner appeared from one of our flanking platoons as we halted for a rest. "Captain," he said to Capt. Kaempfer, "there are some Japs over to our left rear." At the word, our men scattered and took cover. But no Japs developed.

At 10:10 we saw the figure of a man at the foot of a tree, down the path ahead of us. He appeared to be wearing brown clothing. The brown mass did not move as we approached.

Soon we could see that it was a Jap sitting by the tree with a blanket drawn up over his knee. At about fifty yards Capt. Kaempfer leveled his pistol at the man. But the captain did not pull the trigger, for the figure still sat as motionless as stone.

The captain slipped the pistol back into his holster. "Never mind," he said. "He's dead." As we passed the stinking body, the captain pulled the blanket over the puffy face. Evidently the Jap had died of wounds received in our naval bombardment, and the body had been drawing flies for several days.

At 10:17, Capt. Kaempfer halted our column. "There are people ahead of us," he said. He had a good long look with his field glasses.

"I think they're marines," he said. They were: a platoon which had gotten ahead of our advance.

"We thought you were going to open fire on us," said one of the lads as we caught up with them.

"We almost did," said Capt. Kaempfer, with emotion.

We had heard the pompoms firing their scheduled rounds behind us, but when I peeped through the foliage along the shore and had a look in the direction of Matanikau, there was no white flag visible. Not today.

We paused in a clearing where a few tall breadfruit trees stood, chalk white and stately, and a deserted thatch hut squatted in the grass. This clearing, we knew, was quite close to Matanikau. But after the long march without contacting any enemy, and the several false alarms of the morning, we were disinclined to believe we would run into any force of Japs.

I talked with two marines who told me, with great gusto, how they had fought and killed two Japs last night. "We were looking in some tents at Kukum," said Corp. Edward P. Antecki (of Detroit), "when I saw the Japs. I hollered, and we started after 'em. They ran and got in behind a bush and started shooting.

"We charged right at 'em," continued Corp. Antecki. "I only had a pistol, so I had to get right on top of 'em before I could shoot. I fired five or six shots."

Private Reynolds (P.F.C. Terry Reynolds of Philadelphia) was eager to tell his story of the action. "There were two Japs, like stragglers," he said. "They got in a hole. We ran right in on 'em. I used up a whole clip of bullets while we were running up. I had to dive into a hole and get out another clip and load, so I could shoot some more."

I asked Pvt. Reynolds if charging the Japs in the open was not a dangerous procedure. "As long as they're trying to sight on you, you're all right," he said. "If they're aimin' at you, they can't hit you."

There was a little crack at the edge of the clearing where we had halted. A rickety bamboo bridge crossed the creek, and beyond it lay a thick tangle of jungle foliage. The trail which we had followed thus far, however, continued through the jungle—a good, wide swath.

I stood on our side of the bridge and looked down this trail with my field glasses and saw something that made me start. Three or four tense figures of men stood in the center of the trail, several hundred yards away. They were looking in our direction.

Others of our people had spotted the Japs, for Japs they were. But for the moment we were not sure.

There were three or four of us standing in the path, looking at the Japs, and they were squinting at us, not yet sure that we were enemies. (The Jap Navy field uniform looks much like our marine utility suit.)

"Those are our men," said one marine.

"I don't think they are," said another. And in the quick flash of a moment, we were sure and the Japs were sure. "Take cover!" someone shouted, and we hit the ground, while, simultaneously, the Japs vanished from the trail, disappearing as quickly as a frightened school of fish.

After that we formed up quickly and pushed across the bridge and down the trail. Now we kept cautiously to the sides of the trail, using the trees as protection. Squads spread out fan-like to the left, in the jungle, and to the right, along the beach, to protect our flanks.

At 11:10, we heard the cry "Halt," to our left and ahead, and there was a rifle shot, which was in turn answered by another shot of a peculiarly sharp, high pitch. Then there was a burst of machine-gun fire. Then silence, as we pushed forward along the trail.

"What happened?" I asked a marine who looked very nervous.

"It sounded like a Jap .25 caliber to me," he said.

At 11:20 a runner came in from our right flank to say that two Jap landing boats had been found on the beach.

I worked my way to the beach, through a tangle of vines, ferns and stunted pineapple plants, and had a good look at the boats. They were about forty feet long, with gunwales ornamentally curved like a pagoda—not like the straight, powerful lines of our own landing boats. Each had a bin-like hold for troops and a movable ramp, which could be let down to allow the troops passage to a beach, at the bow.

There was a small wheel-house with a shield of metal plate at the stern. But the shield was obviously ineffective, for on one of the boats it was punctured on both sides by bullet holes.

The Japanese had evidently been living aboard this craft. In the little cramped cabin under the wheel-house, we found bottles of saki, cases of hardtack and cans of meat. Also a small envelope containing a spent bullet—obviously one of those which had raked the wheel-house, and had been kept as a souvenir by one of the Japs.

It was 11:40, and we were working our way down the beach at the fringe of the jungle, when there came a sudden spattering of sharp rifle reports to our left and ahead. Deeper-toned rifles took up the chorus, machine guns joined in, and the shower of sound became a rainstorm. Jap riflemen and machine gunners had opened up on our left flank, and our own rifles, sub-machine and machine guns were returning the fire.

The sound of firing was coming from farther down the beach, too, and it took me only a second or two to flop amidst a row of marines who had taken cover behind a long white log which lay athwart the strip of sand.

We lay there a few minutes while the marines fired down the beach and into the jungle on the left, and then I noticed all of a sudden that our lads had pulled their heads down, way down, and were lying extremely flat on the sand. In a minute I knew the reason. A marine on the far end of the log had been hit; he was holding one hand over the lower part of his face.

"Corpsman!" somebody shouted. "Pass the word back for a corpsman. We've got a wounded man here!"

The exchange of firing grew hotter. The marines behind the log had spotted two Japs down the beach. They were firing with automatic rifles set for full automatic fire. The Japs answered with flat-toned, rapid-paced machine-gun fire.

Down the beach one of the Japs had jumped up and was running for the jungle. "There he goes!" was the shout. "Riddle the son-of-a-bitch!" And riddled he was.

There was a lull in the firing. I scrambled for the jungle fringe, and worked my way back to the trail. I had just reached the edge of it, when another fusillade of firing broke out ahead of me. Again I heard the shout: "Pass the word back for a corpsman."

As I crawled along the edge of the trail, in the direction from which the firing had come, a breathless marine told me the news. "Lieut. Gately's been shot," he said.

Again the request for a corpsman came back. There were three of these medical aides near me. I saw one of the three, Pharmacist's Mate Wesley Haggard, get to his feet and start forward. "Hell, I'll go," he said. "Might as well get shot now as any time."

But he did not get shot. For some reason, the Japs were holding their fire for a few moments.

The moments lengthened into minutes. I got up, and followed in Haggard's steps. The Japs did not fire.

The lull in the firing continued, and more marines left their cover and began to walk forward in the open, along the trail. It was a favorite Japanese stunt, as we found out before this day was over, to hold their fire until we got very bold and forgot about cover and then start shooting.

I found Lieut. Gately (John J. Gately of West Roxbury, Mass.) lying on his back and smoking a cigarette. Corpsman Haggard had tended him well. Clean white bandage had been placed over wounds in the chest and one leg.

"How do you feel?" I asked Gately, realizing the question was foolish. But what else, after all, can one say to a wounded friend?

"O.K.," he said, and tried to smile. He motioned feebly toward his chest. "Only flesh wound," he said.

"I saw the Jap sighting in on me," he said. "Thought it was a marine. Said, 'Hold your fire.' Then I saw it was a Jap. We both tried to fire; both had safeties on, couldn't." Gately grinned. "Jap got off the first shots," he said. "I got off burst of five."

One of the shots Lieut. Gately had fired from his sub-machine gun, said a marine, had hit the Jap in the lungs. "He's over there under a tree now," said the marine.

I found the Jap lying on his back with his legs drawn up. He was mute, and his face was expressionless. His beady little eyes blinked a bit, but his breathing was very faint. "Pretty far gone," said Corpsman Haggard, standing next to me.

Back on the trail, I saw another of our wounded, in the grass. A truss of bandages covered one side of his chest. He had been shot through the shoulder.

The man whom I had seen hit on the beach was not badly wounded. Evidently a ricochet bullet had struck him in the mouth.

Now the trail was fairly well filled with marines. And so the Japs began to fire again. First came the crack of a rifle ahead; then several more, apparently coming from all sides, and above.

We took cover before the Japs could score any hits. I crouched amidst some sharp-edged pineapple plants, behind a tree. But the Japs were firing from our rear now. Evidently there were snipers in the trees back there. It was hard to take cover under the circumstances.

I heard a bullet go phffft over my head, and another plop into the underbrush beside me. I moved into a denser part of the jungle—quickly.

Then the firing stopped; our officers held a hasty council of war, and it was decided to return to Kukum, and come back to

Matanikau later with a greater force of troops and clean out the Japanese sniper net. So, sending our wounded back on a jeep, we made the long tedious trek back to base.

At Kukum, we heard "scuttlebutt" about the great sea battle which was fought yesterday to the northwest of Guadalcanal. In that battle, which had kept us aware and worried through much of the early morning, five of our cruisers had been lost, according to the rumor. Five Japanese cruisers had also been sunk in subsequent action yesterday. That was the story. There was no official word on the matter at Marine Corps headquarters, except the announcement that the Australian cruiser *Canberra* had been sunk.

(Later it was learned that we had lost four cruisers in the battle of the early hours of yesterday morning. The ships were the *Canberra*, the *Astoria*, the *Vincennes* and the *Quincy*.)

In the evening I went to a tent camp near the seashore, the camp of Capt. Hawkins, who had been my roommate aboard ship during the approach to Guadalcanal. Capt. Hawkins told me his assault company, which with Capt. Kaempfer's troops had seized the beach-head on Guadalcanal, had encountered *no* resistance the first day. They had captured five Jap laborers, and that was all.

Capt. Hawkins, I found, had achieved the honor of being the first American invader to set foot on Guadalcanal. His boat had hit the shore first. Capt. Kaempfer's boat, the second to touch shore, had been about seventy-five yards behind.

I decided to spend the night in Capt. Hawkins' tent, and was weary enough, after the long day's trek and excitement, to settle down to a good sleep. But just as darkness was setting in, we got word that a submarine had been sighted offshore. That made the business of sleeping difficult, especially in view of the fact that our tent was only some 200 yards from the water's edge.

Would the Jap counter-invasion come tonight? Would the submarine, or submarines, come in close and shell our camp? Whatever happened, we would bear the brunt of it.

The other officers in the tent were jittery. They talked like magpies, without ever a breathing space, far into the night. The favorite topic was home.

Fortunately, there was no landing attempt, no shelling by Japanese submarines, that night.

TUESDAY, AUGUST 11

It was a quiet day. At headquarters, I learned that the transport which I had seen burning so brightly after the air raid of August 8th had been the *George F. Elliot;* that when all efforts failed to bring her raging fires under control, she was torpedoed by one of our own destroyers. The U.S.S. *Jarvis,* a destroyer, was attacked that day (and later listed as lost when the Navy could find no trace of her). But the fact that the Japs had lost all of the attacking planes more than evened the score.

We heard the news from Tulagi that conquest of objectives in that area had been virtually completed, except for isolated snipers. Tulagi, Gavutu, Tanambogo were conquered and thoroughly occupied by our troops. We had a good foothold on Florida (Ngela) Island. About 400 Japs had been killed on Tulagi, 800 on Gavutu and Tanambogo, we heard. Bob Miller—the only other news correspondent on the island—and I made arrangements to go to Tulagi tomorrow.

Our patrols failed to contact any concentrations of Japs on Guadalcanal today. Lookouts along the shore reported seeing several Jap submarines; but there was no shelling of our shore positions, during the day or at night. The night's sleep was undisturbed, extremely welcome.

WEDNESDAY, AUGUST 12

Down at the beach early this morning, and, after considerable delay, finally boarded the small fleet of three motorboats which was to take us to Tulagi. Two of the craft were the regulation type of landing boat. The third was a lighter, filled with drums of gasoline. For armament we had .30 caliber guns, on the landing boats, and .50 caliber on the lighter.

As we set out in the glaring sun, Marine Gunner Banta (Sheffield M. Banta of Staten Island, N.Y.), in charge of our boat, warned our crew to keep an especially sharp lookout for airplanes. Also, he said, for submarines; but I could see that our crewmen spent most of their time anxiously watching the sky; that their principal worry was a strafing attack from the air, which turned out to be a mistake in judgment.

Three times before we reached the middle of Tulagi Bay, Gunner Banta borrowed my field glasses to investigate an object in the sky. Twice, the objects were birds.

The third time there had been an excited warning from Seaman John R. Tull (of Wachapreague, Va.), who manned one of our machine guns. Gunner Banta took the field glasses and focused them nervously.

"It's a plane," he shouted. And our machine guns swung around and angled toward the sector of the sky where he had been looking.

Then, suddenly, we could all see the plane. It was coming straight for us. I suppose in that moment we all realized how helpless is a small boat under the attack of a well-armed aircraft. One felt suddenly very much alone, out there in the middle of the bay, with at least ten miles of water on every side.

"Don't shoot until we've identified it," ordered Banta, as our gunners pulled back their bolts and charged their machine guns. "Remember there's a PBY scheduled to come in today."

So we waited, tensely, while the spot of the plane against the sky grew larger. And then at last we could see the distinct outline of a seaplane hull, the high wing and twin motor nacelles of a P-boat.

"It's ours," said Gunner Banta. And we began to breathe freely again.

The pretty flying boat came toward us for a few miles more, then swung in a slow curve toward the shore of Guadalcanal.

We moved happily on our way. The small green spot that was Tulagi and the rugged blue backdrop of Florida Island were looming larger and more distinctly on our horizon. We had only about four or five miles still to go to reach our destination. The few flecks of spray that came over our bow felt good and cool, and the breeze caused by our movement was refreshing.

"I think that may be a submarine, over there," said someone in the boat. And we looked where he pointed, with a great inclination to disbelieve.

But it *was* a submarine—a long low black shape, with a rise at the center where the conning tower stood. He was moving away from us. But when we spotted him, he also spotted us; slowly he swung around and headed so as to cross our bows.

He was now a mile or two from us, to our port side and ahead. We could see the line of white spray threading along the base of the slim black hull as he picked up speed. We were going to have a *race* on our hands. We knew that then, and I knew that I would not again scoff at the melodramatic formula of Race for Life or Race with Death as being improbable.

In our little boat there was confusion for a few moments as everybody shouted at once. There was some doubt as to what we should do. Should we run back for Guadalcanal or head for the open sea or cut for the eastern, right-hand tip of Florida Island and try to reach it before the Jap cut us off? There was no time for debate. Gunner Banta gave the order to head for Florida, and Coxswain Charles N. Stickney (of Newbury, Mich.) swung our helm sharply to the right and opened the throttle.

Our boat began to jar and pound against the choppy waves as we suddenly picked up speed, and sheets of spray bowled over the bow and drenched us.

The other boats of our little fleet were also pounding along at full speed, tossing plumes of white spray over their cockpits.

But the submarine was gaining. It was evident that he was moving swiftly; that our race with him was going to be close; and that we might have to swim for it, even if we won the race.

There was one item we had not even considered: shellfire. It was a horrifying sight to see geysers of water leaping up between us and the submarine, for we knew then that he was ranging in on us. We heard the sharp bang of the shells exploding, and knew they would soon be coming dangerously close.

Then there were more geysers, closer to the submarine, and we were mystified for a moment, until we heard the booming of gunfire coming from Tulagi shore. We knew then, and were thankful, that a shore battery was opening up on the submarine.

But the shells were not yet falling near the sub. And each time he fired his gun, he ranged closer to us.

I tried to fix my field glasses on the submarine, but our boat jerked and bounced so, and the spray doused the lenses in such steady downpour, that the attempt was futile.

Our clothes were soaking. I started to wrap my field glasses in my field jacket, then undid the bundle. No use trying to keep things dry. We were going to have to swim for it. I could see that. The submarine was gaining on us, and a shell landed only a hundred yards or so astern of us.

Just then we saw that the men in the other landing boat were waving wildly at us. One of the seamen had jumped up on the boat's motor hatch and was trying to send us a message by signal flag. A haze of smoke was coming from the motor hatch of the other boat. We could see that it was in trouble. Our boat swung over next to the crippled one and we bumped gunwales, pulled apart, and smashed together again as the two boats, running at top speed, ran parallel courses. The crew of the other craft fell, slid and vaulted into our boat. Lieut. Herb Merrillat (Herbert L. Merrillat of Monmouth, Ill.), marine public relations officer and ordinarily quite a dignified young man, jumped over from the other boat and landed, a disordered collection of arms and legs, on the bottom of our boat. He was wearing white sox. In the haste of the moment, he had left his shoes behind. Even in that moment, the sight of his descent was humorous.

But we had lost precious time in picking up the other crew. Now the submarine had gained a good lead, and our fate seemed hopeless. I told myself that this was my last day of existence, as it seemed certain to be.

But the splashes of the shore batteries' firing were coming closer to the submarine now. We saw several that appeared to be only a few yards from the conning tower. And one of our crewmen shouted "Smoke, she's smoking!" I could not see any smoke. But it was evident that the shells were now beginning to come too close to the submarine for his comfort. For the sub was turning away from us and toward the open sea to the west. We were saved by the bell. The ordeal was over.

We sailed into the calm waters of Tulagi harbor, down the narrow passage of water walled by greenery and came to a small wooden dock. It was distinctly a pleasure to set foot on land again.

The buildings along the shore did not seem greatly damaged by shellfire, although some of the walls were pocked by bullet holes. We made our way to a frame house where, we had been told, we would find Gen. Rupertus and the officers of his staff.

Gen. Rupertus was a dynamic type, younger than the average general. He showed us to a bare room, where we sat on the edge of a table while we talked. This was his office. There had not been much time to set up the creature comforts on Tulagi.

The general summarized the fighting on Tulagi, Gavutu and Tanambogo. The toughest job, he said, had been to clean out scores of dugout caves filled with Japs. Each cave, he said, had been a fortress in itself, filled with Japs who were determined to resist until they were all killed. The only effective way to finish off these caves, he said, had been to take a charge of dynamite and thrust it down the narrow cave entrance. After that had been done, and the cave blasted, you could go in with a sub-machine gun and finish off the remaining Japs.

The Jap dugouts—"dungeons," the general called them—had been found in great numbers on Tulagi and Gavutu. Exterminating them had been a tedious job, particularly on Tulagi, where only yesterday the last of them had been finished off.

"You've never seen such caves and dungeons," said the general. "There would be thirty or forty Japs in them. And they absolutely refused to come out, except in one or two isolated cases."

The general was enthusiastic about the bravery the marines had displayed in the fighting here. "There should be forty or fifty Congressional Medals awarded to these people," he said.

"I don't know how to express it," he said, and it was plain to see that he was having difficulty putting his admiration into words. "I think the United States should be just as proud of these people who gave their lives," he began, and paused, groping for a sufficiently glorious phrase, but it would not come. He finished the sentence lamely, "Gave their lives in the most wonderful work in our history."

He tried again. "I mean that when it comes to bravery, there isn't anybody in the world that can beat us," he said. "I don't think the United States has an episode in its history that can touch what's been done here."

We talked to Col. Edson (Col. Merritt A. Edson of Chester, Vt.), commanding officer of the Raiders, who had assaulted and taken Tulagi. He was a wiry man with a lean, hard face, partly covered by a sparse, spiky growth of grayish beard; his light blue eyes were tired and singularly red-rimmed in appearance, for he was weary now from long days of fighting, and his red eyebrows and eyelashes, being almost invisible, heightened the effect. But his eyes were as cold as steel, and it was interesting to notice that even when he was being pleasant, they never smiled. He talked rapidly, spitting his words out like bullets, his hard-lipped mouth snapping shut like a trap. Hardly a creature of sunlight and air, he; but I could see that he was a first-class fighting man. (Col. Edson later won two outstanding victories on Guadalcanal, and was awarded the Navy Cross.)

Col. Edson summarized the Tulagi campaign. "The Japs had one battalion, of about 450 men, on the island," he said. "They were all troops—no laborers. All of their defenses were located on the southeast part of the island. Our landing was [at 8:15 A.M. on Friday, August 12th] at the northwest part. There were only small obstructionist groups out there.

"The Japanese casualties were about 400. Not a single Nip gave up. [One prisoner was taken; he had been dazed by a close mortar burst.] In one of the holes there were seventeen dead Japs, when a man went in to get the radio. But there were still two Nips alive. They hit the man and one other who followed him later.

"It was the same in all the dugouts. We found that an officer was alive in one of them. We sent an interpreter out to get him. The interpreter came to the mouth of the cave and asked if the officer wanted to surrender. The answer was a grenade.

"The northwest section of the island, where we landed, was very thick bush—jungle country. There were only a few enemy outposts along the coast in that sector, and we lost only one man, from sniper fire, as we went in to the beach. Our plan was to go inland to a ridge line which ran the length of the island, and then change direction and work along the ridge, giving the men on top of the ridge a position to shoot down.

"The terrain was difficult. It took us three hours to get through a mile and a half of ground.

"As we came out of the jungle, we really ran into trouble. There the Nips had 200 men in dugouts and rock emplacements with snipers scattered around. Even after we got control, machine-gun nests in dugouts held up our advance for several hours.

"It was impossible to approach the Nip dugouts except from one direction. You had to crawl up on the cliffs and drop dynamite inside while you were under fire all the time."

While the right flank of the Raiders was occupied in trying to root out the Japanese dugouts, said the colonel, the center and left flank pushed around the Jap center of opposition and down the ridge which formed the backbone of the island. They met fierce resistance from snipers and machine gunners, and one company suffered 15 percent casualties, including two officers.

"The snipers would lie still until our men passed, then shoot from the rear," said Col. Edson. "There were snipers everywhere in trees or buildings, behind rocks."

Despite opposition and casualties, the Raiders drove down the ridge-back of the island, said the colonel, until they ran into a shovel-shaped ravine with three steep sides. Here they met the stiffest Jap resistance. The walls of the ravine surrounded a flat space which the British had used as a cricket field. Now the Japs had dug innumerable large caves into the limestone walls of the ravine, and from the narrow mouths of these dugouts they fired rifles, automatic rifles and machine guns. There was "continuous crossfire across the ravine," said the colonel.

By the time the marines reached this area, it was dusk and they halted for the night. But the Japs were organizing a counter-attack.

"At 10:30 that night the Japs counter-attacked," said the colonel. They broke through between C and A Companies, and C Company was temporarily cut off. The Japs worked their way along the ridge, and came to within fifty to seventy-five yards of my command post. The Nips were using hand grenades, rifles and machine guns. We suffered quite a few casualties, as our men fought hard to hold the Japs back. One machine-gun company lost 50 percent of its non-commissioned officers. Finally, the enemy was thrown back.

"The next day the Raiders, aided by support troops under Col. Rosecrans (Col. Harold E. Rosecrans of Washington, D.C.), cleaned up the southeastern end of the island.

"The Nips were still in the pocket [in the cricket-field area]. But we had positions for machine guns and mortars on three sides of them. We closed in on the pocket and cleaned up some of the dugouts. By three o'clock that [Sunday] afternoon we had complete physical control of the island. A few groups of snipers and machine gunners remained. It took days to finish them off.

"The Nip defense was apparently built around small groups in dugouts with no hope of escape. They would stay in there as long as there was one live Jap. There was a radio for communication in nearly every one of these holes.

"We pulled out thirty-five dead Japs from one dugout. In another we took out thirty. Some of these people had been dead for three days. But others were still in there shooting.

"In none of these places was there any water or food. The Nips had evidently made a dash for their dugouts when the naval bombardment came, without stopping for provisions.

"In one case there were three Japs cornered. They had one pistol. They fired the pistol until they had three shots left. Then one Jap shot the two others and killed himself."

Col. Edson listed some of the outstanding heroes among his Raider troops. Maj. Kenneth D. Bailey (of Danville, Ill.) had acted with great bravery in trying to knock out a Jap dugout emplacement which was holding up our advance.

"The cave was dug in the ravine," said the colonel. "The enemy fire was so severe that our men could not advance.

"Bailey got on top of the cave by crawling. He tried to kick a hole in the top. When that failed, he tried to kick the rocks away at the foot of the entrance. While he was attempting to do that, one of the Nips stuck out a rifle and shot him in the leg."

Then there was Gunnery Sgt. Angus Goss, a one-man demolition squad. When one Japanese cave had resisted with particular stubbornness Sgt. Goss had tried throwing in hand grenades and these had been promptly returned by the Japs inside. The sergeant then tried holding the grenades for three seconds before hurling them, but even in this case the Japs caught the missiles and threw them back. The patient sergeant then got TNT and thrust it into the hold. But the Japs shoved the TNT out of the cave and the dynamite exploded outside, driving splinters into Goss' leg. He then "got mad" and went into the cave firing full tilt with his sub-machine gun, and killed the four Japs who remained alive. Eight other dead Japs were found in the dugout.

We visited the cricket-field ravine where the toughest Jap resistance had been met. The stink of rotting bodies was very noticeable. We passed several piles of shattered rock lying against one of the limestone sides of the ravine. These were cave-mouths which had been blown in with dynamite.

Some of the cave-mouths were intact. Braving the odor of the dead inside—the Raiders had not found time yet to bury their foes—one could see that the entrances to these Jap strongholds were long and narrow, affording very good defensive positions.

We had to step over six or seven bodies which lay in front of one of the cave-mouths. They were bloated like overstuffed sausages. Other bodies were scattered over the floor of the ravine.

We talked with several other staff officers before we shoved off in a landing boat for Gavutu. One was Lieut. Comdr. Robert L. Strickland (of Enid, Okla.), director of air-support operations. Comdr. Strickland told us how all the Jap planes in the Tulagi vicinity—eighteen in number—had been destroyed before they could get into the air on the morning of August 7th.

"Our Navy fighter planes caught all the Jap planes on the water or on their ramps at Gavutu," he said. "There were nine seaplane fighters, one four-engine bomber and eight seaplanes. They were set afire, most of them sank, and all were destroyed. We had *no* air opposition here."

Flight Officer Cecil E. Spencer, one of the Australian guides who had accompanied our landing forces, told us how his boat had been the first invading craft to touch the soil of the Solomon Islands. The marine troops which he had accompanied had hit the beach at the western end of Florida Island, near Haleta Village, at 7:40 on the morning of August 7th. They were under the command of a Capt. Crane.

They had encountered no opposition in landing, although they discovered traces of Japs in one or two native houses in the village. Leaving an outpost on a hill which commanded Haleta, Capt. Crane, Flight Officer Spencer and the larger part of these marine troops had left the area. They were then ordered to Gavutu to reinforce the embattled troops who had landed there at midday.

"We reached Gavutu at about dusk," said Flight Officer Spencer. "But by that time, Tanambogo was under control. The marines, however, had been unable to cross the narrow causeway leading to Tanambogo. The officer in charge told us to make a landing at Tanambogo.

"We had about five minutes of naval gunfire support prior to landing. As we were coming in, the last shell hit a fuel dump on the beach, lighting up the beach like day. As we came in the Japs opened fire from their dugouts on the Tanambogo hill.

"Only two boatloads of our men had got ashore. The coxswain of the third boat had been hit in the head by a bullet and killed, and there had been some confusion as to who was to take over the wheel. In the confusion, the boat got turned about and all the other boats followed.

"We on shore were jammed between two piers. The only cover we could get was afforded by the side of the pier [the pier was concrete]. As soon as we opened fire the Japs spotted our tracers, and in addition we were silhouetted against the flaming oil of the fuel dump."

One of the two boats retired, taking wounded, and Flight Officer Spencer went with it. He came back to Tanambogo when the boat returned.

"We found only six men in the boat which had been left at Tanambogo," he said. "They said that the Japs had raided our positions along the piers, and that they considered Capt. Crane and the other marines had been wiped out. But Capt. Crane arrived with six of his men. They had escaped from the Japs by hiding in the bushes.

"At nine or ten o'clock two more marines returned, swimming naked toward our boats. Our people fired. But the marines in the water yelled and were saved."

After that, said Flight Officer Spencer, the remnant of Capt. Crane's forces withdrew, and a much larger detachment of marines, under Lieut. Col. Robert G. Hunt, landed the following morning at four o'clock and took Tanambogo.

We talked also with kindly, affable Father James J. Fitzgerald, a Chicago priest who had accompanied the troopers on their attack at Gavutu. The moment he stepped ashore, under enemy fire, said Father Fitzgerald, the man ahead of him had been killed. After that, the priest had led a charmed existence, giving church rites to twenty-seven dead and forty-seven wounded on the open Gavutu beach, despite the fact that snipers were shooting fairly continuously.

We were anxious to visit the Gavutu and Tanambogo battle grounds and secured permission to go. We went by landing boat. Our guide was a sturdy young man in high boots, a Capt. Stallings (Capt. George R. Stallings of Augusta, Ga.). He was the temporary commanding officer.

I noticed that Capt. Stallings' steady blue eyes looked weary almost to the point of being haunted. He spoke in a very low voice, as if he were still under fire and did not want to give away his position through loud talking.

We sat on the floor of our boat en route from Tulagi to Gavutu, for we had to pass on the way through a narrow strait where, said Capt. Stallings, there were still snipers.

When we had landed at the shattered concrete docks on Gavutu, Capt. Stallings gave us a concise outline of the attack there.

Only a few hundred troops had come in on the assault against Gavutu, said Capt. Stallings, because it was expected that Jap opposition would be small. (By far the heaviest opposition had been expected on Guadalcanal.) But it had turned out that there were an estimated 1,370 Japs on Gavutu and the secondary objective, Tanambogo.

Here as everywhere the Japs had been caught by surprise, said Capt. Stallings. The first company of the troops had landed with only sniper fire to harass them. The second company had met heavy fire from a distance 500 to 600 yards from shore, all the way to the beach. The third company had suffered heavy casualties while approaching the shore and landing.

The troopers planned to take Gavutu first, then move on to Tanambogo, said Capt. Stallings. This meant they first had to storm a steep hill, 148 feet high, on Gavutu. This hill, and another 120 feet high on Tanambogo, commanded the docks where the assault troops landed. The hills, and particularly Gavutu Hill, were honeycombed with dugout fortresses like those which had been encountered on Tulagi. The Japs manning these dugouts were well armed with machine guns, rifles and automatic rifles.

"The emplacements had to be blasted with TNT," said Capt. Stallings. "But it was hard to finish off the Japs. A good many of the caves were connected, and made a sort of labyrinth. You'd shoot at a Jap in one hole, and he'd come up in another."

From the dock we had a good view of the two hills, for in fact they seemed to occupy practically all of the land space on the two small islands. It was as if an overgrown beehive or anthill had been planted on each island. The two land bodies are connected by a long, narrow causeway apparently built of sea shells.

We passed several concrete-walled, metal-roofed buildings as we left the dock. They had evidently been storehouses for a certain large soap company. Now the walls and roofs had been riddled by bullets and shell fragments.

One of the larger buildings along the shore had been a company store. The marines had used it as a hospital. "Dr. Burke, Dr. Eisenberg and Dr. Thorne worked here continuously for three days," said Capt. Stallings, "under heavy fire. The Japs took special pains to throw a lot of fire into the place."

Incidentally, said Capt. Stallings, our casualties in the Gavutu-Tanambogo campaign were seventy-seven: twenty-seven killed and fifty wounded. The Japs had probably lost more than 800 troops; a few boatloads of them had escaped to neighboring Florida Island, and "about five" had been taken prisoner. (A later count revealed there were nine.)

Capt. Stallings told us the stories of some of the heroes of Gavutu as we climbed the exceedingly steep hill on the island. One of the first marine casualties, he said, had been Maj. Robert H. Williams (of New Bern, N.C.), who had led the first wave of troops trying to storm this very hill.

But the outstanding hero had been Capt. (now Maj.) Harold L. Torgerson (of Valley Stream, L.I.), who had blasted more than fifty Jap caves with homemade dynamite bombs. His method was to tie thirty sticks of dynamite together, run to the cave mouth while four of his men covered it with rifles and sub-machine guns, light the fuse, shove the TNT in amongst the Japs and run like hell.

In his day's work Capt. Torgerson had used twenty cases of dynamite and all the available matches. His wristwatch strap had been broken by a bullet which creased his wrist. Another grazing bullet had struck his rear end. But that did not stop his pyrotechnic campaign.

On one occasion, said Capt. Stallings, the wild and woolly Torgerson had attached a five-gallon can of gasoline to one of his homemade bombs, "to make it better." That bomb went off with a great roar, knocked Torgerson down and blasted away most of his pants—as well as blowing in the roof of a Jap dugout. Torgerson's only comment, said Capt. Stallings, was, "Boy, that was a pisser, wasn't it!"

Two other troopers had distinguished themselves in disposing of Japanese dugouts, said Capt. Stallings. Corp. Ralph W. Fordyce (of Conneaut Lake, Pa.) had cleaned up six Jap emplacements in each of which there had been at least six Japs. In one case he had dragged eight Jap bodies from a dugout which he had just entered with his sub-machine gun. Corp. Johnnie Blackman had blown in five dugouts with TNT; Sgt. Max Koplow (of Toledo, Ohio) had disposed of the Japs in two dugouts connected by tunnels; he had earlier killed three Japanese who were "playing dead" amongst the corpses on Gavutu beach.

Platoon Sgt. Harry M. Tully (of Hastings, Neb.) had picked off three members of a Japanese machine-gun crew at an extraordinarily long range.

The Japs had fought with almost unbelievable stubbornness. Some of them cached their rifles, then swam out into the water and returned at night to pick up their arms and snipe at our troops.

But the marines had fought with the greatest ferocity. Corp. George F. Grady (of New York City) had charged a group of eight Japs on Gavutu Hill, by himself. He had killed two with his sub-machine gun; when the gun jammed, he used it as a club to kill one more Jap, and then, dropping his gun, had drawn the sheath knife he carried on his belt and stabbed two more of the enemy, before he was himself killed by the three Japs who remained unharmed.

P.F.C. Ronald A. Burdo (of Detroit, Mich.) had charged the hilltop, firing his automatic rifle from his hip, and had killed eight Japs.

There were others in the long chronicle of heroism recited by Capt. Stallings as we climbed and paused at the top of Gavutu Hill, but these were outstanding.

I should have liked to hunt up and talk to some of the surviving heroes of the Gavutu campaign, but our coxswain was anxious to be on the move back to Tulagi before sunset.

"The marines shoot anything that moves after dark," he said.

We had only a little time left, then, so we decided to round up our excursion with a quick trip to Tanambogo.

Climbing down the steep Gavutu Hill, I wondered how the troops had ever succeeded in taking this island. Looking down from that precipitous hill to the strip of docks where the marines had landed gave one the commanding feeling of looking into the palm of one's own hand. I thought then: if I did not know that the marines had taken this island hill, I would have said that the job, especially against a well-armed, numerically superior force, was impossible.

We rode in a boat from Gavutu to Tanambogo, bypassing the long connecting causeway, where the marines had tried without success to effect a crossing. We landed on the Tanambogo docks, where other marine troops had finally come ashore. We passed two burned-out American tanks. These, said Capt. Stallings, were the vanguard of the American landing. The defending Japs had jammed the treads with crowbars, swarmed over the tanks, and set them afire with rags soaked in gasoline.

"The Japs screamed and hollered, and actually beat on the tanks with their fists and knives," said Capt. Stallings. One of the tank commanders, he said, had opened the hatch and killed twenty-three of the swarming Nips with a machine gun, before he was stabbed to death. "I counted the bodies myself," said Stallings.

On a board ramp on Tanambogo shore, we saw the remnants of two of the Zero floatplanes which had been set afire by our strafing Navy fighters.

Then it was time to go back to Tulagi; the sun was beginning to go down and the coxswain of our boat was growing more and more anxious.

Back at Tulagi, there was business to attend to. We were scheduled to leave for Guadalcanal at 4:30 tomorrow morning, and I wanted to make sure that we would have a fast boat for the return trip. I was certain that the Jap who had chased us today would be lying off the harbor entrance, waiting.

We got the boat. For Gen. Rupertus had heard of our narrow escape this morning, and knew our predicament. But the longer I thought about the trip, the more convinced I became that it would be suicidal. I was sure that the Jap would be so placed that it would be impossible to escape from him as we left the harbor. His detector would locate us easily. And, of course, our little boat, with only machine guns as protection, would be no match for the sub.

We bedded down on the floor of a shack very near the Tulagi dock, so that when we moved in the morning we would not have to pass a line of sentries. I lay awake for hours, tortured by the thought that if we were not fools, we would wait until we could make the trip by air. How about the PBY which had flown into Guadalcanal this morning? was the thought that suddenly occurred to me.

I stepped over the sleeping officers in the shack, waked one who would know, and asked if the PBY could be called on to ferry us back. He said no, that the PBY had already left Guadalcanal and returned to base. I suggested that we might wait until air support arrived at Guadalcanal airport. That would make our trip safe.

But we were carrying dispatches back to Guadalcanal, and could not wait an indefinite period of time until our aircraft showed up. We would have to take our chances.

I felt better then, knowing that we had no alternative except to run for it. But it seemed to me inevitable that we would be caught and sunk, for the sub had obviously decided, this morning, that we were some sort of official boat, worth chasing—and worth waiting for.

I sat on the front steps of the shack, under the soft white stars, and thought that this would be my last night of life. I thought that, all in all, it had been a good life, although it seemed to be ending a little early.

THURSDAY, AUGUST 13

We were up at 4:00 this morning, and down to the dock in the dark. The night had turned cold, as is usual in this climate. The sky had been blacked out by a low overcast.

There were to be two boats in our fleet. One was our own landing boat; the other, a small eighty which was to carry Jap prisoners back to Guadalcanal. Now the prisoners, their hands up, were being led into the small hold of the lighter.

There were ten prisoners, three of them Navy troops, the other seven uniformed laborers. They took their places silently, obediently, as if they expected to be taken out into the bay and drowned, and were resigned to their fate. (Two of them later told an interpreter that they had expected to be killed when captured.)

And so we started out, showing a prearranged signal to warn outposts against shooting at us. And once past the line of sentries we crept along at a low speed, hugging the cover of the shoreline. The water was rough and, despite our low speed, we were drenched by spray.

At about five o'clock, we thought the jig was up. A white point of light like a bright star appeared in the sky to the south, and then the star burgeoned into a greater brightness, casting a flickering sheet of light over the whole sky. It was a flare. The sub, we thought, was looking for us.

Another flare, closer and more directly ahead of us, followed a few moments later. We went through certain maneuvers, which for security reasons cannot be described, to confuse the Japs who at that moment were probably listening to our propeller beat and trying to fix our location through their detector.

We resumed our course, some fifteen minutes later, and there were no more flares. But several times more we went through maneuvers designed to throw off the enemy.

It was six o'clock in the morning, and the sky was growing uncomfortably light, when we passed the last protecting shoulder of land and headed out into the open bay. There would be no land within easy swimming distance now until we had nearly finished our trip. This was our dash for life; the coxswain opened the throttle wide and we pounded hard into the short, high, choppy waves. Solid water began to sluice over the bow in sheets. We were drenched anew with each wave, and the wind was chilling, but we did not slow down. This was no time for comfort.

Somewhere, we had lost a lot of time, fallen far behind our schedule. We had planned to be out in the middle of the bay by 6:30. But at that time we were only a few hundred yards away from the shores of the Tulagi group of islands.

But the submarine—we thank our stars—did not appear. We found later that he had been sighted across the bay, along the Guadalcanal shore, at about that time.

Halfway across the bay the coxswain turned to me and said: "Our chances are about one in three of getting there now." But whatever our chances at that moment, they had certainly improved greatly. The high cloud-girdled mountains of Guadalcanal were becoming more and more distinct ahead of us. We would be there soon—if we did not spot a sub.

Then we were close enough to Guadalcanal to see isolated palm trees clearly against the skyline and rows of bamboo shacks; we knew we were going to make it.

Back at Col. (LeRoy) Hunt's command post, where I am billeted, I heard some bad news; that Col. Goettge, Lieut. Cory, Capt. Ringer, and several others of our personnel are missing on an excursion to Matanikau. Also old Dr. Pratt, the incorrigible adventurer, who went along with the expedition for the fun of it.

The story is that a Japanese prisoner (there are more than 100 on Guadalcanal by this time, mostly labor troops) offered to take Col. Goettge to the village, with the contention that the Japs were willing to surrender.

So Col. Goettge took a party of twenty-six officers and men, and set out in a landing boat for Matanikau. The party made a night landing, ran smack into the middle of a Jap ambush. Col. Goettge was the first man hit.

Only three of the party escaped, by swimming down the coast to Kukum. They were Corp. Joseph Spaulding (of New York City), Sgt. Charles C. Arndt (of Okolona, Miss.), and Sgt. Frank L. Few (of Buckeye, Ariz.). Few and Arndt killed three Japs each in the course of the fight.

Sgt. Few is a swarthy, twenty-two-year-old half Indian, vastly respected by the men because he is, as the marines say, "really rugged." This means he is a tough hombre, and Few certainly looks the part; he has fierce dark eyes, a wiry, muscular body, and he moves with the swift ease of a cat. A flashing white smile, sideburns and scraggly black beard and mustache only intensify the effect.

Sgt. Few told me the story of the ill-fated expedition to Matanikau. He was still a little shaky from the experience. "They got Col. Goettge in the chest right quick. Spaulding and I went up to him, but when I put a hand on him I knew he was dead.

"Just then I saw somebody close by. I challenged him, and he let out a war whoop and came at me. My sub-machine gun jammed. I was struck in the arm and chest with his bayonet, but I knocked his rifle away. I choked him and stabbed him with his own bayonet."

Knowing Col. Goettge was dead, said Few, he started back to join our other marines who had landed. Then he suddenly spotted a Jap in the fork of the two trees. "My own gun was still jammed," he said, "so I borrowed Arndt's pistol and shot the Jap seven times.

"I got my gun to working after that, but I couldn't use the magazine. I had to stick a cartridge in the chamber each time I wanted to shoot. I could only fire one shot at a time. Just then I saw another Jap. I let one go, and it hit him in the face. Then I bashed him with the butt of my gun."

When he got back to the main body of marines, Few found they were dug in for a fight. He dug in, too, using his helmet and hands, and there followed a long exchange of shooting.

Several other Americans had been hit, notably Lieut. Cory, the interpreter, with a bullet in the stomach, and Capt. Ringer. The Japs were closing in for the kill when the sky began to grow light with a pre-dawn glow. Spaulding had earlier made a break for the beach, started to swim for Kukum. Arndt followed. And then Few, stripping down to his underclothes, made a dash for the water.

"It was the end of the rest on the beach," said Few. "The Japs closed in and hacked up our people. I could see swords flashing in the sun."

Few had to swim four and a half miles to reach Kukum, and there are sharks in that water, but he made it. When I talked to him only a few hours later, he did not seem physically tired at all.

I went to Gen. Vandegrift's headquarters, where a table, an unusual luxury on Guadalcanal, was available for typing. But it was difficult to do any work; there were three air-raid alarms, which kept us on the run, although no Japs materialized.

Guadalcanal airport, I find, has turned out to be quite a prize. The runways, it is said at headquarters, are excellent. One huge runway is 3,778 feet long and 160 feet wide, and was surfaced with coral gravel and cement, except for a strip 197 feet long, when we arrived.

Shelters for planes had also been set up by the Japs. And they had left behind five steamrollers, two tractors, a large cache of first-quality cement, and a system of electric lights running the length of the runway.

Back at my tent tonight, I felt a loneliness which could not be gainsaid. Lieut. Cory and Dr. Pratt, both of whom are missing and believed dead on the last Matanikau excursion, bunked in this tent.

The rest of us in the tent, Maj. Phipps, Capt. Narder (of Worcester, Mass., now a major) and Capt. Dickson (also of Worcester and also now a major) lay awake talking for some time, and that helped to allay the shock of worrying about and wondering if we had lost our friends.

During the night I awoke and listened, and watched the segment of sky I could see through the tent door. There were flashes of white light, and distant rumblings, coming from the north. I heard the other men in the tent stirring. They too were watching the sky and listening. We lay a long time silently, and then Don Dickson (Maj. Donald L. Dickson of Worcester, Mass.) summed up our thoughts. "It's only a storm," he said. The rest of us had come to the same conclusion. We joked a little about our jittery nerves and went back to a fitful sleep.

IV

EXPEDITION TO MATANIKAU

FRIDAY, AUGUST 14

Enemy aircraft dropped their first bombs on Guadalcanal today. They had been over before, but this was the first time they actually attacked the island.

The time was 12:15, and I was at Gen. Vandegrift's headquarters, attempting to catch up with my writing, when an outpost phoned in to say the enemy had been spotted. There were eighteen bombers, coming in high.

The air-raid alarm, a dilapidated dinner bell, jangled, and there was a general scurrying for protective foxholes. A few of us, however, went to a clearing to watch the excitement (which I later found to be very bad practice).

In a few seconds, someone shouted, "There they are!" and pointed, and we all looked. Then I saw three of the Japs, silvery and beautiful in the high sky. They were so high that they looked like a slender white cloud moving slowly across the blue. But through my field glasses, I could see the silvery-white bodies quite distinctly: the thin wings, the two slim engine nacelles, the shimmering arcs of the propellers. I was surprised that enemy aircraft, flying overhead with the obvious intention of dropping high explosives upon us, could be so beautiful.

Others said they could see fifteen more Jap bombers, but they were not visible to me at the moment. I watched, my glasses frozen on the flight of three planes, while they cruised slowly, leisurely over the airport.

Suddenly, from directly in front of us, came a swift sequence of explosions, and, in an instantaneous reaction, we hit the deck. But it was one of our own anti-aircraft batteries which we had heard. They were firing fast now; we could see the flashes coming from the gun muzzles, hear the quick reports of the firing.

Up in the blue in front of the three silvery planes, we saw puffs of gray smoke, like small clouds, popping into sudden existence. In some of them we could see a slight dash of bright orange. The shells were bursting. Then we heard the soft whoomp-whoomp-whoomp of the explosions, coming to us late over the long distance. And there were more reports from our guns, more little clouds in the sky, more soft whoomp sounds.

But the anti-aircraft batteries were shooting too low. The planes cruised leisurely, and we saw their wings pass along and over the spreading clouds of the ack-ack bursts.

Then we heard a closely spaced series of explosions, sharp and apparently quite near. The sounds were notably loud, and sharper than any I had heard before. And the ground shook under our feet. The Japs had dropped six bombs (which had fortunately fallen into the water) near Kukum. The planes swung in a slow circle with anti-aircraft bursting behind them, and disappeared into the sky to the south.

Tonight at Col. Hunt's command post we were sitting and talking in the dark, and it was peaceful and soothing to sit in close company and hear the voices close by, with only glowing cigarettes to mark the speakers, when the phone jangled. Lieut. John Wilson, one of the staff officers, said, "Oh oh, here we go," as he picked up the phone, and his predilection for bad news was correct. The news was that five Jap destroyers had been sighted, standing in toward Guadalcanal shore.

We decided that the long-expected Jap counter invasion was on the way. But since there was little we could do about it for the time being except wait for further reports, the talk swung to less serious matters. Don Dickson's embryonic red beard, for instance; the raggedness of the foliage brought forth some disparaging remarks.

I had imagined that in such a situation, the atmosphere would be more tense. But now it seemed perfectly natural to be joking about beards, while there was a Jap invasion in the offing.

Then the phone rang again, and this time, there was good news. "The five Japanese destroyers have turned out to be four native sampans and a submarine," Lieut. Wilson reported.

The scare was over. But we did not sleep very soundly. The submarine, a Jap, of course, had been seen standing in toward shore, then submerged. Any time in the night, we knew he might come up and lob a few shells in our direction. As usual, we slept with our clothes on.

The popping of sentry fire in the night did not disturb me. It was becoming more or less routine, like the sound of passing streetcars in the city.

SATURDAY, AUGUST 15

This afternoon, again at 12:15, Jap two-engine bombers swung in over Guadalcanal. Again I could see three of them, as high as before, and again, anti-aircraft opened up and clouded part of the sky with bursts.

The Japs' bombs fell closer this time. There were two sticks of bombs, and they hit near the airport. There was no damage, and only one man was injured. He suffered a slight shrapnel wound in the back.

But the real news came when a jeep dashed up to Gen. Vandegrift's command post with a great burst of speed and skidded to a stop in a cloud of dust. The driver ran to the general and handed him a small red-and-white object. It was a red tassel with a red-and-white cloth streamer attached. It had been dropped, by a Jap plane, said the breathless driver and it contained a map giving directions to Nip troops on Guadalcanal. The enemy planes had also dropped supplies in parachutes, said the driver. Our men were setting out to retrieve some of the bundles, he said.

The map, a mimeograph drawn on cheap paper, was most interesting. It showed the beach and the airport, with an arrow pointing inland to a spot marked in Japanese "broad place." From "broad place," where a cache of food was indicated, a dotted line ran to the airport. The line was marked "six kilometers."

Later in the afternoon two marines brought in two of the packages of supplies which the Japanese had dropped from their planes today; also the news that there had been about fourteen dropped in all. Of these, our forces had recovered more than half.

The packages, wicker containers with cushions on the bottom to break the impact of the landing, contained food and ammunition. There were cans of goulash, bags of biscuits, little boxes of Japanese candy, and .25 caliber ammunition, in clips. There were also more mimeographed sheets, obviously designed to cheer the desperate Japs on Guadalcanal. Capt. Moran (Capt. Sherwood F. Moran of Auburndale, Mass.), the ranking interpreter, made a hasty translation.

One of the messages began, "The enemy before your eyes are collapsing"—which Gen. Vandegrift found an amusing bit of whimsy. And it went on: "Friendly troops: a landing party [marine naval brigade] relief is near," which had a more ominous sound.

Then: "We are convinced of help from heaven and divine grace. Respect yourself. By no means run away from the encampment. We too will stick to it."

Another enclosure for the benefit of Jap morale was headed: "Great East Asia Newspaper, Special Edition," and it gave a highly colored report of supposed Jap naval successes in the Solomons:

"On August 7th and following at the Solomon Islands, the Imperial Fleet inflicted losses upon the American and British combined forces.

"Sunk: battleship (unknown type)—1; armored cruiser (*Astoria* type)—2; cruisers (unknown type)—at least 3; destroyers—at least 4; transports—at least 10."

The "newspaper" also listed as "defeated, crushed, smashed up," two armored cruisers of the *Minneapolis* type, at least two destroyers and one transport. And it was claimed the Japs had shot down at least thirty-two fighter planes and nine "fighter bomber planes." Total Jap losses were listed as seven planes and two cruisers, which we knew was a deliberate lie.

This afternoon a great wave of "scuttlebutt" swept Gen. Vandegrift's headquarters. The topic: a Japanese invasion force is on the way, may strike tonight.

Everyone seemed busy preparing for the supposed invasion. At the general's CP (command post), marines were busy digging extra foxholes. And in the evening troops marched to our treasured airport in a long column to take up defensive positions.

Back at Col. Hunt's CP, my billet, I found the staff officers engaged in hushed consultation. They too evidently expected a Japanese attack that evening.

But the night was quiet, except for the usual shooting on our sentry lines. Despite the Jap message of encouragement, the Nip troops remaining on the island must be growing more and more hungry, more and more desperate. Increasing numbers of them are coming near our lines, possibly looking for food, and being shot or captured.

SUNDAY, AUGUST 16

It was a quiet day, except for the sighting of one submarine off Lunga Point. The sub, lying beyond effective gun range, came in no closer.

At 12:15, as we sat in Col. Hunt's command post, we remarked over the fact that there had been no air-raid alarms all morning.

"What happened to our little yellow playmates today?" mused Lieut. Wilson.

"It's early yet," said Maj. Dickson. "I'll give 'em till 12:30." But 12:30 came and went, and hours after that, and there was no air raid, not even an alarm. We were mystified, but highly pleased.

Col. Goettge, Dr. Pratt, Lieut. Cory, Capt. Ringer and the others who went on the ill-fated excursion to Matanikau have been given up for lost. But another trek into the village is being planned, and this time, the expedition will be in force and out for blood.

This afternoon we were amused to hear a broadcast over the Jap propaganda station, saying that the United Nations' Solomon Islands operations have been a failure; and that in fighting there the first division of marines, our choicest troops, said the Japs, had been wiped out, annihilated, and all our transports sunk. That was such a grotesque statement that it was funny.

MONDAY, AUGUST 17

At 8:30 this morning an outpost of one of our weapons companies called our command post to bring us another alarm. This time, seven unidentified ships had been spotted standing in to shore. "They are supposed to have disappeared behind Savo Island before identification could be made," said Lieut. Wilson, passing on the report.

Once again we thought that at last the Jap invasion attempt was on its way. But at 10:05 the phone rang again in our CP, and Wilson laughed as he told us: "The ships have turned out to be islands."

Living here amidst the constant threat of invasion, one cannot blame the lookouts for being over-zealous. The night-and-day strain is great, especially in view of the fact that we are still without air support—and, if the Japs only knew it, pretty much at the mercy of sea or air attack. But, fortunately, they either don't know or are not yet ready to attack in any great force. We are hoping very hard that our planes will arrive before the Japs do.

The nervous strain of the situation has already told on a very few of the marines, who, including one high-ranking officer, have developed hysteria psycho-neurosis. But except for these very few, our men are showing an exceptionally large amount of good humor amidst distressing surroundings.

Lieut. Snell, whose strength gave out, temporarily, during our arduous second day's march, has come back on the job as Col. Hunt's aide. He is completely recovered from his paralytic stroke and seems in excellent health. He says he refused to be sent home.

This morning there was a call from one of Col. Hunt's headquarters. "Twelve more prisoners today?" said Snell, answering the phone. "Dead or alive?"

Everywhere in our occupied area, prisoners are surrendering in increasing numbers. Most of them are desperately hungry, for, they say, they ran from their camps without stopping even to take food, on August 7th. Some of them have eaten nothing save a few cocoanuts in all the meantime.

The air alert—at Col. Hunt's CP sounded by a battered siren which rather whispers than screams—came at 10:40 this morning. But the enemy aircraft turned out to be only one plane, apparently an Aichi double-float seaplane, which did not drop any bombs, and did not come close to the airport or our positions.

The visit has a rather ominous significance; it means that there must be at least one Jap cruiser somewhere in our vicinity, for the plane is obviously a cruiser type, and could not have reached us from the Jap land bases to the north.

At the prison camp this afternoon I found that Capt. Mike Davidowitch (of New York City), chief of the Military Police, now has 203 Japs under his keep.

Looking at the prisoners, who squatted inside a barbed-wire rectangle like animals on exhibit, brought mixed feelings. One could not but feel at least a trace of sympathy for the group of labor troops, a meek-looking, puny lot, most of them well under five feet in height and physically constructed like children. After all, most of them had been conscripted into service, and had always been unarmed.

But the military prisoners, Japanese naval troops, were different. They were a surly-looking, glowering group, and by no means puny. They were cooped up in a little barbed-wire pen of their own, since they had refused to mix with the laborers. We stared at them and they stared back at us. There was no doubt as to what either we or they would have liked to do at that moment—if we had not remembered our code of civilization or if they had not been unarmed.

Capt. Davidowitch told us the Jap laborers seemed to be happy about the kind treatment given them in this American prison camp. They thrived on American food.

Back at Gen. Vandegrift's headquarters, we found a tall, sturdy blond man joking with the staff officers. He wore the traditional shorts and short-sleeve shirt of the Britisher, and red shoulder marks, the badge of some kind of colonial authority.

He was W. F. Martin Clemens, the British commissioner for Guadalcanal, and he had just come into camp after three months in the bush. He had stayed there during the entire Jap occupation.

Clemens had come into our camp without shoes, and, as he said quite casually, "I had a few tins of food left." He did not say, but it was perfectly obvious, that our arrival had saved him from a difficult spot.

Clemens had retired to the hills a week after the Coral Sea battle began on May 5th, when the Japs had moved into Guadalcanal.

Several times the Japs had nearly found him. Once they had started out with a native guide up the road which led to Vuchikoro, his temporary headquarters. But the guide had turned the Japs off the track, saying in effect, "That very bad road" and leading them up another trail.

Once he had been swimming in a small stream when a Jap plane had flown over low. But by the time the Jap circled and came back to investigate the splashing, Clemens, in the nude, had retired to the safety of the woods.

When the time came for our invasion of the Solomons, the commissioner had emerged from the bush to a ridge 2,000 feet high to "watch the show," he said. From that time on, he had been working his way through the jungle to our camp.

I reached Col. Hunt's CP in the late afternoon, to find the colonel at the center of a rather grim group of officers. They were laying plans for a large excursion into Matanikau, and it was easy to see that they are intent on mopping up the Japs in the village this time. The attack will come off day after tomorrow. The plan is to box in the town from three sides: one company of troops, under Capt. Spurlock (Capt. Lyman D. Spurlock of Lincoln, Neb.) will set out tomorrow morning, cut through the jungles to the rear of Matanikau and work into position for an assault from the land side; another company led by Capt. Hawkins will advance along the shore toward Matanikau from Kukum, bivouac overnight, and be in position to strike from the east when the attack begins; while a third group of troops, under Capt. Bert W. Hardy (of Toledo, Ohio), will make a landing from boats far to the west of Matanikau, beyond the next western-most village of Kokumbona, and attack Matanikau from the west along the shore.

Capt. Hawkins' troops will leave Kukum at one o'clock tomorrow afternoon. I asked him if I might accompany his outfit. "Sure," he said, "come right along."

TUESDAY, AUGUST 18

The time was about 12:45 this afternoon, and I was preparing to go to Kukum to join Capt. Hawkins' troops for the excursion to Matanikau, when the air-raid alarm sounded. We took cover, and at about one o'clock the anti-aircraft guns on the airfield began firing.

It was the first time that I had seen all the enemy planes clearly; they came in two shallow V's of four each, forming two silvery white lines against the cloudless sky, and it was a sort of shock to see them coming so deliberately and steadily in the open.

But our anti-aircraft fire was coming close. The puffs of ack-ack blotted the sky almost directly in front of the leading wave. And suddenly a spurt of smoke came from one motor of the plane on the left flank. Then the spurt became a slender white plume trailing out behind. But the plane did not drop out of its place, and the formation droned steadily on its course. It had not been hit badly.

Then we heard the guttural whisper of the sticks of bombs coming, and all of us who had been watching hit the ground and rested the brows of our helmets against the earth. That was as close to digging in as we could come at a second's notice.

The noise of the falling bombs was louder this time than last, and the carrump-rump-rump of the explosions came close enough to seize and shake the earth under us. There were two sticks, two definite sets of explosions.

The bombs had struck the edge of the airfield, perhaps a half mile from where we lay. We saw dark-brown columns of dust and smoke rising, and the flames of a small fire, apparently in a field of brush.

The Jap planes were swinging in a wide circle toward the south, taking their time, flying steadily. The anti-aircraft fire followed, but it was not close. We watched the plane whose motor was trailing smoke, watched dismayed while the smoke plume grew thinner and then disappeared.

"They're coming back for another run," said somebody, as the planes continued their curving course. But they did not return.

Jim Hurlbut (Sgt. James Hurlbut of Washington, D.C.), the Marine Corps Correspondent, Bob Miller and I set out in a jeep, immediately after the raid, for Kukum, there to join Capt. Hawkins' expedition to Matanikau. The air raid had slowed preparations a bit, and it was two o'clock before we started.

We traced our previous route almost identically, pushing through the same evenly spaced cocoanut palms toward the same grove of white breadfruit trees, and the same little bridge leading to the same thick jungle, as on my last excursion to Matanikau. This time our plan is to march to a spot a few hundred yards from the grove of white trees and the bridge leading to the jungle, and bivouac for the night. Tomorrow morning we will push forward beyond the white trees and several hundred yards through the jungle, to a point near Matanikau. We will halt at that point while our artillery throws a heavy barrage into the village, and then we will move on up to the river and perhaps cross over into the village.

We had started at about two o'clock. At 2:40 our large column was moving through the cocoanut groves, when we heard an outburst of shots ahead.

"We may have some Japs in the bush," said Capt. Hawkins. Then there was more firing, and a few minutes later, as we moved ahead, we passed two small Japanese, evidently laborers, kneeling by the side of the path.

"Oh, look, they've got a couple of goonie birds," said one of the marching marines.

The Japs looked particularly abject. "They look like they're praying," said a marine.

"They probably are," said another.

The lads were in high spirits as we shoved along the trail. By this time, they had done enough marching on Guadalcanal to get toughened up a bit, and now the sense of strength and fitness apparently made them extremely good-natured. Some of them sang "The Band Played On" and other ditties.

At 3:30 we passed the same Jap corpse which we had seen on the last excursion along this trail. Still the corpse sat, bloated and big and motionless, under the tree. Fortunately a blanket covered the face.

"So that's what's the matter with your chow, Rebel," said one of the lads to Sgt. "Rebel" Holmes (Sgt. Alton B. Holmes of Oak Park, Ga.). Sgt. Holmes was the company cook, and the remark was a slighting allusion to the quality of the food he prepared.

"That Jap's been there so long he doesn't even smell anymore," said another marine humorist.

The lads were still in good spirits when at four o'clock, sweaty but not tired, they bivouacked under the cocoanuts. Cheerfully they searched the tangle of grass at the foot of the trees, looking for good cocoanuts. There were hundreds of opened, husked cocoanuts among those which had fallen from the trees; evidently the Japs had been hard pressed for food.

Our supper, which consisted of perhaps a can of "C" ration or a candy bar, inspired the inevitable mockery about the cook's food.

"This stuff is better than that fishheads and rice you've been feeding us, Rebel," said one of his buddies.

"How about a nice fruity Jap for breakfast tomorrow, Rebel?" said another.

"You bring me the Jap and I'll do the work," was the answer.

There was a little group of marines gathered about "Rebel" by this time, for he evidently had a deserved reputation for being a "character" among his fellows. And there is usually, I have found, a circle of admirers about such a character, especially in the idle hour after supper.

At six o'clock the sky had grown dark and threatening. "It looks like rain, eh, Rebel?" said one of the marines.

"The rain ain't nothin' to be afraid of," said Rebel. "You know what the Old Campaigner says, 'Take off your clothes and cover up your weapons—there ain't no soap in the rain.' " The Rebel had been an old campaigner himself, it developed. He went into a yarn about the rain down in the West Indies.

The talk shifted to the subject of Jap snipers and the thesis that they are hard to spot, because of their camouflage, their smokeless powder and the fact that their rifles have no muzzle blast.

"Them guys are the original invisible men," said Rebel.

That brought up the idea that walking in woods filled with Jap snipers was dangerous; that our present mission was dangerous.

"I made out my will before I left, bud," said Rebel. "I said give this package of cigarettes to this guy and..." His idea dwindled into silence. "You know, you're gettin' uglier every day," he said to a buddy.

"It's just that lousy food you've been givin' us. That's what makes it," was the answer.

Rebel resorted to one of the favorite marine words for his answer: the word "gook," which means anything foreign or strange.

"If you didn't get to go on this lousy gook island, bud," he said, "you wouldn't get that lousy chow."

Darkness was closing in on the cocoanut grove. Some of the lads collected palm fronds and arranged them as mattresses, with ponchos atop them. But Rebel's circle remained around him. The talk turned to Jap cigarettes; we had captured hundreds of cases of them in our landing. Rebel remarked that they were pretty dungy.

That suggested to somebody the story about the cigarette salesman, who was quite a demon in disposing of his particular brand of butts. One day, it was narrated, somebody said to this super salesman: "Did you know that Smokos are half dung and half tobacco?"

"Now I'll be more enthusiastic about them than ever," said the salesman. "I thought they were *all* dung."

Rebel said the Jap cigarettes were all dung, and that he had been too proud to smoke them while there were American cigarettes about.

"I smoke 'em now, by God," he said. "I'm gettin' squinch-eyed."

The breeze was still shooting, as the marines say, when I went over to another conversational circle, where Capt. Hawkins and Lieut. Walter S. McIlhenny were talking seriously about tomorrow's job. Crossing the Matanikau was one of their worries. If the Japs had machine guns bearing on the ford, it would be difficult. Another worry was advancing too fast and getting into our own artillery barrage.

I put on my poncho, pulled my mosquito net over my helmet and lay down on a gentle incline. I found that the deep-type American helmet makes quite a comfortable head-rest for sleeping. The hammock which fits around the head inside makes a sort of cushion. If you dig the edge of the helmet into the ground and brace it between two stones, you have a steady head-rest.

The ground felt hard that night, and the grass was lumpy, but I would have slept soundly despite these obstacles if gunfire had not awakened us.

The first salvos, heavy, distant thumpings, began just after ten o'clock. There were two heavy "booms" close together, then another couple, and then a long row of singles. The men lying all about in the cocoanut grove stirred and stood up and looked in the direction of the cannonading. It was coming from the north, toward Tulagi.

The sound seemed to grow closer and louder. The top sergeant, standing near me, was sure the Japs were shelling the airfield. Others knew this was the beginning of the Jap invasion attempt we had been expecting for so long.

Capt. Hawkins sent a patrol out to the beach to see if there were any fires visible on Guadalcanal. One man reported he had seen a fire in the direction of the beach, where we had made our original landing on Guadalcanal. The others could not see it.

"Was it a submarine?" asked somebody.

"I don't know," was the answer. And so we went back to sleep, to the accompaniment of "grousing" about the fact that we on Guadalcanal had not yet received any air support.

WEDNESDAY, AUGUST 19

We were awakened several times after midnight this morning by renewed cannonading, but we did not get up again. At 6:40 A.M., when we were up and on the move, we heard sharper reports of heavy guns, indicating they were closer. A patrol went to the beach to have another look, but reported no ships visible. One man thought he had seen a shape at sea but could not be sure whether it was a fish or a submarine.

We reached the clearing with the white trees shortly after eight o'clock, and halted there to wait for our own artillery bombardment of Matanikau. The bombardment was late. We waited, wondering if the Japs had landed, back near the airport, if that could be the reason for the delay. We still had no word as to the meaning of the gunfire we had heard during the night and this morning.

Lieut. McIlhenny looked down the trail that led to the airport, to the rear. "I believe we'd better query by TBY and see what happened," he said. He called a runner. "Go up and request permission from Capt. Hawkins to radio and find out what happened to our barrage," he directed.

An affirmative answer came, and in a few moments, the tall antennae of the field radio had been set up at the trailside, a generator tied to a tree, and we could hear the steady grinding noise as electric current was wound up.

The operator clicked out his message. "Right on the beam this morning," he said. "They're receipting for it."

We sat and waited for the answer. The air grew quiet. The cannonading from the ocean had ceased. Then we heard the sound of motors, many of them; they were our landing boats, carrying ashore the troops which were going to land beyond Kokumbona and work in toward us, toward Matanikau, and thus close one side of the three-sided vise on the village.

"What's holding up our answer?" Lieut. McIlhenny asked the radio operator.

"He has to give it to the executive officer," said the operator, cheerfully, "and then the answer has to be written out before it can be sent back."

Just then the receiving key of the set began to buzz. "That message may constitute the answer to the query," said the radioman, very officially.

"I don't know whether to move up or not," mused Lieut. McIlhenny. "I might move in there and he might open up with the barrage."

But the answer was reassuring. "Your first message," it read. "Answer: Not due yet."

Lieut. McIlhenny gave the order to move forward, and we passed the clearing with the white trees, crossed the little bamboo bridge over the little creek at the edge of the clearing, and moved on down the wide path into the jungle beyond. We took cover carefully along the sides of the trail as we moved up. We were getting into enemy territory.

It was 8:19 when a marine came from our right flank (which lay near the beach) to report, "I can see a ship."

Just then the guns began booming again. I moved over to the shore and swept the horizon with my glasses, but could see no ship. I went back to our column.

At 8:30 a marine came in from the beach out of breath and said, "There's a Jap destroyer out there." I went to the shore expecting another false alarm and was startled. Like a toy ship on the horizon, but very distinct, moving toward Kukum, in from the sea, was a Nip warship. With my field glasses I could make out turrets fore and aft, the decks characteristically crowded with piles of superstructure, the curved bow, and even an orange flag with a red rising sun at the masthead. Possibly this was the ship which had been shelling our shores. (I later learned that it was. It had passed in close to Kukum, lobbing shells toward shore positions, without doing any physical damage, while another Jap warship bombarded Tulagi.)

I watched the Jap ship as it slowly swung bow on until it pointed straight for the spot where I stood, kept turning and swung broadside to shore. It did not fire, and apparently it lay beyond the range of our shore batteries, for they were not firing either.

A few minutes later, as I returned to our troop column, our artillery opened the expected barrage against Matanikau. We heard the booming of the guns behind us, then the soft sighing as the shells passed overhead, and sharp, loud crashes in quick succession as they landed.

We halted and then moved on while the intensity of the barrage increased until the booms of the cannon, the sighs of the passing shells and the cracks of the explosions overlapped and mingled into a continuous train of sound. When we halted again I worked my way to the sea side to find that only the masts of a Jap ship were visible, projecting just above the rim of the horizon toward Tulagi. The ship was firing, I knew; a thin, dirty cloud of smoke, brownish-yellow in color, floated over her masts. It was the unmistakable smoke that comes with gunfire.

I rejoined our main group of troops just in time to hear a burst of gunfire from our left flank and ahead. There were several bursts of sub-machine gun fire, then a few rifle shots, and then the answering crack of a Jap .25 caliber. I knew that sound by this time, and took shelter in a clump of brush behind a tree. More .25's cracked, in more rapid succession, and firing went on sporadically. I watched the ants hustling through the foliage under my nose. There were three kinds of ants, large and small red ones and medium-sized black ones. There was little to do except watch them until the firing let up.

It was about 9:45 when the firing lulled, and we poked our heads out into the open again to see what went on. Apparently a sniper or two had been knocked out ahead of us. But we moved cautiously. A squad went out on our left, to comb through the bushes. A runner came in from the beach. "I think there are Japs in a boat on the shore," he said. "I saw a sorta head pop up."

The top sergeant sent a squad out in the direction which the runner indicated. I was moving forward, along the fairly open edge of the trail, when I heard a .25 machine gun. The sound was coming from the beach, evidently near the boat which the runner had reported. I heard the heavier tone of the Browning automatic rifle, and the crash of two exploding grenades, from the same area.

Then more Jap .25's opened up ahead; a storm of firing broke and filled the jungle. I dived for the nearest tree, which unfortunately stood somewhat alone and was *not* surrounded by deep foliage. While the firing continued and I could hear the occasional impact of a bullet hitting a nearby tree or snapping off a twig, I debated whether it would be wiser to stay in my exposed spot or to run for a better 'ole and risk being hit by a sniper en route.

I was still debating the question when I heard a bullet whirr very close to my left shoulder, heard it thud into the ground and then heard the crack of the rifle which had fired it. That was bad. Two marines on the ground ten or fifteen feet ahead of me turned and looked to see if I had been hit. They had evidently heard the bullet passing. That made up my mind. I jumped up and dashed for a big bush. I found it well populated with ants which crawled up my trousers legs, but such annoyances were secondary now.

The sniper who had fired at me was still on my track. He had evidently spotted my field glasses and taken me for a regular officer.

I searched the nearby trees, but could see nothing moving, no smoke, no signs of any sniper. Then a .25 cracked again and I heard the bullet pass—fortunately not as close as before. I jumped for better cover, behind two close trees which were surrounded by ferns, small pineapple plants and saplings. Here I began to wish I had a rifle. I should like to find that sniper, I thought. I had made an ignominious retreat. My dignity had been offended. The Matanikau sortie had become a personal matter.

Then it began to rain hard. It rained until we were soaked and the ground was mushy, while the firing continued.

A Jap .25 machine gun, making the characteristically sharp sound in characteristically long bursts of fifteen to twenty shots, was firing again on our right flank and ahead. But the gun had been spotted by our "point" in that direction. In a few seconds we heard the crash of one of our mortar shells, ranging on the Jap. Then a muttered sentence, passed from mouth to mouth, came back from that area:

"Pass the word back, more to the right on the mortars."

A few seconds later I heard the "thwung" sound of the mortar firing, and after the usual long interval of flight, the crash of the exploding shell.

"More to the right on the mortars," was the word that came back. And then again, the thwung of the firing, the crash of the exploding shell—and silence from the Japanese machine gun. (We heard later that this particular nest, hidden in a beached boat, had been knocked out.)

Col. Whaling had come up to our position to see how our advance was going. He brought word that Capt. Hardy's troops had landed beyond Kokumbona and pushed through the town with little opposition. They were moving in now from the west of Matanikau. Capt. Spurlock's troops had also been successful; they had cut a trail through the difficult jungle on the land side of Matanikau and were moving into the outskirts of the village.

Heavy rifle fire, however, still pinned down the movement of our group of marines, under Capt. Hawkins. And there were still machine guns ahead of us, firing intermittently.

It was raining again. We squatted in the mud amidst covering bushes and Col. Whaling, who had come up to our position by landing boat, told us how his boats had been chased by the same Jap warship which we had earlier seen lying off the coast. The ship had fired a few shells at the boats, but fortunately hurt no one.

The word came back from our advance elements, via runner, that our troops were pushing ahead to the village. The firing had by this time slackened considerably. There were only a few stray rifle shots to be heard.

But there were still some Japs to be cleaned up. Suddenly we heard a terrific burst of automatic rifle fire, mixed with the reports of rifles and sub-machine guns, to our left. Then silence. And a few minutes later, a marine walked down to the trail with a small, uniformed Jap in tow.

As the Jap came toward us, there were angry shouts from the marines. "Kill the bastard!" they yelled. "Kick him in the b– – – –!"

This Jap did not have an inscrutable face. Now it was marked by signs of terror obvious even to the Occidental eye. The marine guard explained the reason. "There were four of them," he said. "His three pals were cut in pieces."

Sgt. Hurlbut, Miller and I had agreed by this time to return to headquarters. So it was decided that we should accompany the prisoner to the rear, with Sgt. Hurlbut acting as guard.

It was 11:30 when we started, keeping to the edge of the trail. The jungle around us was silent, and we four, three Americans and the Jap pigmy, were alone. We wondered if we would run into a net of snipers lying in wait for stragglers.

There was one sniper waiting for us. As we came to a bend in the trail, he fired from behind us. We heard the crack of the rifle and the whiz of the bullet, but it did not sound very close. However, we broke into a run, while Hurlbut goaded the Jap along with his .45. The Jap was very obliging. He ran faster than we did; probably he was thinking how happy one of his own people would be to kill him, now that he had disgraced himself by being captured.

We got around the bend in the trail before the sniper could fire again. And we met no more of his disagreeable ilk.

But the excitement of the day was not yet over. As we neared Kukum, we saw a group of landing boats moving in toward shore. They were far enough from the beach so that it was hard to tell whether they were American craft. And just then we heard the sound of an approaching plane, and a B-17 came in over the water and swooped low over the landing boats. The combination was too much for some of the jittery shore outposts. To them, the B-17 appeared to be strafing—and that positively identified the boats as Japanese.

"A Jap landing party!" they shouted. And the handful of marines standing about ran madly for cover.

For a second we were swept by the feeling of excitement that filled the air. But I stopped to fix my field glasses on the supposed enemy landing boats. They were our own.

Miller, Hurlbut and I were not yet sure. The Japs might have captured our boats or manufactured some like them. This might actually be a landing party, and the B-17 might have been strafing.

"If it is a landing party, what shall I do with the prisoner?" said Hurlbut, motioning toward the Jap with his gun.

The Jap now looked utterly disconsolate. It was plain that he understood our alarm and expected to be dispatched immediately.

But we had been watching the landing boats with our glasses, and now we could make out that there were several figures of men visible in each boat. If the boats had been carrying Japs, they would have appeared to be empty, save perhaps for the coxswain, for the Japs would have been crouching below gunwale level. Thus we reasoned, at any rate. And we were right.

The B-17 had passed on toward Tulagi, and now we saw her turning. Through glasses, one could make out the masts of a ship, projecting above the horizon, directly below the bomber. We knew the aircraft had dropped bombs, for we saw a mushroom of dark-brown smoke rising from a point just aft of the rear mast, and a steady torrent of smoke followed.

The masts came up higher on the horizon, and we could see the stack of the ship and the superstructure. It was a Jap heavy cruiser, and her fantail was afire. The B-17 had scored a direct hit.

We could hear the sound of heavy anti-aircraft firing coming from the Jap, see bursts in the sky. But the bomber had done his job; now he climbed up into the sky and headed for home.

The Jap was crippled, but not stopped. He made full steam for the passage that leads to the sea, between Florida and Savo Islands. Clouds of brown smoke were still rising from the fantail.

Back at Col. Hunt's CP, later in the afternoon, I heard the official news that Matanikau and Kokumbona had been taken. Gunner Edward S. Rust (of Detroit, Mich.), an officer attached to Col. Hunt's staff, came in to tell an exciting tale of the Matanikau attacks. Rust had accompanied Capt. Spurlock's troops—the group which closed in on Matanikau from the jungle or land side—and had seen plenty of action. Capt. Spurlock's forces had run into Jap entrenchments, good defenses in depth which had been hard to take. They had killed sixty to seventy of the defenders, and a handful had escaped.

THURSDAY, AUGUST 20

Awakened this morning by the sound of cannonading, coming from the direction of Tulagi. Getting to be a routine occurrence. I quickly went to Kukum, where a group of marines stood on the beach looking toward the north.

"A damn Jap cruiser was in, shelling Tulagi," said one of the watchers. He pointed to a Flying Fortress which cruised slowly over the horizon. "That B-17 scared him away," he said.

News this morning that the number of Japs killed on our expedition to Matanikau yesterday is about 100. Of these, Capt. Spurlock's troops are officially credited with sixty-five to seventy-five; the remainder were finished by Capt. Hardy's company, coming in from the west, and Capt. Hawkins' company, which Miller, Hurlbut and I had joined for the expedition. Our own casualties, killed and wounded, totalled fewer than twenty-five.

I dropped in at Capt. Spurlock's CP this morning to hear his story of the Matanikau raid. He said the hardest part of his advance had been the push through some 600 yards of intrenched positions on the village outskirts. The Japs, he said, had built a system of trenches reinforced with logs. They had a number of machine guns, including a heavy weapon of about .60 caliber. When the enemy trenches had been cleaned out, one by one, the Japs made a last effort to win, said the captain; they made a bayonet charge.

"That was when a few of them got away," said Capt. Spurlock. "But most of them were killed. Our men took pretty careful aim and knocked them off. Some of our people even stood up and fired off-hand at the Japs in the middle of the charge."

Gunner Rust, said the captain, had been one of the heroes of the advance. He had thrown hand grenades from the phenomenal range of a few yards, an almost superhuman feat, to blast a Jap machine-gun nest. And when a platoon leader had been killed, Rust, although he was acting officially only as an observer, had taken over the disordered platoon and held it in a skirmish line.

Probably the outstanding hero of the attack, however, had been P.F.C. Nicholas Sileo, a tough scrapper from Brooklyn. Sileo was a Browning automatic rifleman who had been doing excellent work in cleaning out Jap snipers during the approach to Matanikau. When the stiffest resistance was encountered on the outskirts of the town, he set to work on a Jap machine-gun nest, but exposed himself while working into position, and was shot three times; one bullet hit him in the chest, a second in the groin, and a third shattered his hand, ripping two fingers clean away. That might have knocked out a lesser man, but not Sileo. He kept on firing his gun, using his good hand to pull the trigger.

Capt. Spurlock said he had lost one of his best friends, and one of the finest marine officers, in the Matanikau fracas. The friend and officer was Lieut. George H. Mead, heir to the Mead Paper Company fortune, and famed as a former polo player at Yale. Lieut. Mead had taken over the "point" platoon when the N.C.O. in charge was killed, and had led the platoon brilliantly, disregarding Jap sniper fire until, finally, a bullet hit him in the face, killing him instantly.

At Gen. Vandegrift's CP today, I heard the news that a patrol led by Capt. Charles H. Brush (of New York City) caught a Jap patrol, about twenty-five strong, near Koli Point (east of the airport) last night, and killed eighteen of them in a short, savage fight.

The Japs, said the general, were Navy troops, well armed and equipped. Apparently they had been landed from a Jap warship to make a reconnaissance.

One of the Nip lieutenants had been wounded in the exchange of firing, and when Capt. Brush approached him, he put his pistol to his head and killed himself. (Here was one Jap who had lived up to the hara-kiri tradition of death before dishonor—in contrast to our Jap prisoners, who apparently enjoyed American hospitality without thought of suicide.)

This afternoon the marines on this island enjoyed a long-awaited treat; it was the pleasure of seeing our air support arrive. We watched the flights of fighter planes and dive-bombers swing over the airport, then come in for a landing. The powerful roar of their motors was reassuring. It seemed almost unbelievable that we did not have to dive for shelter at the sound.

"That's the most beautiful sight I've ever seen," said one marine.

And I heard an officer say: "Morale's gone up twenty points this afternoon."

V

TENARU FRONT

FRIDAY, AUGUST 21

At about 2:30 this morning, we were awakened by the sound of heavy machine-gun fire coming from the east. There were several long bursts, and then rifle fire joining to form a waterfall of sound. But then the firing slacked, and we decided the disturbance had been only a brush between one of our listening posts and a Jap patrol.

At 4:30, however, we were waked again, and this time we knew it was no mere patrol action which we had heard. The sound of the firing was loud now, and it sounded as if hundreds of rifles and machine guns were firing at once. And now the firing of smaller arms was augmented by loud, heavy reports that could be only artillery or mortars. We hurriedly got dressed and went to Col. Hunt's field office, where a group was already gathered. Considering the fact that the firing we had heard probably marked the long-awaited Jap invasion attempt, everyone seemed in high good humor. Possibly the coming of our air support yesterday was responsible.

We sat in the darkness, listening to the sounds of the firing. We heard one extremely long burst of machine-gun fire.

"That fella's finger must have stuck to the trigger," said one of the voices in the dark.

"Another belt, another barrel," said another.

"Dear Mom," said Col. Hunt, "please send me another barrel."

"With accessories, G.I.," said another voice.

We listened while the firing swelled in volume. "Sounds like a pretty fair-sized engagement," said Col. Hunt.

We could see red flares, then white, then red flares rising against the sky in the direction of the beach. "Mebbe some Jap landing party," suggested Lieut. Wilson.

At about five o'clock, we heard the heavy, loud crashing of artillery fire. We could hear the guns going off, then the explosions as the shells hit. But the explosions sounded farther away than the gun reports. We decided it was our own artillery, ranging on the Japs.

In Col. Hunt's CP, the good-natured banter continued, but there was frequent and slightly anxious reference to the fact that dawn was approaching. "Wait until our planes get up and hit those babies," said Lieut. Snell. "Won't they be surprised?" He glanced at his watch. "About forty minutes to go before sun-up," he said.

The talk shifted to yarns about marine yesterdays in Nicaragua and China, and about this or that famous marine character, but the approach of the dawn was carefully clocked every ten minutes or so.

At about six o'clock the sky was beginning to lighten in the east, when we heard the sound of airplane engines.

"Ah," said Lieut. Wilson, "airplanes!" And he rubbed his hands, as before a feast. Our planes were warming up.

We had been trying to get through a call to Gen. Vandegrift's headquarters, to find out what was happening. Now Lieut. Wilson tried again, and got an answer.

"The firing was all prearranged barrage," he reported. "The enemy front line is the Tenaru."

It was a slight shock to hear the news, for if the enemy front lay on the Tenaru River, then probably a formidable invasion force was only three or four miles from the airport, to the east, trying to break through our defenses.

The sound of airplanes grew louder. The engines were being revved up now, preparatory to takeoff.

Col. Hunt was talking earnestly on the phone. "Apparently they tackled somebody this time," he said. He hung up. "Tell the reserve outfit to get ready to move," he told Lieut. Wilson. "They may need help on the Tenaru."

Immediately after breakfast I went down to Gen. Vandegrift's headquarters to seek out Col. Jerry Thomas, operations chief and the sparkplug of our troops in the Solomons. I wanted to check the matter of the Jap invasion with him. I still found it hard to believe that a large-scale assault had begun.

Col. Thomas confirmed the story. The enemy had apparently landed in force and made their way down the coast from east to west until they reached the Tenaru River. There they had run into one of our outposts. A fierce exchange of firing had followed, and the Japs had charged across a narrow spit of sand which closed the mouth of the Tenaru. Fortunately, the Japs had run into barbed-wire entanglements and been slowed down by the wire and our own fierce resistance until more troops could be brought into the gap.

Now our artillery was ranging on the Japs. There was the usual doubt as to the enemy's precise armament, which is natural in any such engagement. Col. Thomas told me all this in short sentences. The phone rang fairly often to interrupt him. He snapped quick orders to the different commanding officers in the sectors under stress.

"I'm going down to Col. Cates' CP now," he said. "Do you want to come?"

Col. (Clifton) Cates was the commanding officer of the group of troops which held our front line along the Tenaru. I said that certainly I would like to go.

We jumped into a jeep and hurried along the road to a tent camp. Col. Cates was a quick-moving, quick-speaking, very trim man of middle years. I knew that he had won honors in the First World War. He and Col. Thomas went into a quick huddle on the battle then going on. Col. Cates unfolded a map and pointed to it with a pencil. The scene was very calm, considering that a battle for Guadalcanal was going on only a short distance away.

We could hear the rattle of rifle and machine-gun fire, and an occasional heavy explosion: mortar or artillery fire.

Col. Thomas said: "We aren't going to let those people [the Japs] lay up there all day."

"We've got to get them out today," said Col. Cates.

A grizzled man with a lined face and light-blue eyes came up. He was wearing breeches and high, laced boots, and his shirt was wet with sweat. Evidently he had been out in the bush. He was Col. L. B. Cresswell of College City, La.

Col. Thomas nodded. "You know this terrain, L.B.," he said without further ado, pointing to the map. "How's the chances of getting tanks in there?"

"Yes," said Cresswell. "There's dry land in through these woods."

"Good," said Col. Thomas. He turned to Col. Cates. "We'll give L.B. a platoon of tanks," he said.

We heard the booming of our artillery firing, heard the explosions of the shells landing at the front. An artillery liaison officer stood nearby, talking into a phone. He had a direct connection with a spotting post, another with the batteries.

"How is it?" he asked.

He listened, then phoned the batteries. "It's right on," he said. "Give G Battery up 200." The shells were apparently falling amidst the enemy positions.

Cols. Cresswell, Cates and Thomas bent over the map. The plan was developing as they talked. It was to send Col. Cresswell with a strong force of troops around the flank of the Japanese positions.

Col. Thomas marked out the rough Jap position on the map. The enemy forces were evidently concentrated in a fairly small area running along a strip of Guadalcanal's northern shore. Their front was the Tenaru River, which runs roughly north and south in Guadalcanal. The shoreline runs east and west.

Col. Cresswell would take his troops—and tanks if he could get them through—and move around the southern flank of the enemy position. Then he would drive northward, pushing the enemy toward the sea.

Meanwhile, the American marines who held the line of the Tenaru River (they were under the command of Lieut. Col. Alvin Pollock) would prevent any further enemy advance. The enemy would be boxed in from two sides.

"I want you to get in there and pin these people down," said Col. Thomas to Col. Cresswell. "It's between you and Al [Col. Pollock].

"Once in there don't hold back. Drive in there like Brush [Capt. Brush, whose men wiped out the Jap patrol the night before last] did."

Col. Cresswell began moving immediately. He shouted to an aide who stood nearby, "Tell B Company to move right down there and wait for the rest." And he was gone.

"How many casualties?" Col. Thomas asked Col. Cates.

"Hard to tell yet," said Col. Cates. "There were two ambulances came back loaded and a third being loaded. They have to load between bursts."

The artillery liaison officer was talking on the phone. "Five volleys per battery."

We heard a series of explosions, sounding like bursting mortar shells coming from the direction of the Tenaru River front. Col. Thomas and Col. Cates stopped talking for a moment to listen.

"Ours or theirs?" said Col. Thomas.

"I don't know," said Col. Cates, taking a puff from his long cigarette holder. "That's the trouble with this war," he said with a smile. "You never know."

"In the last war we used to know where the enemy was," he said.

Col. Thomas laughed and started for his jeep. But a marine came out to the car and said an air-raid warning had gone up. "There's a large number of enemy planes on the way," he said.

Our own Grumman fighters were taking off. We could see them swinging up into the sky, reaching for altitude. A few minutes later the warning changed to urgent.

"All right," shouted Col. Cates to all and sundry around his CP, "stand by your holes."

But the Japs did not show up. At 11:12 the "all clear" signal came. (We heard later that the Japs had been Zero fighters, who were driven off.)

We could hear another long series of loud "bomp-bomp" sounds like mortar shells exploding, in the direction of the Tenaru.

Col. Cates explained it. "The damn Japs are throwing rifle grenades into our positions," he said.

It was 11:15 when Col. Cates got a radio message from Col. Cresswell. "Col. Cresswell says he is beginning to attack," he said. "His right flank is on the Ilu River [the Ilu is east of the Tenaru and runs roughly parallel to it]. There are no tanks." Evidently the tanks had been held up by some obstacle in terrain.

Col. Thomas had climbed into his jeep again and was starting back to the general's headquarters. Did I want to go back? Col. Cates had just taken a telephone call. "Good work," he was saying. "A white flag, eh?" he turned to me. "The Japs are coming across with a white flag," he said.

"I'll stay here awhile and maybe go up to the front," I told Col. Thomas.

"O.K.," he said. "Good luck."

His jeep ground into high speed.

"Hold your fire and tell the men to take them prisoner," Col. Cates was saying into the phone. He hung up.

"It's just one man coming over with a white flag," he said. He called Capt. Wolf, the interpreter attached to his troops. He instructed the captain to go up to the Tenaru front and talk to the prisoner, who was wounded. I started out for the front with Wolf.

We walked several hundred yards through a former cocoanut grove until we came to an advanced command post. The firing sounded quite loud here and the men of the command post were stretched out flat on the ground.

"Better get down," said one of them. We squatted in the dirt.

One of the officers was talking on the phone. "All right," he said, "we'll send a couple of men out to check it."

"Our line to Col. Pollock is out," he said. "Probably mortar fire clipped it. Who'll go?"

Two marines, looking scared but resolute, offered their services. "We'll show you the way to where Col. Pollock is, if you'll follow us," they said.

So we started out, moving fast, keeping low, halting behind trees to look ahead. The marines found the break in the line, and set to work to repair it.

"Col. Pollock is up that way," they said, pointing toward the Tenaru. "He's right out on the point."

Now we moved with even more caution than before, running bent from the waist as we made our way from tree to tree. Snipers were firing occasionally. We heard the crack of their guns, and bullets ricocheting among the trees. Our artillery was still ranging on the Jap positions on the far side of the Tenaru. And the Japs were throwing rifle grenades over to our side. We could see one of the bursts ahead, a spray of dirt rising where the explosive hit. Occasionally we heard the bursts of sharp-sounding Jap machine-gun fire: the light .25 calibers.

We pushed ahead, moving between bursts of firing, until we

could see the river, and the long curving spit of gray sand which closed its outlet into the sea, and the shadowy cocoanut grove across the river where the Japs were.

We were crouching behind a tree when Col. Pollock, looking quite calm and walking erect, came over. "The prisoner's up there," he said. He pointed to a group of three or four men lying prone around a foxhole about fifty feet away.

We made a dash for the foxhole and flopped beside it. In the foxhole on his back, with one of his arms wrapped in a red-stained swath of bandage, lay the Jap prisoner. He looked dazed and unhappy.

Capt. Wolf immediately began talking to him in Japanese. But the prisoner's answers were slow and apparently not very satisfactory. A marine told me the prisoner had got up from a foxhole and walked across the intervening no-man's-land all alone. "Like a ghost," he said. "Or somebody walking in his sleep." Evidently it had been an awful spectacle.

The Jap said he did not think the others would surrender. When asked how the invaders had arrived on Guadalcanal, he was very vague. He either knew nothing or would say nothing about the ships on which they had arrived on Guadal. (One reason for his confusion became apparent later, when it was learned from other prisoners that the troops, new arrivals, were not told where they were or where they were going. Some of them did not even know they were on Guadalcanal.)

It was only about a hundred yards from the foxhole, where the prisoner lay, to the front line of the Tenaru River.

Snipers began to range on us from across the river. We heard the ping-ping-ping of their .25's, and bullets began to whir fairly close. I lay for a few moments while the firing continued, thinking what a wonderful target we were, gathered so close together in a small circle, and then two of the other onlookers and I got the same idea at the same moment; we headed for cover.

A pink-cheeked captain shared my cocoanut tree. He told me while we watched the shadowy woods across the river that it was his unit which had been doing the fighting in this particular sector. He said that his name was James F. Sherman, and that he came from Somerville, Mass. "Lots of Boston boys in the outfit," he said. Then we heard the crackling of a light .25 caliber machine gun, and it was no effort at all to duck and stop talking.

When the firing let up a little, the captain waved a hand at a point of land which marked the seaward extremity of the Tenaru's west bank. "That's Hell Point," he said. "That's where the Japs tried their crossing. Some of our men moved up onto the point to get a better field of fire, and the Japs put up flares that were as bright as daylight. We lost some people in there. But," he added, "we stopped the Japs."

One did not have to look hard to see that he was understating the case. I worked my way, crawling between volleys of firing, flopping close to the earth when a mortar shell or grenade burst, to Hell Point, and looked out on hundreds of Jap bodies strewn in piles.

It was easy to see what they had tried to do. A sandbar, about fifteen feet wide and ten feet above the water level at its crest, shut off the mouth of the Tenaru from the sea.

The Japs had tried to storm our positions on the west bank of the river by dashing across the sandbar. Many of them had come close to reaching their objective. But they had run into unexpected rows of barbed wire at Hell Point, on our side of the Tenaru.

"That wire maybe saved the day," said a marine lying next to me.

I looked across the river into the shadowy cocoanut groves, where only 150 yards from us the advance elements of the enemy were located. We could hear the crack of rifle and machine-gun fire from there, and the occasional crash of our own artillery shells falling among the Jap positions. But no Japs were visible—and that, I had learned, was a perfectly normal condition in this jungle warfare.

I heard the report of a sniper's rifle coming from the right very close, on our side of the riverbank. The sound seemed to come from above. I saw a marine run, crouching, from one tree to the foot of another, and stand peering up into the tree, with his rifle ready.

Then, silently as a ghost, he beckoned to another marine, who then zigzagged his way to the foot of the same tree. The second marine had a tommy gun. The first marine pointed up into the foliage, and the second followed the gesture. Then the marine with the tommy gun made his way to a nearby stump, and crouched behind it, watching the tree top. I resolved to watch him ferret out the sniper and bring him to earth, but my attention was distracted by the sound of a .25 caliber machine gun coming from the sandbar that closed the mouth of the Tenaru.

"There's a bunch of Japs on the lee side of the bar," said the marine next to me. "They open up every hour on the hour from behind it. We can't spot 'em."

I could see how it might be possible for Japs to hug the lee side of the bar without being seen by our people. The bar was curved in a gentle arc toward the sea, and the bar had steep shoulders like an old-fashioned road. The result of this combination of circumstances was that at certain places there was excellent cover.

The machine gun snapped out at us again in a long burst. "If we could spot that guy we could lay mortar fire right on him," said my informant.

The battlefield is full of distractions. Now I was distracted by heavy firing from our own rifles, coming from my left. I saw a line of marines, lying close together behind sandbags, firing out to sea.

Out in the glassy blue water I saw globs of water jump up where the bullets struck. "They've got a Jap out there," said my friend. "He's trying to swim around and get in behind us. We've killed a lot of 'em that way."

A veritable sheet of bullets was smacking into the water. The marines apparently were all anxious to shoot a Jap.

I worked my way back to Capt. Sherman, who was standing behind a tree with Col. Pollock. Pollock still looked calm and efficient as he trained his field glasses on the patterned rows of cocoanut trees across the river.

There were bright-yellow explosions in the grove now, a series of them. A haze of white smoke drifted among the trees. And apparently from the back of the grove came heavy fusillades of rifle and machine-gun fire.

Col. Pollock looked at his watch. "Probably Cresswell's coming in," he said.

Machine guns began to clatter on our right. "They must be trying to cross the river down there," said Capt. Sherman. He told me how, in the darkness of the early morning today, some of the Japs had tried to cross the Tenaru lagoon by swimming.

Some of them, he said, had reached our side and hidden themselves in an abandoned tank which lay on the sloping riverbank. They had set up a machine-gun nest in the tank and it had taken some hours' effort to get them out. I could see the gray bulky shape of the tank up-angled on the slope.

"That machine gun in the tank made it tough for the marines to man that field piece," said Capt. Sherman. He pointed to an artillery piece on the riverbank. "They could take that thing in cross fire," he said. "Every time somebody moved into position to fire the gun, he got shot."

I remembered then that during the first heavy outburst of firing during the early morning I had heard the loud bang-bang-bang of the field piece, slower and heavier than the fire of a machine gun, and then not heard it again for an hour or two.

At about 1:15 Col. Pollock said, "Our people are coming in at the rear now. I can see 'em. Keep your fire down." He walked erect along our front firing line, saying, "Keep your fire down. Those are our people coming in the rear." Rifle and machine-gun fire still cracked on the other side of the river; grenades and mortar shells were still bursting among us, but Col. Pollock was as cool as if he were leading a parade-ground maneuver.

The volleys of machine-gun and rifle fire, from the depths of the grove across the river, grew louder. Col. Cresswell's people were rolling the Japs toward us.

Suddenly I saw the dark figures of men running on the strip of beach that bordered the palm grove. The figures were far off, possibly a half mile down the light ribbon of sand, but I could see from their squatness that they were Japs. There was no time for any other impression. In a few seconds the black, violently moving blobs were squashed down on the sand and we heard a fusillade of rifle fire. The Japs did not get up again. It was the first visible evidence that Cresswell's men were completing their maneuver of encirclement.

We knew that from this time on things were going to grow hotter along the Tenaru. It was possible that, as the Japs were pushed in from the rear, they might charge our positions on the west bank of the Tenaru, might again try to take the spit of sand across the Tenaru mouth.

Two ambulances had come up and stopped well back of our front line. The bearers were now picking up casualties on stretchers, loading them on the ambulances. Col. Pollock said to me: "The ambulances are going back. You can ride if you want to." I decided to stay and see the excitement.

The colonel passed the word along the line that there should be no firing unless a specific target was visible. The men had one of those a few moments later when a single Jap jumped out of the underbrush, just across the Tenaru in the edge of the cocoanut grove, and made a dash for the beach. A storm of firing burst from our line, and red streaks of tracers zipped around the Jap. He dropped to the ground, and for a moment the firing ceased, and then again he was up and running wildly for his life, and the firing was louder than ever. This time he fell violently, on the beach, and did not get up again.

Now the .25 caliber Jap machine gun which had been shooting at us for hours from the lee side of the Tenaru was opening up again. As usual, it had the effect of making us keep cover and to a certain extent pinning us down. But this time we spotted the Jap. A sharp-eyed marine saw a hand move above the level of the top of the sandbar, and made a mental note of the exact spot.

One of our mortars went into action. We heard the "thwung" sound of the piece discharging, waited the usual long seconds while the projectile arched into the air, then felt the ground shake as the explosive struck the sandbar and blew up.

We could hear a marine shouting, apparently giving the mortar crew directions on the matter of correcting their range. Then again, the "thwung" and the shattering explosion.

"That's better," called a marine. "Up fifteen."

The mortar went off again, and just after it was discharged, the figure of a Jap popped up from behind the spit of sand. He was less than 150 feet from me. I saw him take about three fast steps, and then the mortar shell landed almost directly on top of his helmet. The explosion of the shell was a canopy of dirty gray smoke and debris shedding over the Jap from above, and then swallowing him altogether.

The puff of the explosion expanded over the ground, and as it spread and thinned, we saw three more Japs, evidently members of the same machine-gun crew, leap up and start to run for the far end of the Tenaru sandspit.

They had gone only a few feet when they were in clear view of our troops, and bullets, including tracers from our machine guns, were winging all around them. Two of them fell as the fusillades of firing rang out and one kept running, then dived for cover.

But when he jumped up again, our men were waiting for him. Apparently he sensed this, for he ran desperately, turning in a fast hundred yards in his dash for the far end of the spit. Before he reached it, however, the bullets caught him and knocked him down.

I was not sorry to see the end of the last of this machine-gun crew. War takes on a very personal flavor when other men are shooting at you, and you feel little sympathy at seeing them killed.

A rumbling of powerful motors came from behind us. We turned to find a group of four tanks moving down the trail through the cocoanut palms heading for the Tenaru and the spit of sand across its mouth.

The plan, evidently, was to send the tanks across the spit and into the Jap positions at the edge of the grove.

On our (west) bank of the Tenaru the tanks halted for a few moments, then plunged on across the sandspit, their treads rattling industriously. We watched these awful machines as they plunged across the spit and into the edge of the grove. It was fascinating to see them bustling amongst the trees, pivoting, turning, spitting sheets of yellow flame. It was like a comedy of toys, something unbelievable, to see them knocking over palm trees which fell slowly, flushing the running figures of men from underneath their treads, following and firing at the fugitives. It was unbelievable to see men falling and being killed so close, to see the explosions of Jap grenades and mortars, black fountains and showers of dirt near the tanks, and see the flashes of explosions under their very treads.

We had not realized there were so many Japs in the grove.

Group after group was flushed out and shot down by the tanks' canister shells.

Several times we could see our tanks firing into clumps of underbrush where evidently Japanese machine-gun nests were located, for we could hear the rattling of the guns, in answer to the heavier banging of the tanks' cannon.

I saw a bright orange flash amidst a cloud of black smoke bursting directly under the treads of one of the tanks, saw the tank stop suddenly. It was crippled. The other tanks moved in protectively toward it. I learned later that they were taking off the crew, who escaped uninjured.

The three remaining tanks continued to roar and rattle amidst the palm grove for a time that seemed hours long. Everywhere they turned in their swiveling course, their cannon spewing sheets of orange flame. It seemed improbable that any life could exist under their assault.

I remember seeing one Jap in particular who was flushed out from under the treads of one of our tanks. I saw him jump up, and run hard toward the beach, with the tank following. I thought the tank would run him down or hit him with machine-gun fire, but it turned off quickly and headed back into the heart of the grove.

The Jap, however, continued to run. He was heading for the beach. All along our front line, rifle fire banged and machine guns clattered; the tracers arched around the running Jap.

Then the Jap sank into the underbrush, took cover, and Col. Pollock shouted: "Don't shoot. You might hit our own tanks."

The Jap jumped up and ran another forty or fifty feet toward the shore, then sank down into cover again. Despite the warning, several rifle shots were fired at him. As usual, each marine was eager to kill his Jap.

"One man fire," shouted Capt. Sherman. He designated a grizzled, leather-faced marine to do the shooting. I noticed that the man wore the chamois elbow pad and fingerless shooting glove of a rifle-range marksman. The marines told me he was Gunnery Sgt. Charles E. Angus (of Nashville, Tenn.), a distinguished marksman who had won many a match in the States.

We watched Sgt. Angus, as if he were the spotlighted star of a play, when the Jap jumped up again and began to run. Angus was nervous. He fired several shots, working his bolt fast, and missed. He inserted another clip of cartridges, fired one of them. But then the Jap had sunk down into cover again.

It was a little disappointing—but only for the moment. The Jap had flopped on the beach. He was evidently heading for the sanctuary of the water, hoping to swim for it. But now he started to get up again—and that was as far as he got. He had reached only a crouch when Sgt. Angus, now quite calm, took careful aim and let one shot go. The Jap sank as if the ground had been jerked out from underneath him. It was a neat shot—at about 200 yards.

Now the tanks, their job finished, were rolling out of the grove, heading for the spit. There were only three of them now. One sat very still and dead in the grove.

In a few minutes the tanks were behind our line. I followed them back until they stopped a few hundred feet west of the Tenaru, and the tank captain, his face grimy and his shirt soaked with sweat, climbed out. He said his name was Lieut. Leo B. Case (of Syracuse, N.Y.).

Col. Pollock had come back to talk to Lieut. Case. The colonel said, "Man, you really had me worried." He laughed. "But what a job!"

The colonel told me that his orders to Lieut. Case had been only that the tanks should run up and down the beach, on the far side of the Tenaru, and do a sort of reconnaissance. Turning into the grove, where close-spaced trees made it difficult for tanks to maneuver, and blotting out the Jap positions with point-blank fire— this had been Lieut. Case's own idea.

I went back to our front line, for firing was growing heavy again. Across the river Jap after Jap jumped up from the underbrush and dashed for the shore. It was their last hope for escape, with Col. Cresswell's troops coming in from behind. Most of the Japs were knocked down by our fire as they ran, long before they reached the beach. Some of them, however, reached the beach and tried to swim away. Their heads, small black dots amongst the waves, were difficult targets to hit. But our men relished the firing. Whenever we could see the head of a swimming man, a small storm of little waterspouts rose around him as our bullets smacked home.

Now we could distinctly see a few green-uniformed marines, noticeably bigger than the enemy, popping into view, then disappearing, in the grove across the river, far back among the even lanes of trees. And the sound of rifle and machine-gun fire accelerated, telling us that there must still be considerable Japanese resistance in the grove.

There were more of our troops on the beach at the edge of the grove, far down across the Tenaru. They were visible for a few seconds at a time, as they moved forward, then took cover, then repeated the process.

Our artillery fire, which had been pounding into the grove constantly in the earlier part of the day, had now halted. But Col. Cresswell's people were using mortars to finish off the Japs. The flashes of the explosions were like huge orange flowers scattered through the edge of the grove, just across the Tenaru. We simply kept our heads low and watched the excitement. There was no firing from our side of the river, for we were afraid of hitting our own men. And the Japs were too occupied with fighting our people closing in the rear to bother with those of us on the west bank of the Tenaru.

From time to time a live Jap stirred from among the dead piled on the Tenaru River spit and dived into the water. But at such point-blank range, these would-be escapers did not get far. From Hell Point, on Col. Pollock's end of the spit, volleys of firing sprang out and the Jap was killed as he swam; even the kindliest marine could not let the swimming Jap escape, for he would be apt then to swim around our rear and throw grenades as several Japs had done earlier in the day.

There was bitter fighting now in the grove across the Tenaru. We realized that the tanks had not "mopped up" completely, for we could still hear the snapping of Jap machine-gun and rifle fire. But Col. Cresswell's people were closing in fast. A large group of them advanced steadily but cautiously down the beach bordering the grove. Several groups moved simultaneously among the rows of palms scarcely 300 yards beyond the Tenaru. We kept our heads low, for the bullets of Cresswell's marines might accidentally strike among us.

And then the fighting, suddenly, seemed to have ended. We saw marines at the opposite end of the Tenaru spit, three of them, swiveling their heads about, stepping tensely with rifles at the ready—all set to kill any Japs who might try one last stealthy act of resistance.

Several times, as these three leaders moved across the spit, live Japs stirred among the piles of dead—I was told later that some of them tried to throw grenades at our people—and were killed for their trouble.

Jap dead are dangerous, for there are usually some among them alive enough to wait until you pass, then stab or shoot you. Our marines had by this time learned to take no chances. The dead were shot again, with rifles and pistols, to make sure.

More marines trickled out of the cocoanut grove, from the other side of the Tenaru, following the three leaders, advancing just as cautiously. More of our men moved out from our (Pollock's) side of the Tenaru to move across the spit and help in the brutal but necessary re-butchery of the dead. I watched our men standing in a shooting-gallery line, thumping bullets into the piles of Jap carcasses. The edge of the water grew brown and muddy. Some said the blood of the Jap carcasses was staining the ocean.

I followed our men out onto the Tenaru spit. At the far end I talked to some of Cresswell's men; they told me there were hundreds of Jap dead in the grove and beyond, and some wounded prisoners—a few.

Just then came a recrudescence of rifle fire rattling in the cocoanut grove, then a few of the unmistakable sharp cracks of a Jap .25. Snipers were still operating in the grove. We spread out a little on the spit. The strip of sand was not yet a safe meeting-ground.

But the Battle of the Tenaru was to all intents and purposes at an end. The detailed sequence of the fighting was not yet clear. But we knew that a major Japanese attempt to break through our lines and seize the airport had been stopped, and we knew too that this must have been one of the most crushing defeats the Japs had yet suffered. Our own casualties, I found, were only 100, twenty-eight killed and seventy-two wounded; whereas the Japs had lost an estimated 700 killed. (I found later that the actual count of the Jap bodies in the Tenaru battle area was 871.)

SATURDAY, AUGUST 22

This morning I went down to the Tenaru with Lt. Col. Buckley and Capt. Moran, the interpreter.

The stench of bodies strewn along Hell Point and across the Tenaru spit was strong. Many of them lay at the water's edge, and already were puffed and glossy, like shiny sausages. Some of the bodies had been partially buried by wave-washed sand; you might see a grotesque, bloated head or twisted torso sprouting from the beach.

It was not pleasant to look at the piles of bodies on the spit. But that carnage was a pale painting, compared to the scene in the grove across the spit. That was a macabre nightmare. We saw groups of Jap bodies torn apart by our artillery fire, their remains fried by the blast of the shells. We saw machine-gun nests which had been blasted, and their crews shredded, by canister fire from our tanks. The tread tracks of one of our tanks ran directly over five squashed bodies, in the center of which was a broken machine gun on a flattened bipod.

Everywhere one turned there were piles of bodies; here one with a backbone visible from the front, and the rest of the flesh and bone peeled up over the man's head, like the leaf of an artichoke; there a charred head, hairless but still equipped with blackened eyeballs; pink, blue, yellow entrails drooping; a man with a red bullethole through his eye; a dead Jap private, wearing dark, tortoiseshell glasses, his buck teeth bared in a humorless grin, lying on his back with his chest a mess of ground meat. There is no horror to these things. The first one you see is the only shock. The rest are simple repetition.

Walking among the clustered dead of the grove, we could see why it had been difficult to spot the Japs from across the river. They had been well dug in, with excellent foxholes. It had taken our tanks to flush many of them from their holes.

We found some interesting Jap equipment: several flame-throwers, which evidently had not been used; a small Jap field-piece on a little cart; bangalore torpedoes, long pipe-like bombs used to blow up barbed-wire impediments. The Japs' packs contained canned heat, rice, cookies, soap; an extra pair of shoes and gas masks were strapped on the outside. And all the equipment was new; the Japs had been well equipped.

We saw our tank, which had been stopped by a Jap grenade or mortar. It was undamaged, except for the fact that one tread was broken clean in two. The machine was being towed away by a truck.

The snipers who remained in the grove yesterday afternoon had been almost completely cleaned out. Patrols were setting out to finish off the remainder. We could hear scattered shots coming from the eastern part of the grove.

Back at the airport, I found some long-nosed fighter planes, painted army brown, coming in for a landing. They were pursuit ships, the first Army planes to arrive in Guadalcanal. The planes bore bright insignia and spectacular individual crests. One plane carried in large letters the legend "The Flying Pole." The plane's aerial had been painted like a barber's pole, carrying out the motif. And the pilot, inevitably, was a young man of Polish extraction, named Lieut. Edmund E. Brzuska, who came from Chicago. The leader of the group was Capt. Thomas J. J. Christian, whose father is a brigadier general at Camp Sutton, N.C.

At Gen. Vandegrift's headquarters, we heard the story of a native police chief named Vouza. Vouza, it seemed, had been caught by the Japs on a scouting expedition, and tied up and held prisoner when his captors found a small American flag in his possession. The flag had been given to him by marines.

Vouza said that the leader of the Japs who caught him was a notorious Jap agent named Ishimoto. Ishimoto had been a carpenter on Tulagi for years, ostensibly, while he carried on as an agent for the Japs. When the Japs had taken Tulagi, May 5th, Ishimoto had been given a rank in the Jap land forces. He had apparently commanded at least a part of the troops which our forces turned back yesterday at the Battle of the Tenaru.

Vouza, according to the story, was tied to a tree and questioned by Ishimoto as to the American strength and positions. When the middle-aged native refused to talk, the Japs, he reported, stabbed him with bayonets. Still, he would not talk. Finally the Japs left him hanging from the ropes, with gushing wounds in his chest and throat. But the native, nothing daunted, chewed through his bonds with his teeth and walked twenty miles back to our lines. He was hospitalized. (The doctor who tended him told me later that as soon as the bad gash in Vouza's neck had been sewed up, he asked for something to eat.) Vouza told our officers that Ishimoto had seemed certain of victory over our forces; Ishimoto, he said, had bragged about his force of more than 1,000 Japs, said they would "mop up" our people.

I stopped at Col. Pollock's command post and talked with him about the officers and men of his outfit who had distinguished themselves in yesterday's battle. There were many, but several were outstanding:

Pvt. Joe Wadsworth had occupied a foxhole on Hell Point at the time early yesterday morning when the Japs made their all-out effort to cross the Tenaru sandbar and penetrate our lines. He had fired at them with his automatic rifle, killing several, until his gun jammed. Then he had picked up a Springfield rifle and fired with that, and finally, when the Japs had come close, he had jumped up and run to meet them with his bayonet. Then he had been struck by a bullet which knocked him down. But he had refused to be evacuated until the more seriously wounded had been cared for.

Lieut. George Codrea (of Akron, Ohio), whose platoon formed the foremost firing line in the furious fighting during the early morning hours, had been hit twice in the left arm by grenade fragments at 4:30 A.M. But he had stayed on the spot and continued to direct his men, although his wounds were very painful, until 11:30 when the pace of the fighting slackened a bit.

Corp. Lawrence A. DiPietroantonio, when the Japs took one of our field guns in cross fire and killed or wounded the crew and replacements, took over the gun single-handed and operated it as a one-man crew until others could join him.

I stopped at Col. Cresswell's headquarters and he told me more tales, in practically endless sequence, about the marines under his command who had done heroic things in the Tenaru battle. One of them was Corp. Raymond A. Negus (of Peabody, Mass.), who had been wounded in both arms, the abdomen and left thigh as Cresswell's people closed in on the Jap positions from the rear.

Two of his comrades had picked up Corp. Negus on a stretcher, but he had climbed off and told them to take cover, as they were exposed to devastating fire from Jap rifles, mortars and machine guns. And then he had crawled to a safer spot without assistance, despite his wounds.

Pvt. Roy L. Barnes (of Cincinnati, Ohio) had shot a grenade out of the hand of a Jap as the Jap was about to hurl it at Barnes' platoon. When Lieut. Maurice F. Ahearn (of Boston, Mass.) was wounded, a Navy Corpsman, Pharmacist's Mate Third Class Richard J. Garrett, had deliberately placed himself between the wounded officer and the enemy riflemen; he had used himself as a human shield.

Those were the outstanding among the scores of stories I was told by Cols. Cresswell and Pollock. But they were typical. The Battle of the Tenaru had been a first action for many of the marines involved. But they had stood up to the enemy like more seasoned troops.

VI

BOMBARDMENT

SUNDAY, AUGUST 23

There is no laundry on Guadalcanal. It was one of the things the Japs forgot to provide. Apparently they did their own, as we must now do.

I turned to this morning with a wooden bucket and a cake of laundry soap and scrubbed several dirty items. After some hours of effort, I found the clothes were at least a tattletale gray, whereas they had formerly been a darker shade.

It was a pleasant morning. And noontime came and still there had been no air raid. It began to seem that we were going to enjoy one day of rest.

But in the afternoon there came a disrupting surge of "scuttle-butt." A slew of Jap ships were on their way to Guadalcanal.

I checked the story with the best-informed sources, and found it was true. Our patrol aircraft had spotted a large Jap naval force, 150 miles off, heading in our direction. There were transports, cruisers and destroyers to a total of about fourteen ships.

A striking force of our dive-bombers went out to hunt the Japs. But before they could reach the enemy, the weather closed in so that they were unable to make contact. I was at our airport operations center when the pilots came back, looking brokenhearted about the matter.

"I feel like hell about it," said the squadron leader, checking in with the operations chief. "But we just couldn't get in there."

"I never saw anything like it," said another dive-bomber pilot. "I came back from Tulagi two feet over the water, trying to get under the overcast. Even then I couldn't see anything."

There was nothing more to be done about the matter, for the moment, except to leave our shoes on when we went to bed that night. Which we did.

MONDAY, AUGUST 24

The expected Japanese task force did not show up during the night. But a Japanese submarine came up off Kukum at about two o'clock this morning and threw shells into Guadalcanal.

When we heard the sound of the cannonading, Capt. Dickson, Capt. Narder and Major Phipps, my tent mates, rose up in the dark with a swift reflex and sneaked for our dugout, I with them.

It was some time before we discovered what was happening. We could see that the sky over Kukum was illuminated by white light while the shelling went on, and judging from the suddenness with which the light snapped off and on, we estimated it was a searchlight.

The sounds of cannonading were not alarming; we could hear the sound of the shell exploding *before* the whistle of the projectile passing through the air. And that was a good sign. It meant the shells were falling far short of us.

Ten minutes after it had begun, the shelling stopped. But the alarm was not yet over. We could hear the low-toned muttering of motorboat engines coming from the direction of Kukum.

Lieut. Wilson checked on the phone. "Jesus," he said, "they ain't ours. All our boats are beached, all crews inland."

We sat in the CP, waiting and talking while the usual cigarettes glowed in the darkness. It was a scary situation, sitting in the dark, listening to the sound of motorboats, and wondering if that sound marked the coming of the much-expected Jap landing party. But humor does not desert Americans in such situations. We sat, waited and exchanged wisecracks.

Maj. Gannon (James J. Gannon of Philadelphia, Pa.), however, brought news which dampened our spirits for a few minutes. "Number four gun had almost a direct hit," he said, tragically. "I lost two men and two wounded." Our spirits sank. "It's too bad," he said. "But there it is."

But later it developed that this first estimate, like a good deal of first news about casualties, was overly gloomy. We heard the verified fact in the morning: that only one man had been seriously wounded in the shelling.

I visited the spot in the morning with Col. Phipps. Three of those who had been slightly wounded were still on duty at the scene. They told me they still carried pieces of shrapnel in various parts of their arms and legs.

I asked one of the wounded, a husky lad named Kagle (Pvt. George R. Kagle of Abilene, Tex.) if his wounds did not hurt.

"Sure, they hurt some," he said cheerfully. "Like a bee-sting. But outside of that they're O.K."

I looked at the spot where the one marine who had been seriously injured had been lying asleep at the time of the shelling. It was a squat shelter constructed of wooden boxes which were now partially splintered. There was a small, oval-shaped hole in the sand less than ten feet away. Here the shell had struck, sending a shower of fragments into the marine's shelter.

"If he didn't have the little house, he'd of been a dead duck," said Pvt. Kagle.

At about 2:30 in the afternoon, our air-raid siren sounded, and we watched our swift fighter planes zooming into the overcast sky. They were straining to "get upstairs" before the Japs arrived.

I went to an open spot at a bend in the Lunga River to watch the fighting. I could see no planes for a few minutes, ours or theirs. But I distinctly heard the tat-tat-tat of machine guns, the tortured sound of zooming motors.

A plane swooped suddenly out of the sky, streaked over the tree-tops to my right. Then another behind it. The second was one of our Grumman Wildcats. His guns rattled and stopped, then rattled and kept rattling. The first plane, I realized, must be a Jap fighter. Was he strafing the airport? I had time to think only that, and then both planes were gone.

Then we heard the swishing sound of bombs falling, and a sharp, ground-shaking "crack-crack-crack" as they struck. From somewhere up in the gray continent of sky, the Jap bombers had dropped their sticks.

I went to the airport immediately after the "all clear" and waited for our fighters to come down. Most of them seemed almost hilariously elated as they taxied in one by one and jumped down from their cockpits. For most of them, it was a first victory over the enemy—although a few had made contact with some Zeros on the 21st.

A smiling, handsome lieutenant told me how he and another fighter pilot had knocked down two enemy bombers apiece. The pilot was Lieut. Ken Frazier (of Burlington, N.J.). "I took the left side of the formation and Carl [Lieut. Marion E. Carl of Hubbard, Ore.] took the right. I let one have all my guns and he exploded. Then I moved my sights up a little and let go at the second guy. A sheet of flame came out of one of his motors."

Lieut. Frazier had, quite naturally, been excited by the experience. He could not say surely how many enemy bombers there had been or whether they were one or two motored craft.

A blond lad with very white teeth laughed as gaily as if he had been given a much-desired present, as he told his story. He was Lieut. J. H. King (of Brookline, Mass.).

"That bomber was flying along like a fat and happy goose," said Lieut. King. "I dove at it and it just exploded at the first burst."

He told me, laughing as if it were a huge joke, how he had been chased by a flock of Zeros. "I ducked into a cloud," he said. "Each time I came out I found them sitting there buzzing around and waiting."

Col. Fike, the graying executive officer of the marine fliers, was taking notes on their stories, arranging a tally of victory. The memo on his notebook pad showed a total of ten bombers and eleven Zeros shot down in the fight.

Two of our fighter planes were still unreported when we left the airport. Another pilot had been seen to bail out over Tulagi Bay. The rest had returned. It was not a bad score at all: three of our men missing, in exchange for twenty-one Japs shot down.

We drove across the airfield on the way back to our camp. The Japs had missed it completely, although the runways were obviously their target. In a neighboring meadow, we saw two fairly regular lines of large craters churned into the black earth, where sticks of bombs had struck.

A large trailer truck lay on its side, apparently overturned by the bomb blast, and the cab had been riddled, windshield shattered, by bomb fragments. But it was a captured Jap vehicle, and no one, said bystanders, had been in the cab at the time.

There were the usual rumors, this afternoon, that a large force of Japs were on their way in to attack Guadalcanal, and most of us went to bed again with our shoes on, and our helmets within easy reach. But I decided to be comfortable for once, despite the rumors, and took off pants, shirt, shoes and socks.

TUESDAY, AUGUST 25

My taking off my clothes last night, with a view to sleeping more comfortably, turned out to be a great mistake. Just after midnight this morning, my sleep was shattered by explosions coming very close. The instant reflex action took me out of bed and onto the ground, flat. I knew that the others were leaving our tent, dashing for the dugout. I fumbled for my helmet and couldn't find it.

I could hear heavy gunfire, in a sequence that I knew instantly was ominous: the metallic, loud brroom-brroom of the guns going off, then the whistle of the approaching shells, then the crash of the explosions, so near that one felt a blast of air from the concussion.

I ran for the dugout, not stopping even for slippers, but hit the deck and stopped dead still just inside the tent flap when I heard more shells on the way. The crash of the explosions dented in my eardrums, and I could hear the confused sounds of debris falling.

Col. Hunt and I arrived at the dugout at the same moment. We bumped into each other at the entrance and then backed away and I said, "You go first, Colonel." He said politely with a slight bow, "No, after you." And we stood there for a few moments, arguing the matter, while the shells continued to fall. The colonel too had decided to sleep comfortably last night and now wore only his "scivvie" drawers and shirt. We must have made a comical couple, for I took a riding for the rest of the day about the Alphonse-and-Gaston act performed in underwear and under fire.

But the humor of that moment was soon gone. When the barrage halted, we could hear a blubbering, sobbing cry that was more animal than human. A marine came running to the dugout entrance to say that several men had been badly wounded and needed a corpsman. And the crying man kept on, his gurgling rising and falling in regular waves like the sound of some strange machine.

I edged around a smashed tent toward the sound and found myself amidst a scene of frightfulness. One gray-green body lay on its back. There was a small, irregular red hole in the middle of the chest.

Nearby lay the wounded man who had been crying in the night. A big, muscular fellow, he lay on his right side, while a doctor bandaged the shredded remains of one leg, and a corpsman worked on the twisted, gaping mouth of a wound which bared the other leg to the bone.

His face and shoulders lay in the center of a sheet of gore. Face wounds rained blood on the ground. A deep excavation through layers of tissue had been made in one shoulder. The other shoulder, too, was ripped by shrapnel. I could see now how he made the terrible noise. He was crying, sobbing, into a pool of blood. The blood distorted the sound of his wailing, as water would have done, into a bubbling sound. The sound still came in cycles, rising to peaks of loudness. One of the wounded man's hands moved in mechanical circles on the ground, keeping time with his cries.

There were others wounded. Two dim lights, set in a square dark shape, marked an ambulance, standing by. Corpsmen were loading it. The squeak of the stretchers sliding into place, a sound much like that of a fingernail scratched across a blackboard, I shall never forget.

Next to the smashed tent stood the splintered trunk of a palm tree. The top of the tree had fallen onto another tent, squashing one side of it. The tent walls which still stood had been torn by flying shell fragments.

Back at Col. Hunt's headquarters shack, I found Capt. Hodgess, the Australian guide, telling how the treetop had fallen onto his bunk. He found humor in the matter. "First time I ever had a tree in bed with me," he said. He was uninjured.

When the wounded had been carted off, we went tentatively back to bed. And we were glad to hear our planes taking off, obviously in an attempt to attack the Jap ships which had been bombarding us.

In the calm morning light, we found that our damage and casualties in the shelling had been amazingly slight when one considered the possibilities. Only the one shell, which had come so close to my tent, had caused any injuries. That missile had exploded when it struck the top of the palm tree. The downward blast of the explosion had killed the one marine who had died instantly. The marine whom we had heard crying in the night had also been hit by that shell. He had died of his injuries before morning. Two others had been seriously wounded but would not die. About ten had suffered slight wounds from the flying fragments. The damage had been confined to the two tents, a few holes in surrounding structures, and the broken palm tree. We made up for the tree to some degree by serving the hearts-of-palm, a choice part of the branch, for lunch today.

In general, it seemed amazing that the enemy could throw so many rounds of ammunition into our camp and do so little damage.

We had word from our shore observation posts this morning that the force which had shelled us consisted of three destroyers. Evidently the destroyers had been carrying troops which were landed at a point to the west of the airport, well beyond our lines. Then the small armada had swung along the shore to pay us their respects with high explosives.

At the airport operations headquarters, Lieut. Turner Caldwell (of San Diego, Cal.), the leader of a squadron of naval dive-bombers, told me that the marauding Jap ships had been spotted by our planes and a possible hit scored on one of the destroyers.

"Anybody that flew over the spot today could see an oil slick about twenty-five miles long," he said. "It might be we sank the destroyer."

While we were talking, there was an almost continual roar of planes taking off from the airport. They were going out to attack the large Jap task force of warships and transports which had been hovering in this area. More bombing flights went up all through the day. The results were encouraging: the Jap forces had been turned back and dispersed and one of their cruisers and two transports badly damaged.

At the aviation bivouac, I found a group of marine dive-bomber pilots sprawling under a tent canopy. They seemed exhausted, and most had wiry incipient beards and dirty faces; they had been flying since midnight this morning. Some of them told me they had slept in their planes.

They told their stories cheerfully. Maj. Richard C. Mangrum (of Seattle, Wash.), leader of the group, told me smilingly about the unusual way in which he had hit one of the Jap transports.

"I dived on the cruiser in our original attack," he said. "But my bomb got stuck and wouldn't come off. I didn't know about it at the time.

"When we were flying back home after the attack was completed, the other guys told me my bomb was still on. So I left the formation and went back. I saw a transport then that we hadn't even seen before. I guess it had been under a cloud."

Maj. Mangrum's radioman and rear gunner, Corp. Dennis Byrd, described the hit the major had scored. "The bomb seemed to hit near the fantail," he said. "A big column of smoke and water went up." Byrd said he was sure the steering apparatus of the ship must have been damaged.

The pilots said it is always hard to see your own hit, if you are a dive-bomber, because by the time the bomb strikes, you are too busy pulling out of your dive, and dodging anti-aircraft, to take time to look behind you. A radioman–rear gunner, who faces the rear, or a squadron mate, however, often has an excellent view.

Lieut. Lawrence Baldinus (of Yuma, Mich.) had not been able to see the hit he scored directly amidships on the largest Jap transport, which incidentally carried the large red flag of a Jap general or admiral, and might have been a flagship. But Lieut. Don E. McCafferty (of Hempstead, L.I.) said he had enjoyed a "fascinating view" of Baldinus' bombing.

"The bomb hit right by the bridge," he said, "and everything went up as if it was made of wood—like a model in the movies. I veered over to watch it, I was so fascinated, just everything spraying up and coming down."

Maj. Mangrum said he had seen Baldinus' transport, which was a big ship of about 14,000 tons, burning fiercely, and seen indications that the crew were abandoning ship. "There were small boats all over the water," he said.

I found Lieut. Fink (Chris Fink of Gray Bull, Wyo.), the naval dive-bomber who had hit the enemy cruiser, a new vessel of the *Jintsu* class. He was a slow-speaking Westerner, and said, as the other pilots had said, that he had not had a chance to watch his bomb hit. But his radioman, Milo L. Kimberlin (of Spokane, Wash.), told the story: "The bomb hit right on the bridge and a sheet of flame and smoke went right up to the clouds. I could see the stack and bridge lift out of the ship and go kerplunk into the ocean. She was still burning when we left. You could see the smoke and flames for about forty miles."

I was skirting the airfield en route to Col. Hunt's CP this afternoon, when the air-raid alert sounded, and a few moments later, we heard the impressive sound of many powerful engines, and saw the usual thin silver line of Japanese bombers spanning the sky.

There were twenty-one of them, this time. I counted them; then, as they were almost overhead, I dashed for shelter behind a huge limestone rock. I heard the bombs coming down, and the swishing sound of their descent was louder than I had ever heard it before. I forgot technique—forgot the approved method of taking bomb cover, which is to support yourself a little on elbows to avoid concussion—and instead burrowed as deeply as possible into the ground. The crash of the stick of bombs was loud, and I felt the earth jerk with the impact. Clods of dirt came showering down. When the last "carrummp" had sounded, I waited a few seconds, then got up a bit shaken and looked across the grassy field at a row of fresh, clean-cut, black bomb craters. The ground everywhere around was strewn with small, cube-shaped clods of earth. I measured off the distance between me and the nearest crater. It was not much more than 200 yards.

Tonight I heard cheerful reports of an action between our naval forces and the Japs', somewhere near Guadalcanal: our torpedo bombers from a carrier had attacked the Jap carrier *Ryuzyo* and probably sunk it; at the same time, eighty-one Jap planes had attacked one of our carriers and seventy-one had been shot down. Our bombers had scored hits on other Jap warships of unspecified number and type.

WEDNESDAY, AUGUST 26

Bob Miller and I were standing at the edge of the airfield today when the now-routine Jap air raid occurred. We now have the timing of these matters pretty well organized. We know about how long we can afford to watch the bombers coming before taking cover. Today we heard the bombs screeching down as loud and close as they were yesterday. Then we piled into a small foxhole. This time I remembered to support myself slightly on my elbows, to avoid concussion, in case one came too close. Some of our people have been so badly shaken by close ones that they have suffered shock and prolonged bleeding from the nose.

The worst time in a bombing is the short moment when you can hear the bombs coming. Then you feel helpless, and you think very intensely of the fact that it is purely a matter of chance whether or not you will be hit. The chances vary with your location: the Japs are bombing such and such an area, so many acres; the circles of fragments from their bombs will cover a certain proportion of the total acreage. You wonder if your portion of the acreage will be overlapped by the acreage of the bombs.

If you are caught on the airport by a bombing, you can figure your chances for escaping injury are much fewer than elsewhere, for the airport always seems to be the Japs' target. But even in other parts of the island, where odds may be greater, say, nine out of ten that you won't be hit, you wonder if you will be the unlucky tenth case.

You will also think about those who have been cruelly wounded or killed by previous bombings, and in your imagination you suffer the shock of similar wounds. You also wonder why, instead of getting into a shelter which has a sandbagged roof, you stayed around to gawk and left yourself only time to get to an open foxhole or nothing at all for protection except the flatness of the earth. When you have nothing but the earth and your lack of altitude to protect you, you feel singularly naked and at the mercy of the bombs.

These thoughts pass very swiftly through your head during the short time that seems so long, the time when you hear the bombs swishing and rattling through the air on their way down to you. And while your mind is racing through these thoughts, your ears, without any conscious effort on your part, are straining to gauge the closeness of the bombs from the swishing and the rattling of them.

After the sticks have hit, you wait a few more minutes, suffering from a disinclination to get up immediately; you watch the ground, close in front of your eyes, very patiently, and wait to see if there will be another stick or more sticks. Usually, here on Guadalcanal, there are no more sticks after the bombers have made one run. They do not come back then because they are too busy trying to fend off our fighters.

When you finally get up to look around, you have butterflies in your chest and your breath is noticeably short and your hands feel a bit shaky. Those feelings do not seem to be avoidable by any conscious effort.

This morning Miller and I jumped up rather quickly after the sticks had cracked down, and before the dust columns of the explosions had settled saw reddish flames leaping into spreading brown smoke at the far edge of the field. Some of the bombs had hit one of our oil dispersal dumps. But there did not seem to be any other damage.

Gen. Vandegrift passed us in his jeep. He was anxious to see what damage, if any, the bombs had done to the airfield. Miller and I hitched a ride with him, and we dashed over toward the fires; but as we came close we could see that only a few barrels had been hit.

"I can see those Jap pilots turning in a report about how they turned the airport into a holocaust," said Miller. "How they could see the flames for forty miles, etc." We laughed, because undoubtedly that was just what the Japs did—those who got back.

Somewhere up in the sky the crescendo, protesting wails of zooming and diving motors could be heard, and the chatter of machine guns. We knew many of the Japs would never get back to make any report at all.

The general turned his jeep to another part of the airport, and that was fortunate, for a delayed-action bomb, a big fellow, blew up near the spot where we had turned, a few seconds after we left.

Miller and I hopped off at one of the shelter pens, the skeletal type of hangars the Japs had built on the airport, and waited for our fliers to come down.

Marion Carl came in, grinning happily, to tell us that he had shot down his fifth and sixth planes—both Zeros. The lads call him "the Zero man," literally a very unflattering title, but in this connotation quite agreeable to Carl.

The other pilots seem to have great respect for Carl. They don't mention it to him, but one of them told me today: "What a pilot! He's a natural. Always relaxed."

Carl was with the marine fliers on Midway, during the great battle, and shot down one Zero there. I asked him how the Zeros he was meeting over Guadalcanal compared with those at Midway.

"I dunno why," he said, "but we got shot up a lot more there than we do here. Maybe the pilots were better than these."

Capt. John L. Smith (of Lexington, Okla.), Carl's squadron leader, is a more quiet type. He has the steadiest eyes I have ever seen; they are brown and wide-set and you fancy they would be most at home looking out over the great plains of the West.

Smith is a prairie type: tanned face, wide cheekbones, the erect head of a horseman, a thick neck set on square shoulders, a big, sinewy body. You get the impression that life must have a calm, elemental simplicity for him.

Capt. Smith did not say so, but he is the ace among the fliers on Guadalcanal. Already he has shot down nine enemy planes. And that success does not seem to have excited or perturbed him at all.

Back at my tent, I found Don Dickson and Lieut. McLeod (William J. McLeod of St. Petersburg, Fla.) sitting on a bunk, deep in conversation. They seemed to be working over some sort of document. Dickson, who usually has a wonderfully good temper, said rather curtly: "We have a little private matter here."

I felt a little cut, but later found out what the conspiracy was. P.F.C. Tardiff informed me that I was under arrest, and two marines with fixed bayonets took me in tow. Dickson came by and said with mock gravity, "You're a prisoner of war."

Capt. Hodgess, the Australian, was also brought along under military guard. We stood side by side—"Stand at attention, Pvt. Tregaskis," snapped Lieut. Wilson—while Col. Hunt marched out and gravely read a long "citation" for each of us. This document honored us for our speed in getting to a dugout amidst a bombardment and drafted us for membership in the "Lunga Point Shell-Dodging Marines."

Don Dickson, who had been an artist and cartoonist in civilian life, had embellished our citations with comic drawings. Making them had been his "private matter" in the tent. The documents were embellished with official-looking seals made from Jap beer-bottle labels.

Col. Hunt solemnly pinned captured Japanese medals on Viv Hodgess' chest and mine. It was the Eighth Order of Palenowa. "We found a case of those in the Jap tent camp," said Col. Hunt. (Later he told me: "We had to put on some kind of show for the boys. They were getting a little bit glum.")

Tonight was quiet. The Jap submarine which visits us nocturnally—we now call it "Oscar"—did not show up. Nor did the cruisers and destroyers which have often bothered us.

But I was not to have any rest this night, despite the quiet of the evening. I was awakened by the unpleasant symptoms of a local epidemic, which the doctors call gastro-enteritis.

THURSDAY, AUGUST 27

I thought I could sleep off my illness, but that was impossible. This was a formidable assault of the ailment. I generated a dizzying fever and nausea.

This morning the air-raid alert sounded. I felt too sick to move from my cot, whatever happened. Don Dickson came in and said the warning had become urgent, and asked if I wanted help in getting to the dugout. I told him I would stay where I was.

I heard the drone of planes in the sky and got my helmet and put it on, then turned face down on the cot. That way, I figured, I would have a maximum of protection.

But the bombers did not make a run today. They jettisoned their bombs somewhere in the backwoods. Evidently they are growing chary of our fighters. (Yesterday, according to the official count, our fighters downed seven Jap bombers and five Zeros.)

For some time I lay abed, feeling dizzier and sicker by the moment. I could hear the booming of cannon-firing batteries. Don Dickson told me it was our own batteries I heard. They were shelling the Matanikau-Kokumbona area. The Jap forces which had been landed piecemeal at nighttime had filtered back into those villages. We were going to blast them out. The artillery was softening the positions. Then a large body of troops was going to move in, later in the day.

Dr. Hopkins (Henry Hopkins, of Hyannis, Mass.) came in to give me some medicine; my nausea quickly disposed of it. After that, I was carried off feet first. I remember hearing the familiar squeak of the stretcher as I was put into the ambulance, the jouncy ride, losing my sense of direction, and reading, several times, the red letters "USN, MC" painted on the stretcher above mine, being placed on a cot that was too short for me, as most of them are, and then suffering through four or five hours of tortured sleep and being conscious that my fever was rising and nausea increasing. I had a bad case.

(Gastro-enteritis is marked by a combination of nausea, vomiting, diarrhea and high fever. The organism, if there is one, has not been isolated. The doctors on Guadalcanal knew little of the cause of the matter, were too busy with more serious matters to bother about pathological research into this local plague.)

It was dark when I became conscious of movement and talking at the entrance to the tent. I heard the shuffling of feet, and somebody said: "His clothes are wet. Better get 'em off." They had brought in a casualty. I was too sick to be interested. But the voices kept on.

"What's the matter with him?"

"Sunstroke."

Then I heard grunts and groans. They were moving the man from the stretcher to bed.

"He's a big 'un," said a voice.

A doctor spoke in a pleasant, soft voice. "Were you out in the sun?" he asked.

The man spoke as if it were difficult to summon wind enough for words. "Chees," he said. It was a sort of gasp. Then he said, "Chees," again, and finally: "I've got a platoon. On the ridge."

"You're in the hospital now," said the doctor. "I'm Dr. Lynch." (Dr. George Lynch of Boston, Mass.)

The man said "Chees" again. And then, sick as I was, I recognized the voice. It was Lieut. Donoghue, of Jersey City, one of my shipmates on the transport which had brought me to Guadalcanal.

Finally the corpsmen brought Lieut. Donoghue to, and he told, between gasps of "Chees," a foggy story of having been out on a ridge with his machine-gun platoon. They were advancing on Matanikau with the other troops, he said, when the commanding officer ordered him to take his platoon up onto a steep rocky ridge. "My men pooped out," he said, "after we got up. I went down to look for Capt. Hawkins. I asked where he was. Next thing I remember, Dr. Claude giving me a drink. . . . Chees."

Another of the men in the tent, a young lieutenant who was recuperating from gastro-enteritis, wanted to chat in the evening. He and the corpsman in charge talked about the fight for Matanikau. The corpsman said there had not been many casualties in today's attempt to get into the town. He said there were some killed and wounded, but the wounded weren't being brought here; they were being taken to another hospital.

FRIDAY, AUGUST 28

Lieut. Donoghue repeated his story this morning. He said he felt better, but he talked as if thinking and speaking were a great effort.

The young lieutenant who is recuperating talked with the corpsman about how good the "chow" was at this camp. The lieutenant said he wished he could stay awhile. Possibly by accident, he smoked a cigarette just before his temperature was to be taken. This upset the corpsman, who accused the lieutenant of gold-bricking, which, after some confusion, the lieutenant cheerfully admitted.

Lieut. Donoghue, at the opposite extreme, begged the doctor to let him go, as his mind cleared at about midday. "I hate to lie down in one place, Doc," he said.

I still suffered from nausea and vomiting and fever, and was not inclined to be interested in any of these goings-on, or even curious when later in the afternoon a lot of our planes took off, and there was a great, excited passing of "scuttlebutt" about a huge Japanese task force which was supposedly on its way to attack Guadalcanal. (I got the news next day that a force of one small Jap destroyer and three larger ones had been spotted by a patrol of our dive-bombers near Santa Isabel Island. The dive-bombers had attacked the small destroyer and set it afire. And a striking force—the other planes which we had heard taking off—had found the small destroyer listing and burning, and had attacked two of the others. Both of these had been hit; one exploded and sank, and the second burned and was apparently heavily damaged.)

Lieut. Donoghue talked about the advance on Matanikau. He said that en route he had passed the mutilated body of a young woman lying by the side of the trail. He said that the girl had been raped and her torso hacked.

Tonight the other patients in the tent, who were with one exception in better shape than I (the exception was a sick officer who was being checked for possible malaria), spent an interminable time yarning about the Solomons campaign to date. Some of the stories were fairly interesting; like the one about the Jap who, in the first night on Tulagi, was challenged by a marine sentry. The Jap said in English that he was the corporal of the guard. "O.K., bud," said the marine, and opened up with his pistol. There was no such thing as a corporal of the guard in that organization.

Another story, which I had heard before, was about the Japs in one of the dugout caves on Tulagi. An interpreter went out to ask them, in Japanese, to surrender; one of the Japs had stuck his head out of the entrance and answered in colloquial English.

That led to other yarns about the Japs' ability to speak English, and the alleged fact that many of the dead wore American high-school rings. Then, there were stories about the American mementoes that had been found on Jap bodies. American cigarette

cases, etc. Then the yarning turned to our first days on Guadalcanal, the large amount of shooting at shadows during the first few
nights ashore and how, allegedly, the general had issued an order
that no shots should be fired, that only the bayonet should be used,
and that this measure had cut down the unnecessary firing—that
was the story.

And so the yarning went on, and finally somebody told the
classic story about the two marine jeep drivers on Guadalcanal,
supposedly a true story, very true, anyhow, in its essential American psychology. It was about two jeeps passing in the night, one
with proper dim-out headlights, the other with glaring bright
lights. So the driver of the dim-light car leans out as they pass and
shouts to the other driver: "Hey! Put your f— — — — —g lights out!"
To which the other replies: "I can't. I've got a f— — — — —g colonel
with me!"

SATURDAY, AUGUST 29

This morning at about four o'clock I heard somebody shout "Air
raid!" and slid out of bed and through the folds of my mosquito net
and onto the floor just as the bombs came swishing down. The
crack of their explosions, however, was not loud, and I surmised
they were small ones. We found after the excitement was over that
some Jap floatplanes had made a sneak attack. The bombs had
fallen far from the airfield and caused only a few casualties.

From 9:30 on, we spent the morning dragging ourselves to a
dugout and back; there were three air-raid alarms. The shelter was
crammed with sick people. The feverish, emaciated wrecks, most of
them suffering from gastro-enteritis, were a pitiful sight.

The Japs did not show up until noontime. Then there were
twenty-four bombers with an escort of twenty-two Zeros. I climbed
out of the murky air of the dugout—I was feeling well enough to

haul myself around without help by this time—and watched our anti-aircraft bursting in the sky. Then came a shower of bombs, and I could see the dark-brown smoke of their explosions rising above the treetops.

Our fighters caught the Japs. I heard the familiar sound of diving or zooming motors and rattling machine guns in the clouds. And then one plane came tearing down out of the sky in the most awful power dive I have heard. The sound accelerated and rose in a crescendo that filled the sky. I never saw the plane, but it seemed a certainty that it was coming down directly on top of us. But I heard the plane crash some distance away, and a cloud of black smoke edged up over the trees to the south.

It was a Jap bomber. Visitors who came later in the day to our tent said that the plane had come down vertically and must have been going well over 600 miles an hour when it hit the ground, and that it disintegrated like a bomb on impact. Apparently the pilot had been killed, and in his dying efforts, had jammed the controls forward. The total tally of our pilots for the day was three Jap bombers downed and four Zeros. We had lost no planes in the fighting.

A marine who came in to bring some clothes to one of the in-mates of our tent told us that Matanikau had been successfully oc-cupied by our troops, but that the resistance indicated that the Japs had been landing troops and supplies. And the impression had been confirmed by the discovery of large stores of fresh ammunition and food cans.

It is rather easy for the Japs to build up strong forces, piece by piece, on other parts of this island—if the transporting ships can reach our shores unharmed, which they have been able to do.

We hold a tiny strip of this island, a toehold, a piece about seven miles wide and four miles deep, centering around the airport. The Japs can move about the remainder of the island, which is ninety miles long and thirty miles deep, almost at will.

SUNDAY, AUGUST 30

We were roused at 1:30 this morning by an alert, and went over to the air-raid shelter in the moonlight. But no aircraft appeared, and at 1:45 we went back to bed. I helped a feverish gastro-enteritis sufferer from the steaming dugout and found his arm hot to the touch. I was glad that I had shaken the disease.

After breakfast I got my discharge from the hospital and went down to Kukum. Two ships were lying offshore, one a freighter, the other the auxiliary transport *Calhoun*.

We had an air-raid alert soon after, and the two ships up-anchored and hustled off to sea, where they would have more room to maneuver evasively if attacked.

Lieut. Comdr. Dexter told us we would have a good view of the raid from the beach. "We have the best spot on the island," he said. "We see the approach, the anti-aircraft fire, watch the bombs drop, see the dogfights, and send boats out to pick up the aviators who get shot down."

But today there was a low ceiling of heavy, dark cumulus clouds, and a beneficent rain-squall covered the *Calhoun* and the freighter. They were blotted out of sight even from shore.

No bombers appeared, but we heard the sounds of a furious dogfight coming from the high banks of clouds. It lasted for about ten minutes.

At the airport, we talked to the fighter pilots as they came in from the raid. Capt. Smith told us he had had his biggest day of fighting, had shot down four Zeros, three of them, he said, in a minute and a half.

"I dove on one, shot him down, and saw another on my wingman's tail," he said, calmly. "I slewed over and picked off that one. Then I saw one coming at me from below and ahead. I nosed over and dove right at him and let all my guns go. I had a tough time avoiding crashing him head on. I could see the prop shatter, and I came so close I could see his damned head—his helmet and goggles. He was trying to climb out of the ship then, and I guess he used his chute."

After that, said the captain, he had ammunition left for only one gun. He lit out for the airport, trying to sneak in low over the water. "I was flat-hatting along the beach at about fifty feet," he said, "when I saw two Zeros ahead and to the right. I made a run on one of them with my one gun and saw him fall off and dive into the water. The other one took off as fast as he could go. I did too, because I'd used up all my ammo."

Capt. Carl also had a good day's dogfighting; he told us happily that he had shot down three more Zeros, making his total score nine, to date.

At Gen. Vandegrift's headquarters, we got the official word that eighteen of the Zeros encountered that day had been shot down. Gen. Vandegrift was happy about it. Today, he said, interception had been perfect; the bombers were driven off and most of the Zeros destroyed.

But the afternoon was not yet over; suddenly we got word of a surprise air raid and raced for cover. Then we felt the ground shake, from deep down, as if there were an earthquake. There was a succession of tremors, and we heard deep, dull booming sounds coming from the direction of Kukum. I raced for the open and saw a towering black cloud mushrooming over the trees in the direction of Kukum.

The cloud of smoke mounted higher into the sky, and then we heard the news: the *Calhoun* had been hit by Jap bombers. They had come in three waves, a total of sixteen bombers, and the little auxiliary transport had been hit squarely by three bombs. She had sunk almost immediately.

Miller and I set out for Kukum immediately in a jeep, but it was impossible to get there. The roads were jammed with trucks bringing in survivors and wounded. We gave up the project of getting to

Kukum, and I contented myself with talking to Dr. Bill Duell (of Hackensack, N.J.), who had seen the bombing.

The deep explosions which we had felt shaking the earth, he said, had been caused by depth charges. A submarine had been hovering in the vicinity at the time the bombers attacked the *Calhoun*. One of our destroyers had dropped a series of depth charges at the same time the *Calhoun* was being bombed.

"I saw a lot of little puffs traveling along the surface where the depth charges were going off," he said. "You could feel the ground shake; it was terrific, out there on the beach. And then the black bow of the sub just reared out of the water like a whale and sank back."

Losing the *Calhoun* seemed like a terrible tragedy at the moment. But later in the evening, we heard that the loss of life aboard the ship had been slight. We had recovered about 100 of the crew, lost only about thirty-eight.

Tonight there was none of the usual "scuttlebutt" about an enemy task force being on its way into our island, but late in the evening we heard the sounds of many of our planes taking off and surmised that some sort of contact had been made.

SUNDAY, AUGUST 31

This morning at operations headquarters on the airport (which now, incidentally, is being called Henderson Field after the heroic marine flier of the Midway battle), we heard that four Japanese troop-carrying destroyers had been spotted last night trying to land forces at Koli Point, about twenty miles to the east of our positions.

The two fliers who had spotted the ships were on patrol at the time. They had dropped their bombs, but the visibility was poor and they were undergoing heavy anti-aircraft fire at the time; the combination had made it hard for them to observe the effects of their bombing.

After that the patroling pilots had called by radio for supporting aircraft, but the striking force which we had heard taking off had failed to intercept the enemy. Evidently, they had hauled out of the area after the attack of our two patrol planes.

I heard that one of the two patrol fliers had been wounded. Then I learned that he was an ensign whom I had met on a previous Pacific war adventure, "Spike" Conzett (Elmer E. Conzett of Dubuque, Iowa). I went down to the field hospital to see "Spike."

One of his long legs was bandaged, in the region of the knee, and he looked a bit drawn. He said he had a chunk of shrapnel in there, and that it pained a bit now.

"I didn't even see those birds until they opened up with anti-aircraft, and I got this," he said, motioning toward his leg. "They shot out my instrument panel, filled the cockpit full of holes, and scared the hell out of me."

Spike said that the other flier up with him, a Capt. Brown of the marines (Capt. Fletcher L. Brown of Pensacola, Fla.), had spotted the enemy ships before he did. Brown had dived on one of the ships.

"The weather was pretty thick up there," said Conzett, "but I made an approach and dived and let my bomb go, too.

"On the way back here I got lost and thought I'd never get out of it. I was trying to fly by what instruments I had left, and that didn't work out very well. I got into a spin and spun down from 8,000 to about 4,500 before I could pull out of it. My radioman said he was figuring on getting out and hitting his chute. It was that bad."

But after he got out of his spin, said Spike, things straightened out a bit and he found his way back to Guadal but, he added, "I was pretty feeble when I reached here, and I couldn't find the runway. I was lucky to get in at all."

There were three air-raid alarms today. But none of them developed, and enemy planes reached Guadalcanal only on the second alarm. They were frightened by our fighters and jettisoned their bombs in the jungles to the southwest and then retreated precipitously.

The longest air-raid alarm lasted from 12:30 to 1:30. I picked out a comfortable foxhole by a bend in the Lunga and lay on my back, watching the sky. It was pleasant there, lying beside the swift-moving water, infinitely preferable to the hot dugouts where most of our people go for such occasions.

TUESDAY, SEPTEMBER 1

Good news today that our coast defenses are being strengthened by extra artillery of large caliber. This news heightens the general air of optimism, which is engendered by a combination of other circumstances.

The fact, for instance, that for the last two days the Jap bombers have shown themselves to be frightened and cautious; they have turned back and unloaded their bombs.

And then the fact that last night was particularly calm, with no shellings either by "Oscar" or the usual force of Jap destroyers or cruisers.

Furthermore, things have been quiet along our land fronts, and large numbers of Japs have been coming in to surrender. Apparently their food is getting short.

Increased numbers of ships have been coming in with supplies of late, including food as well as ammunition. Soon, we hope, we may be able to start eating three meals a day, getting away from our present scanty schedule of two meals.

We are also becoming a little more comfortable in our island quarters. A few elementary necessities like privies have been slammed together, mostly made from prefabricated Japanese housing sections which we captured here.

Our privy, at Col. Hunt's command post, is called "McLeod's Masterpiece," after Lieut. McLeod, who built it. A rope set on stakes has been constructed leading from the command post to the masterpiece, so that one may find his way in the dark. Lieut. Wilson has labeled this the "McLeoderheim Line," and set up a poster celebrating the fact.

We also have an oven which has been fashioned from a captured Japanese safe, so that Juan Morrera, our cook, can make bread. Bread, however, is still so scarce that it is received with whoops of joy and eaten with as much relish as if it were cake.

It is startling to think how one's standards of values change under the continued impetus of living conditions such as ours on Guadalcanal. Things like bread and privies, considered the barest necessities at home, become luxuries. One thinks of warm water, the smooth water-closet seat of civilization, and a bed with sheets as things that exist only in a world of dreams.

Miller and I went to Kukum at about noon today to watch for an air raid. There was an urgent alert, but again the Japs did not appear. We went for a swim in the beautiful clear water along Kukum Beach. The swimming was superb, but would have been more enjoyable if we had not found it necessary to look out for sharks. Sharks are the principal hazard of swimming in salt water hereabouts—that and the hazard of getting fungus infections in the ear, just as crocodiles impinge on one's contentment while swimming in the Lunga River.

This afternoon trucks came to dump a pile of gray canvas sacks at Col. Hunt's CP. It was mail—the first to reach the troops since we landed on Guadalcanal! Each man seemed as happy as if you had given him a hundred-dollar bill at the mere thought of getting mail. And that evening was an orgy of reading. Most of the men had three or four letters each; they sat about in circles and read them several times, and read pieces of them to each other.

Guy Narder dashed into our tent with a letter in his hand and shouted: "I'm a mother!" The girl's name, he said, was Geraldine, and she had been born on the 27th of June.

Don Dickson stood at the tent door, watching more mail being sorted out for delivery. "Mail should have priority before food," he said.

Col. Hunt had three letters. "They're from Dear Mom," he said, "and no bills."

Sgt. Charlie Morris had a bill, however. It was from the Book-of-the-Month Club.

I saw a circle of marines clustered about one of the lads who had a reputation for being a demon with the gals. These, he said, were letters from his Number One girl.

"That's the only dame he could never make," said one of his admirers good-naturedly. "He wants to *marry* her."

The Sheik only chuckled. "F– – – you, Mac," he said, indulging in the marines' favorite word. "The trouble with you is you never met a virgin."

WEDNESDAY, SEPTEMBER 2

Guy Narder, who is a communications officer, waked me at 2:30 this morning to ask if I wanted to come to the radio dugout.

"They've got an enemy contact," he said. "Want to listen to the calls?"

"They caught some ships that were landing troops," he said, as we probed our way through the night.

We climbed down into the lantern-lit dugout and Narder gave me an earphone. The set was tuned to our inter-air frequency.

We could hear planes taking off from the airfield. But there was no sound in the earphones, except the crackling of static. Nearly an hour later, we heard the message:

"To all planes from control. Plane Two is in the target area. He will drop flares. He will drop flares."

A few minutes later: "Over enemy ships dropping flares"—a report from Plane Two, on the job.

But the other planes were having trouble trying to spot the enemy.

"I am down to 1,000 feet trying to pick up enemy. Visibility very poor."

I had begun to realize before this how difficult are flying weather conditions around Guadalcanal, how hard it is for our planes to spot enemy ships at night unless the moon is very bright.

Now we heard some of the planes, having difficulty in the thick overcast, calling Control in an attempt to find out the exact enemy position.

One pilot heard the calls and reported: "During initial dive on the cruiser it was heading due east. That was fifteen minutes ago. She was making twenty knots. I haven't located them since."

"How many miles east of the field?" asked Control.

"Twenty miles," was the answer.

"The enemy is landing troops at Taivu Bay, twenty miles east of the airport," reported Control to all planes.

A few minutes later we heard inter-air conversations of pilots who were evidently on the scene but could not locate the enemy.

"Let's go down to 500 feet," said one voice. "They should be directly under us around here." But there was no contact. Weather conditions out there must have been abominable. I took off the earphone and looked out the dugout door. The night was black; there was no trace of a moon.

It was after four o'clock when we heard the news of a contact relayed to headquarters: "Control from Plane Three: three large landing boats sighted east of Taivu Point."

Plane Twenty-seven corrected: "One mile *west* of Taivu Point." But the weather was evidently too thick for interception.

I gave up the long night watch at about 5:00 and went back to bed. I was just getting to sleep when I heard the sudden rattle of bombs on their way down. I shouted, "Hit the deck!" and the others in the tent were so well trained that we all landed on the tent floor at about the same moment—the moment that we heard the crack of the bombs exploding.

Fortunately, they were not close to our camp, and fortunately the Jap attackers did not make another "run" on our positions. But there came salvos of gunfire a few minutes later, which apparently landed far down our shores to the east.

Miller and I hustled to the headquarters building at the airport to find out whether any damage had been done to the Jap ships which were apparently landing troops at Taivu last night. Col. Fike said misty weather had interfered with the contact, but added that three large Jap landing boats had been strafed by our Navy and marine fliers.

An Army captain came in to report that his flight of Pursuits, which had just returned from a patrol, had found six large Jap landing boats on the beach near Taivu (the Pursuits went back later in the day to strafe the boats). He reported there was no activity in the area, no people visible, and no sign of the Jap ships which had launched the boats.

Col. Fike said there was no definite information as to the number or type of ships. But probably they were several of the now-familiar, troop-carrying type of destroyer, and probably at least one cruiser, for the two planes which had come over and dropped bombs just before daylight this morning had been cruiser-type aircraft.

At Col. Cates' CP we heard that there had been only one casualty in this morning's early raid, and that casualty had been a man who lost his leg in the explosion of a delayed-action bomb. Our people are becoming more expert at taking cover; with the exception of those who stay out to watch the show, few are being injured or killed.

Two more correspondents have come in to Guadalcanal. They are Tom Yarbrough and Tillman Durdin. They have glamorous fresh uniforms and make Miller and me feel like street urchins, for our hand-washed clothes are scarcely clean and our faces stand in need of a good scrubbing with hot water.

This afternoon we had two air-raid alerts, and after the second, eighteen Jap bombers appeared and dropped their sticks. Three bombers and five fighters were shot down in the mêlée that followed.

For a few minutes after the bombers had dropped their sticks, we heard the rattle of small arms fire and heavier explosions sounding like mortar or artillery shells, coming from the direction of the Tenaru. We wondered if the Japs were making another attempt to break through our lines, but Lieut. Wilson checked by phone and looked contented as he reported: "It's only a small ammo dump. Bombs set it afire."

Col. Hunt has one of the few desks in the Solomons—an item captured from the Japs. Some of the officers of the Raiders came into the CP this afternoon and asked if they might use the desk. Then they spread out maps and started a deep discussion. I found they were laying plans for an expedition to Taivu, where the Japs last night apparently landed troops and supplies, and where, according to our scouts, there is now a good-sized task force. That should be an interesting excursion. I may go along.

THURSDAY, SEPTEMBER 3

We were awakened at fifteen minutes after midnight this morning by guns booming offshore, from the direction of Kukum. I sat outside the dugout and watched the flashes lighting the sky, heard the haughty voices of the cannon. The shells were not coming in our direction at all this time. Others came out of the dugout and we watched the firing.

Lieut. Wilson checked with Kukum, and told us the beach watchers had spotted three subs lying off Savo Island (which is off the western end of Guadalcanal). One of the subs, which lay closest to Guadalcanal, was doing the shelling. Comdr. Dexter said that there were small fires burning along the shore near Matanikau, apparently signals to the Jap subs.

The shelling lasted about ten minutes more, then stopped. And Wilson said, "Oscar's tired." So were we. We went back to bed.

There were several air-raid alarms this morning, and Miller and I went out to Kukum to watch. But the Japs did not come. They were growing exceedingly timid, and that was encouraging.

Back at Col. Hunt's CP, I found the Raider officers at work over their maps. But, they told me, their plans, for the time being, had been changed; they were going to make a landing at Savo Island first, and put off the Taivu expedition until after that.

It seemed that mysterious fires, possibly signal fires, had been seen on Savo Beach of late. And one flier thought, but was not sure, that he had been fired on by a machine gun as he flew over the island. A large group of Raiders were being sent to conduct a reconnaissance in force. They were leaving this afternoon.

Miller and I stopped in at Col. Edson's CP (he had moved his people from Tulagi to Guadalcanal) and got permission to accompany the expedition to Savo.

The auxiliary transports *Little* and *Gregory* were going to carry this group of Raiders to Savo. Miller and I were told to be at a certain embarkation point at four o'clock to get aboard one of these ships. But we were late. The ships were pulling out as we arrived.

Col. Edson was standing on shore at the time. He was not going along on this trip. Lieut. Col. Sam Griffith, Edson's executive, was leading the show.

Col. Edson said: "You're too late." But he was helpful. "Get aboard the cargo ship," he ordered, "and you can get aboard the transports later.

"Better get going," he snapped, "or you'll miss it." We did not understand at all how we could get aboard one ship, which was leaving, by getting aboard another which was not leaving. But Col. Edson was the leader; we obeyed his instructions.

The mystery became clear soon after we went aboard the handsome cargo ship. She was going to put to sea in a few minutes, and later in the night would have a secret rendezvous with the two transports. Then we would be able to change over to the *Little*.

We were not sorry to be aboard the cargo ship. She was clean and brightly modern. A friendly officer showed me to his bath and gave me a clean towel, and I was able to wash in hot water for the first time in five weeks. It was balm.

I had dinner in the ward-room afterward, and felt like the country-mouse come to visit his sophisticated cousin. I found my values had grown so primitive on Guadalcanal that I was dazzled by the white tablecloth and shining silverware. I wondered if unconsciously I would put the silverware into my pocket after the meal, for on Guadalcanal, one carries his own spoon, and knows that if he loses it, he will probably have to rely on his fingers for feeding purposes.

We got aboard the *Little* later that night, according to plan. The leader of the excursion, Col. Sam Griffith, and his officers received us hospitably in the ward-room.

Col. Griffith, a handsome young officer, tall and broad-shouldered, with reddish mustache, cursorily went over the plans for the expedition. A warhorse from 'way back, with a distinguished record in Nicaragua and China, and also at Tulagi, he did not seem at all nervous about tomorrow morning's landing.

The other officers shared his calm. Evidently they did not think we would meet much opposition on Savo.

Our plan, said the colonel, is to land at the northern tip of the island. There we will divide into two groups, one of which will reconnoiter the eastern half of the island; the other the west, and the two will meet at the southern tip after the work is done.

The island, said the colonel, who expresses himself well and easily, is shaped like a walnut, with the points at the north and south extremities. It is about nine miles from northern to southern tip along either shore. That hike should take all morning and part of the afternoon. "If," said the colonel, "we don't run into any Nips."

The captain of the ship, who did not share the colonel's suave good nature, viewed Miller and me with suspicion. He asked for our credentials and told us not to talk to any of the crew of the ship. He seemed upset because we had no written orders to make the trip. Miller and I had visions of ourselves in the brig, but the prospect did not bother us. By this time we were past being annoyed by the idea of physical discomfort.

Finally the matter with the captain was straightened out, and he unbent and became quite friendly. We decided that he had merely been carrying out routine procedure. We—the captain, the colonel, some of the other officers, Miller and I—sat in the captain's little office, yarning.

FRIDAY, SEPTEMBER 4

After a wonderful hearty breakfast, up to the bridge to find that we are zigzagging. "Stand by for depth charges," was the word that crackled from the ship's speaker system.

We were making full speed. The crew went tensely, hurriedly about the business of preparing to fire depth charges.

"We've sighted a periscope," the officer of the deck told me, "dead ahead."

But before any "ashcans" could be fired, the ship slowed and the air of tension relaxed. "It's only a mast of one of the ships we lost out here," said the O.O.D. "Every time we see it, we think it's a periscope."

We were getting near to Savo Island. I went below and got my gear together and came back up on the bridge. We all stood silently watching the small, humpbacked island grow larger. The regular "bong, bong" of the depth finder was a hollow, eerie sound in the stillness.

General quarters sounded, and the speaker system droned, "Man your boats. Stand by, all boat crews."

I went to my assigned boat and climbed aboard, jamming my way among tight-packed marines. Our engines rumbled and coughed, then started, and we were off for shore.

It seemed odd to be going through the same experience of landing on a strange shore again, as I had done at Guadalcanal. The movements were the same—our sitting low in the boat, our strung-out lines of landing craft streaking in toward the beach, and even the growing distinctness of the island, as palms began to stand out against the sky and thatch huts became visible, seemed something like routine. But there remained the breathless suspense, wondering when and if machine guns would open up on us from the shore, and in those moments of wondering, as usual, one imagined the arrival of bullets and the prospect of men being hit in the boat.

But none of these things happened, and we came to shore and made our landing without having been fired on. We advanced cautiously up the beach, but there were no Japs and no shots fired.

We came almost immediately to a row of bamboo and thatch huts which constituted a village. The houses sat amidst wide-spaced palms, and in the grove black natives stood and watched us as we advanced. Most of them wore only bright-colored loincloths.

An Australian guide who accompanied us set to work to secure some native boys who would lead us through the trails around the island. The big chief of the island was not in the vicinity, but one black man who spoke the Solomon Islands pidgin English was soon located. Like the rest, he wore a bright flannel loincloth and his hair was crinkly—and red. (I found later that native dandies dye their hair with lime-juice.)

The native's manners were mild. He raised his hand in greeting and smiled, showing stumpy teeth thickly covered with tartar and stained reddish-brown by betelnut.

While the Australian and the native talked, marines crept out into the surrounding woods with guns at the ready. We did not want to be ambushed in the village by the Japanese.

A line of five or six natives stood behind the black man who spoke English. They smiled childishly. Some of their black bodies were tattooed. One of them wore a necklace of bright-colored beads.

"Me fella lookum Japanese man," began the Australian.

But the native shook his head and smiled benignly. "No Jap'nee man island," he said.

We must have looked incredulous, for the row of natives behind their spokesman raised their right hands, shook their heads, and smiled, reinforcing his argument.

Our aviators on reconnaissance had spotted roads and objects resembling tents on Savo Island. The Australian brought up the matter.

"This fella Jap'nee have tent," he said. "You savvy tent?"

The native looked mystified. "Him small house, him calico," explained the Australian.

But the native insisted there were no Japs on the island. Four Japs, he said, had come to the island some time before in a small boat. But they had left on Sunday.

But we would have to see for ourselves whether or not the native was telling the truth. The Australian explained that we needed two guides.

"Big master want sendum half man go around this way," said the Australian. "Half sendum round this way. Me fella need two good boys, savvy?"

Two native boys who spoke pidgin were soon located. The Australian gave them instructions. "If you lookum Japan man you fella no run all about quick time," he said, "but all same stop and we fella killum."

The two natives nodded enthusiastically. "Byumby you fella getting good chow long government," he promised.

I chose to go with the group of Raiders who were covering the east coast of the island. They were being led by Capt. John W. Antonelli (of Lawrence, Mass.).

The guide assigned us was of typical native pattern: stumpy, dirty teeth, red hair, childish manners—and he smiled apologetically when he spoke. He told us he had learned English on Tulagi, where he had been a cook for an Englishman. He had come back to Savo to get married. He said his name was Allen-luva.

As we started out through the coastal cocoanut grove, working along a trail, Allen-luva told us the Japs who had come to Savo (which he pronounced "Sabu") "take bananas, fowl, pumpkin, everything." A large group of Japs had come in July, he said, in two "launce" (launches), and had been here two weeks.

"Him speak English?" we wanted to know.

"Like drunk man," said Allen-luva and laughed. "Him talk 'aeroprane' and 'guadarcanar.' "

We passed through a succession of native villages as we pushed along the coast. They were similar: each located amidst wide-spaced cocoanut groves, looking out over a lovely vista of beach and aquamarine-colored sea; each with rows of neat bamboo-walled, thatch-roofed houses; each with a larger bamboo structure serving as a church; some of these churches with handsome altars neatly woven in two-tone fiber, white and black—which had all the elegance of ebony inlaid with ivory; but the effect was spoiled by cheap, colored religious prints pinned to the walls.

There were song and prayer books in these churches, on the crude benches. Allen-luva told us that the islanders went to church twice a day. There were two sects, Anglican and Roman Catholic.

We passed through the villages of Septatavi and Pokelo, and then we found the first of the debris. It was the debris of ships—life rafts, oil drums, life-belts—our ships which had been sunk in the great battle of the night of Aug. 8–9 (now called the Battle of Savo Island).

The debris was washed up on the beach, and even now, nearly a month after the battle, the water's edge was still stained with oil. Stones and branches farther up the beach were still coated with oil, some of it a quarter or half inch thick.

Allen-luva said the battle had occurred close to shore. Evidently he had been greatly frightened by it, for he looked scared as he mentioned it now, and all he would say was, "Fires, great fires."

Farther to the south, we found debris strewn more thickly along the shore: an oil-coated, rubber life-raft from the *Quincy,* a soggy notebook kept by an officer on the *Astoria,* the propeller of one of the catapult planes which the *Canberra* had carried, crates marked "Australia," more pieces of wooden life-rafts, more life-belts, inflated and uninflated. But there were no Japs, although our men were constantly on the look-out for them.

At about noon we had traversed about half the distance from north to south. We halted for a short rest. The jungle had grown thicker as we progressed south, and the trail ran up and down many steep hills. We were dripping with perspiration. It was time to take a swallow of water—and a salt pill (a necessity in the Solomons).

We heard the sound of many airplane engines in the sky. Capt. Antonelli looked at his watch. "Time for the daily air raid," he said, and grinned. "It's going to be good to watch one from a distance, for a change."

But the planes were ours. Soon we saw them swinging north past Savo Island, a large formation of our dive-bombers, probably heading for Bougainville or Rekata Bay or Gizo, Japanese bases.

In midafternoon, we met the other group of troops, who had traversed the other side of the island. We had reached the southern tip, walked our nine miles.

Col. Griffith, who had led the other group, said they had run into no Nips anywhere. But they had found an abundance of debris, and oil, along shore, as we had, and had passed the grave of the captain of the *Quincy.*

The sea grew rough in the afternoon, and the sky overcast, and we had some difficulty in getting back to our transports. But the childish natives gave us a hand, and waved, grinned and shouted "Cheerio!" as we started for the ships.

When we reached Guadalcanal, there was some debate as to whether we should stay aboard the *Little* and *Gregory* that night. There was a possibility, it seemed, that we might be going down to Taivu tomorrow. But it was finally decided that we should go ashore.

SATURDAY, SEPTEMBER 5

At one o'clock this morning we were routed out of bed by the sounds of heavy, close shelling. The guns were cracking close off-shore in the direction of Kukum, and the shells sighed over our heads and seemed to be crashing far back in the woods.

I sat on the edge of the dugout and watched the bright flashes of light rising high in the sky, heard the haughty, metallic voices of the cannon. Sitting like this, virtually in the lap of a shelling attack, one felt as if he were at the mercy of a great, vindictive giant whose voice was the voice of thunder; the awful colossal scale of modern war has brought the old gods to life again.

The shelling continued for about five intense minutes, and then, suddenly, stopped. A few seconds pause, and the sounds and flashes of cannonading began again, doubled and redoubled in volume.

But the shells were no longer passing over our heads, no longer directed against Guadalcanal. We surmised then that a naval engagement must have begun.

Ten minutes later, the cannonading continuing at a furious pace, we heard the sound of an airplane motor. Then a pinpoint of green light appeared over the beach to the east. The light grew brighter, then became a bright sheet of green-white, flickering over the whole side of the sky. It was a flare.

More flares followed, east and west, while the blasting of the guns continued, and then a white light snapped the sky over Kukum suddenly into illumination. It was a searchlight glare, probably from naval vessels, ours or theirs, illuminating the opponents.

The gunfire kept on, and the searchlight went out as suddenly as it had come on. Then it started again. And there was more cannonading.

These wonders continued until 2:08, when they ceased sharply, and there were no more sounds, no more flares, no more searchlights.

From Kukum, by phone, we heard the "dope": that there had been a furious naval engagement off Savo Island, with about five ships participating. That two ships had been hit and were still afire. But we did not then know whether they were ours or theirs.

With daylight I hurried to Kukum to see what had happened. En route I passed several ambulances going the other way. They were loaded.

Comdr. Dexter told me the *Little* and *Gregory* had been sunk. Boats were out now, bringing in survivors.

I found survivors scattered all over the beach: some on stretchers, with doctors working busily over them; some with lesser wounds, sitting dejectedly on the sand, waiting treatment; others, in scant, torn clothing, many of them still smudged with oil, standing in silent groups.

Boats lined the shore and wounded were being taken from these on stretchers; other boats dotted the water a few hundred yards offshore, moving like busy waterbugs.

At the back of the beach they were still loading ambulances. Some stretcher bearers passed me with inert, white-bandaged wounded.

I talked with one of the "walking wounded," who sat in his underwear on a pile of gear while a gash in his lower leg trailed a small trickle of blood on the sand. He had been hit by a chunk of H.E.

A corpsman came up and said to the sailor: "You better get that fixed."

"I'll wait until *they*"—the sailor motioned toward a badly wounded man on a stretcher, now being tended by a doctor—"get through."

The sailor told me he had been on the *Little*, and was a chief bosun's mate. His name was Ralph G. Andree and he came from Wheelersburg, Ohio.

He spoke dully, stoically, about the action in which his ship had been sunk. "We only got about three or four rounds out of each gun," he said. "And the Japs shot through us like paper. They couldn't have been more than a couple of thousand yards away.

"The first shot they fired hit a fuel tank and set us afire. Then they turned the searchlights on and kept on firing until they had us afire all over.

"Then they went over and sank the *Gregory* and it looked like they came back and gave it to us again after that."

A young lieutenant, wrapped in a blanket, a little blue from the cold but otherwise unharmed, told me he had been officer of the deck aboard the *Gregory* at the time of the sinking. He was Lieut. (JG) Heinrich Heine, Jr., of San Diego, Cal.

"Judging from the searchlights and the gunfire," he said, "I'd think there were about five Jap ships. There was at least one cruiser because they were firing three at a time—salvos.

"It was like about forty kinds of hell breaking loose. Put 'em together and you get the picture."

Lieut. Heine gave a very coherent account of the events of the fight as he had seen them.

"We were patroling offshore and about to make a turn," he said, "when somebody dropped flares. Then there were searchlights, and then hell.

"The Japs opened fire with the *Little* as a target, until we opened fire. Then the Japs shifted to both ships.

"One of our four-inch guns and two smaller-caliber guns fired on the Jap astern. We put out the searchlights. But they came on again. And by that time we were ready to abandon ship.

"I was stationed at Boat No. 3. I tried to get one of our machine guns to bear on the Jap searchlights, then realized that was foolish. I saw several hits on the bridge, and went there to see if there were any wounded. I found only one officer.

"Then I went to the well deck to see what could be done about extinguishing the fires. I then went back to the boat stations and lowered No. 2 and No. 3 into the water."

Lieut. Heine talked as formally as if he were writing an official report. "I collected approximately twenty men," he said, "and we launched a life raft. I had all hands in the water swim to the raft.

"The Jap continued to fire. He was at the time about 100 yards from the *Gregory,* on the side opposite from ours. Several shells came over the ship and landed twenty to twenty-five yards from the raft.

"The ship was burning amidships. She had taken a shot through the fire room. But a member of the fire-room crew had pulled the fires and secured the main steam stop, and prevented the ship from blowing. He was John Maar, water tender, first class."

One of the few survivors who appeared energetic and chipper was Lieut. (JG) Paul F. Kalat, of Worcester, Mass., who had been the engineering officer on the *Little*. After his ship had sunk, he had spent some eight hours in the water, and the Jap warships, he said, "just missed me by a whisker—about twenty-five to thirty feet." Lieut. Kalat said he believed the Jap ships were cruisers, and that they were new vessels. Ensign William M. Newton, of Gastonia, N.C., said there were two cruisers and a destroyer, at least.

We went back to Gen. Vandergrift's CP and from there to airfield headquarters to see what damage the dive-bombers, which we spotted yesterday, heading north, had done. We found they had bombed and strafed thirty-six landing boats which had been spotted bringing Jap troops into Cape Esperance.

Dive-bombers and Army and marine fighters had gone out this morning to strafe fifteen Jap landing boats trying to get ashore at dawn.

Apparently both groups of boats—those at Cape Esperance and those at Taivu—were badly damaged, and many Japs killed in the attack. But the discouraging fact remains that some Japs are getting through our cordon and landing. (Later we found that the Japs were using small boats to transport troops all the way from Bougainville to Guadalcanal—nearly 500 miles. The boats moved at night in small jumps from Bougainville to Choiseul to Santa Isabel. In this way, by constant effort, they were trickling forces into our island. Eventually those landings, coupled with the landings being made from larger ships, would mount up—unless we could find some way to stop them. But in any case, our air activities did have the effect of making such landings difficult.)

We were still at headquarters on the airfield when an air alert was sent out. So we of the Guadalcanal Press Club—Miller and I plus the two new members, Yarbrough and Durdin—climbed into a jeep and sped down to Lunga Point to watch the show.

There was a radio available here. Miller clamped on the headphones and listened in on the interplane messages, calling them aloud so that we had a blow-by-blow description of the fighting.

The first exciting call came at 12:32:

"Planes off the starboard bow..."

Then, "Morrell [a call to Lieut. Rivers J. Morrell of San Diego, Cal.], have you sighted the enemy?" And Morrell's answer:

"They are up on the left side above you. See 'em?"

"I'm going in, going in," called Morrell, signaling his attack.

Then other groups of fighters spotted the enemy, in quick succession:

"There are twenty-six bombers coming in from the south."

"I'm going over there where the mess is going on."

"I'm starting to go in."

"There are Zeros with those bombers. Watch out."

"Watch it, there, watch it."

"Six Zeros just passed over us. Look out for 'em."

We heard the sounds of dogfighting in the sky but the planes were too high in the clouds to be seen. We also heard booming explosions, which we at first took for anti-aircraft, but later realized were bombs. We found out later the Japs had jettisoned their bombs after interception and fled without making a run.

"We got one bomber," called one pilot. "Bracket!"

Then one of our casualties called in, "I'm in trouble and I don't mean maybe. I'm going down." A few moments after, we saw him coming in, his motor streaming smoke and his propeller sitting still on the nose of his plane. A "dead stick" landing.

"Hope he makes it!" shouted Miller.

Back at the airport, we found that this flier *had* made it, and that our fighters had shot down two of the Jap bombers and one Zero.

This afternoon, at about four o'clock, we heard scary news on the "scuttlebutt" circuit: that thirty-three Jap ships were on their way toward Guadalcanal, off Lord Howe Island, and at their present rate of speed would be here at four o'clock tomorrow morning.

Before we went to bed, however, we heard that the alarm was another false one. The root of the report had been a radio message from a B-17, which had spotted *three* Jap ships heading *north* near Lord Howe Island. The message had simply been misunderstood.

Still, the night was not to be calm. At nine o'clock, I woke up to find my cot shaking, as if someone had a grip on one end and was trying to jostle me. It was an earthquake—which, they say, is a fairly common occurrence hereabouts.

Later, we were awakened by the sounds of machine-gun and rifle fire, and there were two louder explosions which sounded like mortar shells. Had the Japs broken through? I wondered. But after a while one grows bored with the incessant repetition even of thoughts like these. I went back to sleep.

SUNDAY, SEPTEMBER 6

This morning we heard at Col. Hunt's CP that the Japs *had* fired mortar shells into the tractor camp last night. But when our men had answered with heavy fire, the Japs had withdrawn. Apparently they were a small patrol trying to feel out our positions.

We arrived at the airport this morning just in time to hear the tail end of an address by a general to the pilots. They were gathered in a circle around him. And the general was saying: "And I don't want you to think that those people back there at home don't appreciate what you are doing. They do appreciate it."

"What was the rest of the speech about?" I asked one of the fighters.

"You heard it," he said, disconsolately. "It was that last sentence, repeated a few times." What the fighters would *like* to hear, obviously, is news of some relief. Some of them have been flying eight to ten hours almost every day under combat conditions, for the last three weeks. And their rest is disturbed by the Japs practically every night. They would like a little rest in some relatively peaceful country.

Col. Fike gave us the results of today's raid by our dive-bombers. The target for today was the Jap base on Gizo. The dive-bombers found no aircraft or ships there, but bombed a group of buildings, and probably destroyed a radio station.

Some of our pilots lost their way in the "soup." Ensign Walter W. Coolbaugh (of Clarks Summit, Pa.) could not even find Gizo, because of the thickness of the overcast; but, nothing daunted, he *did* find Santa Isabel, and bombed that.

Lieut. Richard R. Amerine (of Lawrence, Kans.), a marine flier, came wandering into our lines today, thin as a ghost, to say he had been out in the jungles, dodging Japs and existing on red ants and snails for seven days. He had parachuted from a fighter plane when his oxygen apparatus went out, a week ago, and had landed at Cape Esperance on the northwest corner of the island. Trying to find his way back, he had run into a large group of Japs. He had found one Jap asleep by the side of a trail, killed the Jap by beating his head with a boulder, taken the Jap's pistol and shoes, killed two more Japs with the butt and one with a bullet, and finally reached our lines safely. Having once studied entomology, the science of bugs, he was able to subsist on selected ants and snails. He knew which were edible.

There's a tide of "scuttlebutt" tonight that relief is on the way for the marines here on Guadal, that a huge convoy of ships is en route carrying enough Army troops so that the marines will be able to ship out and perhaps go home.

There is also a less credible rumor that President Roosevelt has promised in a fireside chat—which nobody heard—that the marines on Guadal will be back home in the United States by Christmas. The fact of the matter seems to be that Walter Winchell said something to that effect on one of his broadcasts, but he did not mention the President or link him to the "tip" in any way. So "scuttlebutt" groweth.

VII

BATTLE OF THE RIDGE

MONDAY, SEPTEMBER 7

This morning Col. Edson told me that he is planning to make an attack on the Jap positions in the Taivu Point area tomorrow. If I wanted to go along, I was to be at a certain embarkation point at 3:45 this afternoon.

It was pelting rain when I arrived. But the Raiders, who seem to love a fight, were in high spirits. I had been assigned by Col. Edson to go with Col. Griffith aboard a tiny diesel-engined ship which was acting as an auxiliary transport for the occasion. As we stepped aboard, one happy marine said, "This is the battleship *Oregon*, I presume?"

The captain of the little craft was a jovial Portuguese who had formerly been a tuna captain on the American West Coast. His name, Joaquin S. Theodore. He still spoke in interesting Portuguese constructions, despite his rank as captain of a naval ship.

"We'll have it coffee for everybody in the morning," he said. Kindly, he warned against smoking on deck. "Tal your men I don't like to smoke it on deck," he said.

He wanted to clear away a space in the small ship so that the tight-packed marines might have a little more room. He pointed to a clothes line and said to his first officer, "Whoever this clothes belongs to I want it out of the lines."

The ship was a tiny thing, with only limited supplies of stores. But Capt. Theodore passed out grub and all available cigarettes to the Raiders, and shared his little cabin with Col. Griffith.

As we put out onto a rough sea, the pink-cheeked, hearty Portuguese told me proudly about his two " 'lil kids" back home and about the exploits of his ship.

Col. Griffith later went over the plans for our expedition: we are to land our troops to the east of a small village called Tasimboko, in the Taivu Point area, and advance from that direction on the town. Tasimboko is supposed to be the bivouac of a large group of Jap troops—estimated to number from 1,000 to 3,000. But the Japs are supposed to be lightly armed.

A bombing and strafing attack on Tasimboko, and shelling from the sea, will be timed to fit in with our attack.

Getting to sleep was a terrible job. The ship's steaming hold, full of the noise of the engines, was crammed with marines; no room to sprawl there. Every nook about the deck seemed to be filled as well.

Finally I found a spot on the deck, which was partially shielded by a hatchway, and curled around it. But the ship rolled heavily, and rain began to fall. I found another spot on the forecastle deck and pulled the edge of a tarpaulin over me. The rain fell more heavily, and the wind grew cold. I stumbled along to the captain's cabin and lay down on the floor in the stuffy room. It was better than sleeping in the rain.

TUESDAY, SEPTEMBER 8

Despite the hardships of sleeping aboard Capt. Theodore's tiny tub, the Raiders were fresh and ready to go this morning when the time came for us to climb into our boats and shove off for shore.

Just as we were starting, there came a fortunate happenstance: a small convoy of American cargo ships, escorted by warships, passed very close to our own transports. They had no connection with us, and were bound for a different part of Guadalcanal; but the Japs, seeing our ships and the others together, evidently got the impression that a mass assault was coming. And so, fortunately, many of them ran.

But we naturally had no way of knowing this as we dashed for shore in our landing boats. We were ready for a real struggle, and a bit puzzled when there were no shots from shore.

We were more mystified, when, a few minutes after landing, as we were pushing along the trail toward Tasimboko, we found a fine, serviceable 37 mm. field piece, with the latest split-trail, rubber-tired carriage, sitting at the edge of the beach. It was complete with ammunition, and surrounded by Japanese packs, life-preservers, intrenching tools, new shoes, strewn in disorder on the ground.

As we moved along, we found more packs, more shoes, and life-preservers, and fresh-dug slit-trenches and foxholes in the underbrush. We also found another fine 37 mm. gun, which like the other was unmanned. This second gun was pointed toward the west, indicating we had possibly, as we had hoped, surprised the Japs by circumventing their positions and attacking from the east.

Or perhaps this was only the entrance to a trap. The Japs are supposed to excel at such tactics. We moved on cautiously, circled a small pond and crossed a ford in a river, wading in water up to our waists.

Beyond the ford, we passed a pile of clam shells, evidently freshly opened. "I'm thinking they've gone up for breakfast and knocked things off," snapped Col. Edson with his humorless grin. But he did not relax. He moved his troops ahead fast, barked at them when they failed to take proper cover.

We heard the sound of approaching plane motors, then saw our dive-bombers come out of the sky and slant westward. A few seconds later we heard the thud of bombs falling.

There were strafing planes, too, the long-nosed Pursuits flashing overhead, and we could hear their guns rattling as they dived.

We moved along the shore through an overgrown cocoanut grove and in the brakes of underbrush; we found more foxholes, carefully camouflaged with palm leaves, and caches of food and ammunition.

Shortly after eight o'clock, we made our first contact with the Japs. I saw our people running in numerous directions at once, and knew that something had happened. I ran to the beach and saw what the others had seen: a row of Jap landing boats lying on the sand some distance away, and amidst the boats, a small group of men in brown uniforms, looking our way—Japs.

The colonel called "Nick," quietly, and Maj. Nickerson (Floyd W. Nickerson of Spokane, Wash.) anticipated the order. "Open fire?" he said hopefully.

The colonel nodded his head.

"Nick," who is as lean and hard as the colonel, called, "Machine-gun runner." And when the man came up, which was almost immediately, he gave him the order. Within two minutes our machine guns were firing.

"Red Mike" (as the Raiders call their colonel for the obvious reason that he has red hair) is most taciturn. I asked him, at this juncture, what was happening.

"I think we might have caught a few," he snapped. And that was all he said.

Now the Japs were answering our fire. I heard the familiar flat crack of the .25 rifle, and the repetition of the sound in long bursts of light machine-gun fire. Others of our men joined in the firing, and it swelled in volume. In the midst of the outburst, we heard the crash of a heavy explosion. I was lying on the ground under a bush, near Red Mike, taking thorough cover.

"Sounds like mortar fire," he said, concisely.

The burst of firing stopped, and there was a lull for a few moments. Red Mike was on his feet immediately, moving ahead. He sent a message up to Maj. Nickerson, who was leading the advance elements of our troops.

"Nick's got to push right on up," he said, low-voiced. Then he was gone, tending to some military business in the rear. A few moments later he was back again, still moving fast. I had found the colonel to be one of the quickest human beings I had ever known.

Rifle and machine-gun fire burst out again, the Jap guns standing out in the chorus like a tenor in a quartet. The bullets were closer this time. I crawled under a wet bush and kept my head down.

A man was hit over to our left. I heard the cry, "Pass the word back for a corpsman," felt the sickening excitement of the moment in the air. Our first casualty.

Then there came another loud crash from ahead, close and loud enough so that the earth shook under us. I was lying next to a private. "Sounds like a 90 mm. mortar," he said.

Now the blasting concussion of the explosion was repeated, and we heard the furry whistle of a shell passing over our heads, heard it explode well to the rear. Was it a mortar or a field piece ahead of us? There was more than a possibility, it seemed, that we had run into a heavy Jap force, equipped with batteries of artillery.

I was more certain of it when the explosion was repeated. Again we heard a second crash a fraction of a moment later, well behind us. Now it seemed evident that these were artillery pieces firing, probably several of them.

The Jap artillery was answered by the lighter-toned firing of our own mortars, and another chorus of rifles and machine guns. The Jap guns crashed again, and then the firing stopped.

A runner came to Col. Red Mike, who was sitting for a brief second in a clump of underbrush. "Nick says to tell you there are people across the stream," he said. A small stream ran parallel to the beach at this point, and that stream marked off our left flank. The Japs apparently were moving through the jungle on the inland side of the stream, planning to cut off our rear. "We can't see 'em yet, but we can hear 'em," said the runner.

The colonel called Capt. Antonelli. "Tony," he said, "Nick says there's somebody working back across the stream. Take a patrol. Flank 'em if you possibly can."

There was other business for Red Mike: he wanted to check on the exact location of our companies; he got the "walkie-talkie" into action, sent runners out. He checked on the wounded by making a personal tour. Then he was back in time to get a report from Col. Griffith that a Jap field piece had been captured, unmanned.

"Shall I go with Tony or get the gun?" asked Col. Griffith.

"Go get it, take it down to the water and shoot it," said Red Mike.

Next, Red Mike disappeared into the foliage ahead. Now we were out of the cocoanuts, getting into thicker growth. But the colonel still moved like the wind. I followed and after a struggle found him at our foremost position, talking to Maj. Nickerson.

"I'm trying to locate that firing up ahead," said Nick.

Our planes came in again, and dived and strafed the Jap village ahead of us. The Japs were not firing. We moved ahead.

We passed through a jungle brake which looked just like any other from the outside, but inside we found stacks of cases filled with medical supplies. "Opium," said a marine, but I made note of the labels on some of the boxes and checked later. Most of the boxes contained "Sapo Medicatus," which is a blood-coagulating agent.

The foxholes were growing more numerous as we progressed. They were everywhere, carefully camouflaged with leaves. And caches of supplies were also more numerous: crates of canned meat, sacks of crackers; there were more groups of new field knapsacks, with shoes strapped to them, and scores of gray life-preservers, indicating the Jap troops who had been here were probably freshly landed from boats.

Something moved in the bush ahead and to our left. "There are troops going through there," said the colonel. "Find out who they are."

Seven minutes later, firing burst out again. I flopped into thick cover, and none too soon. A bullet snapped into the underbrush very close behind me. I picked out the sounds of Jap .25's, our automatic rifles and our machine guns. There was a torrent of Jap .25 machine-gun firing from the left.

"The boys got on the other side of us," said the colonel, with one of his wry smiles.

Now came a terrific blast from only a few yards ahead. It was so loud it made my ears ring, and the concussion shook chips of wood on my head from the trees above. We heard the shell whiz just over our heads and burst a few hundred yards to the rear. We knew then that we must be right smack up against the muzzle of a Jap field piece.

The piece fired again, and again, and then there was another outburst of machine-gun fire, ours heavy-toned against the Japs' cracking .25's. Then silence.

Maj. Nickerson came back to tell the colonel that our men had "killed the gunners on a Jap 75. It's only 150 yards ahead," said Nick. "It was covered by machine-gun fire. We got the gun."

But the Japs had more guns. We advanced only a slight distance, and another opened on us, as close as the last had been. At the time I was squatting in a thick jungle brake, a tangle of vines and dwarf trees, but the crash of the firing so close was scary, despite the good cover. Each time the gun went off, one felt the blast of hot air from the muzzle, and twigs rattled down from the trees above. But we knew we were safer here than back where the shells were falling. We could hear the explosions of the shells well behind us.

There was quite a cluster of us in this jungle grove: marines, squatting or sprawling unhappily in the green wet underbrush. Then it began to rain, and the rain came in sheets and torrents. The firing kept on. There were Jap riflemen around us too. (I later found that there had been one, not more than fifty feet from us. We found his body. Why he did not fire at us I don't know.)

Nick shouted at the little group in the jungle brake. "Spread out," he said, with the proper blistering expletives. "We lost one squad of the second platoon with one shell. One of those might come in here."

I moved off to the right, to try to get a look ahead, and then moved back to the rear to see what damage the Jap shells were doing. I passed a marine who was lying on his back in a foxhole, his face very gray. His upper torso was wrapped in bandage, and I could see there was no arm where his left arm had been, not even a stump. A 75 shell had done the work.

A runner came back to report to Col. Red Mike, at 10:45, that a second Jap 75 had been put out of action and the crew killed.

It began to look as if we might have tackled a bigger Jap force than we could handle. The colonel was concerned about the Japs who might, he thought, be sneaking around our flank, cutting us off from the beach where we had landed. The colonel called for naval gunfire support.

A group of destroyers which had come down with us swung in close to shore and began to shell Tasimboko. I went out to the beach to watch the yellow flashes and the geysers of smoke and debris rising where the shells hit.

Then I went forward to look for Nick. Firing broke out again, torrents of it; but there were no more of the heavy crashes of artillery fire this time, only rifles and machine guns firing, and most of them, according to the sound, ours.

It had stopped raining. When the firing stopped a great quiet fell on the jungle. And in the quiet, we heard the desperate shouting of a man who was evidently in great trouble. He was shouting something like "Yama, Yama!" as if his life depended on it. Then the voice was smothered up in a fusillade of machine-gun and rifle fire. It was a Jap. But we never found out what he was shouting about.

The tide of our action seemed to be turning. We heard no more artillery, and a runner came back from Capt. Antonelli's troops with the happy word, "We solved the problem, took the village." Nick's men sent back word that more Jap 75's had been captured, unmanned.

Appropriately, the clouds were clearing and the sun was coming out. Fresh reinforcements for our troops were landing. But now we did not need them.

We marched on into Tasimboko without any further resistance. We found many more cases of Japanese food and sacks of rice, and ammunition for Jap machine guns, rifles and artillery pieces, totaling more than 500,000 rounds, Col. Griffith estimated. We burned the ammunition and destroyed the village of Tasimboko, including a radio station which the Japs had established there.

Looking over the bodies of the Japs who had been killed (about thirty), we found some interesting items: pictures of Javanese women, American ammunition with labels printed in Dutch. And we found that the gunsights with the 75's were of English manufacture, and that some of the Japs had been armed with tommy guns. It seemed that some of these soldiers who had run so fast had been veterans of the Jap campaigns in the East Indies, and possibly Malaya too. Perhaps this was the first time they had been surprised. Or perhaps they had heard too much about what happened to the Japs who tried to cross the Tenaru.

Most of the loot we had captured was destroyed. But we transported the medical supplies back to headquarters, and our men helped themselves to large stocks of British cigarettes, bearing a Netherlands East Indies tax stamp.

The sun had set and there was only a faint reddish glow on the clouds over the horizon to light the darkening sky, when, in our transport ships, we reached a point offshore from the Tenaru River. We were heading toward home.

But the day's excitement was not yet over. We got word that twelve Jap aircraft had been spotted. Our fighter planes were rising into the twilight sky.

The transports went into evasive maneuvers, and, fortunately, the sky grew quickly darker, and was black, except for high streaks of silver gray, when the Japs arrived.

They did not come to Guadalcanal. For once, they picked Tulagi as their target, and we saw cup-shaped bursts of bright white light rising from the direction of the island, just over the horizon rim. We heard the distant thudding of the bombs a few seconds later, and wondered if the Japs would spot our wakes in the dark. But they did not.

WEDNESDAY, SEPTEMBER 9

Shortly after 12:30 this morning, I heard the others in my tent dashing for the shelter. Maj. Phipps shouted to me to come along, and I heard cannonading coming from the north, but I was too tired to move.

At breakfast this morning, I heard that a small group of Jap destroyers or light cruisers had shelled Tulagi—and hit Capt. Theodore's little ship and set it afire.

Later in the day, I heard that Capt. Theodore had been wounded through the chest in the course of the engagement. But he had beached his little craft, and saved it from sinking, despite his wounds. I am glad to hear that he is expected to live.

This is the second time that I have left a ship in the evening and it has been attacked and lost before morning. This fact gives rise to the thought that my luck has been good, so far.

There were two air-raid alarms today. But the Japs never appeared. It was a quiet afternoon. We sat in Col. Hunt's CP after lunch, talking of the reunion we will have ten years hence, and the tales we'll tell about Guadalcanal, then, and how by that time our imaginations will have magnified our deeds immeasurably, and we will all be heroes.

Col. Hunt told us about some of his narrow escapes in the World War, when he commanded the Sixth Marines. Our casualties were very high, then, he said, and gave the figures. But the fighting at the Tenaru battle, he said, was about as concentrated and intense as in any engagement of the World War.

Tonight we were awakened, just before midnight, by the sound of heavy firing in the jungles. There were machine guns, rifles and, occasionally, the crash of a mortar.

We lay awake and listened. And then cannonading started, to the north. We went to the dugout, and I sat on the sandbagged entrance with Maj. Phipps. The guns, we knew, were big ones, because of their heavy tone and the brightness of the flashes against the sky. But Bill Phipps was sure they were firing in the Tulagi area, not off our shore. He had measured the interval between the time of the flash and the time the related boom of the gun reached us. That interval, he said, was ninety seconds. Multiply the 90 by 1,100, the number of feet sound travels in a second, and you get 99,000 feet, or about twenty miles. Tulagi is twenty miles north of us.

Star shells glowed in the sky. The Japs were illuminating the Tulagi shore. One of our observation posts phoned in the report that there were three Jap ships, probably cruisers, and that they were firing salvos.

THURSDAY, SEPTEMBER 10

This morning we heard that the Japs had shelled Tulagi harbor last night and again hit Capt. Theodore's ship, which was still beached.

I went to the CP of Maj. Nickerson (the Raider officer) and talked to some of the men who did outstanding work on the excursion to Tasimboko, day before yesterday. Among them, two young corpsmen, Pharmacist's Mate Alfred W. Cleveland (of South Dartmouth, Mass.) and Pharmacist's Mate, second class, Karl B. Coleman (of McAndrews, Ky.). They told me how they had used a penknife to amputate the ragged stump of one Raider's arm after it had been shattered by a 75 explosion; the wounded man had been the one whom I had seen, lying in a foxhole, just after he had been treated and bandaged. These two lads, Nick told me, had saved the wounded man's life by amputating the remnants of his arm; the medicos themselves had said that the man would have died if the two lads had not done such a good and quick job in the field.

Pvt. Andrew J. Klejnot (of Fort Wayne, Ind.) told me how he had picked off one of the crew of one of the Jap 75's.

"There were only two men on the gun," he said. "I picked off one, and the other went and hid behind some boxes in a little ammunition dump. I fired into the dump and set it afire."

I moved my worldly possessions from Col. Hunt's CP out to Gen. Vandegrift's headquarters today. The general has moved into the "boon-docks," as the marines call the jungles; and the new spot is too much of a trek from Col. Hunt's headquarters.

A tent has been put up for us correspondents, near the general's headquarters. The members of our "press club" now are Bob Miller, Till Durdin, Tom Yarbrough, and there is a new arrival, Carlton Kent.

The Japs air-raided us at about noontime; twenty-seven of the usual silver-colored, two-engine type, flying lower than usual today. But the sticks of bombs fell a long distance from our location at the time.

The general's new CP is located in the thick of the jungle. Sui, pet dog of the commissioner, Martin Clemens, proved it tonight by dragging an iguana, a small dragon-like lizard, into plain view as we sat at dinner over the crude board table tonight. Sui had unearthed the iguana at the jungle edge, which stands up straight and dense as a wall only a few feet from our mess table.

The tent which has been put up for correspondents is one of a number located at the foot of a ridge, facing the jungle. The general's tent is atop the ridge. Tonight we were told to be on the alert, since the Japs had been reported infiltrating the jungle which we faced. We were told that if an attack came, we should retire up the ridge to the crest, where a stand would be made.

"I wish I had a pistol," said Yarbrough, as we correspondents lay in our bunks, after dark. And the rest of us were nervous, and not anxious to go to sleep. We kept up a clatter of conversation to help our spirits.

The situation was not without an element of humor. For, as we lay awake, the mackaws sat overhead in the trees and bombed our tent. The plopping of their missiles was loud and frequent. The birds seemed to have singled out our tent for the heaviest bombardment. Maj. Jim Murray, the general's adjutant, chided us about the fact. "Those birds have got the correspondents' number, all right," he said.

FRIDAY, SEPTEMBER 11

The Japs who were supposed to be investing the jungle in front of our tent did not put in an appearance last night. There was not even any firing out in the "boon-docks."

In today's air raid—by twenty-six Jap two-engined bombers—I had my closest escape from a bomb explosion. When the air-raid alert came in, Miller, Durdin and I went to the top of the ridge and walked down it, looking for a good high spot from which we could watch the bombers.

We found three or four men at work building a shelter at a spot several hundred yards away, where the ridge was bare of any foliage except grass, and one had a wonderful view of the sky. The incipient shelter, now only a pit, was just what we wanted in the way of a box seat for the show. It was deep and wide. We could sit on the edge until the bombers were just overhead, then still have plenty of time to dive for cover.

We did just that. The planes came as usual in a wide line that was a very shallow V, stretching across the sky. As usual, the anti-aircraft guns put up bursts in the vicinity, and as usual the bombers plowed on steadily, holding their formation and course.

Then the bombs came. When we heard them rattling down, we piled into the pit, layer upon layer of humanity, and waited. The bombs made a slightly different sound this time, perhaps because they were closer than before. Their sound was louder and more of a whistle. And the explosions were deafening. You could hear fragments skittering through the air over the top of the pit, and in that second all of us must have known that if we had been lying on the bare ridge we would have been hit and hurt.

Till Durdin said, "Hot." I saw that he was touching the sole of his shoe. He pulled a piece of metal out of the leather and held it gingerly between two fingers. It was a bomb fragment, still warm from the explosion.

Miller and I were anxious to see how close the craters had been this time. We spotted a small crater about forty yards from our pit. It was this missile, probably, that had thrown the fragments over our heads.

Beyond the small crater were other, larger holes. One of them must have been thirty feet across. That one lay about three hundred yards from our pit, fortunately beyond effective range. It was one of an irregularly spaced line of craters that led into the jungle beyond the grass.

Now, from the jungle, we heard excited shouting, and cries for a corpsman. We knew that meant that there had been some people hurt down there. We saw several being brought out on stretchers.

Our fighter planes were already avenging the casualties. We heard the sounds of a dogfight in the sky, and later came word that they had knocked down six of the bombers and one Zero.

Later this afternoon, our dive-bombers came in from a trip to Gizo. This time they had found a small ship, a patrol-boat type of craft, lying off the base, and had sunk it. They had also bombed the buildings of the base again.

At air-operations headquarters I found a box which had been sent me by plane, from my shipmates on a former task-force excursion. It included cans of beans, brown bread, salmon, peaches. Miller, Pvt. Frank Schultz, who drives our jeep, Jim Hurlbut (the Marine Corps correspondent) and I went down to the Lunga, taking the box along, and had a swim in the swift, clear water. Then we opened the cans and had a feast.

SATURDAY, SEPTEMBER 12

This morning, as an urgent air alert was flashed, we of the Press Club decided to go down to Lunga Point to watch the show for today. So we piled into a jeep and our driver turned out one of the fastest cross-country records such a vehicle has ever achieved. He was not inclined to be caught on the road when the bombers arrived.

At the Point, Miller put on the headphones of the radio set and began calling out the interplane conversations of our fighters, who were by that time rising to search for the foe.

At 11:42 Maj. Smith called: "Control from Smith. They're coming in from the south—a big squadron of 'em." And then we saw them, the usual impressive span of two-motored silver bombers, Mitsubishi 96's, moving like a slender white line of cloud across the blue sky.

This time the planes were set against an almost cloudless sky, and had a long course of blue to traverse before they reached dropping point over the airport. That chance gave the anti-aircraft an unusually good opportunity to range on them.

At first, the puffs of ack-ack fire were too high and ahead of the Japs. We saw the silver-bodied planes pass under the spotty cloud formed as the bursts spread out and merged. And then the AA began to come on the range. The flashes of the bursts came just in front of the silver-bodied planes; then one bomber in the left side of the formation was hit. We saw the orange flash of the explosion just under his wing, under the starboard motor nacelle, and then the motor began to trail a pennant of white smoke and the plane pulled off and downward, and left the formation.

Just as the plane pulled clear of the formation, another anti-aircraft shell burst directly under the belly of one of the planes at the center of the formation. A tongue of flame spread across the middle of the plane, then receded and was swallowed in a torrent of black smoke, and, in an instant, the plane was nosing straight down toward the ground. Now I saw one wing sheer off as if it were paper, and flutter after the more swiftly falling fuselage. Then the plane simply disintegrated, chunks fluttering away and falling, while the center part of the plane plunged at ever-accelerating speed toward the ground.

By this time the remainder of the Jap bomber formation had passed on out to sea. But one of the planes, possibly crippled by anti-aircraft fire, had become separated from the rest. One of our fighters was quick to pounce on him.

There was quite a group of us on the Point this day, watching the "show." Now they were cheering like a crowd at a football game. "Whoooo-ee," shouted someone, "look at that fighter. He's got him."

The tiny speck of the fighter, looking like a bumblebee in comparison to the bigger, clumsier bomber, was diving now. And we heard the rattlesnake sound of his guns. The bomber slewed, came up in a whipstall, and fell off in a steep dive toward the ocean.

The other bombers had disappeared somewhere in the blue, but we could hear our fighters going after them.

In the beautiful amphitheater of the sky, the kill of the isolated bomber by the fighter was continuing. We saw the bomber diving straight toward the sea, vertically, but the fighter, like a malevolent mosquito, hovered about the larger object, watching for signs of life.

The bomber dived a few thousand feet, and then, suddenly, pulled out of the dive and climbed straight up into the sky, up and up, like an animal gasping for air in its death struggle.

Quickly, the fighter closed and its machine guns rattled again, for seconds on end in a long burst. And then the bomber paused, fell off on one wing and with spinning wings fluttered vertically toward Tulagi Bay.

A few seconds later the spinning plane hit the water, and from the spot where it struck came a great backfire of ruddy flame and black smoke. And the watchers on the shore cheered madly, as if our side had made a touchdown.

Back at the airport, we found that the final score for the day was ten bombers and three Zeros; another goodly addition to a total that is mounting much too fast to please the Japs.

Capt. Smith came in to report that he had downed his fourteenth and fifteenth planes today; he did not say so, but it was told at the airport that he has been promoted to the rank of major, an award richly deserved.

We found that Lieut. Ken Frazier (Kenneth D. Frazier of Burlington, N.J.) was the pilot who had destroyed the crippled bomber so spectacularly while we watched from Lunga Point. He had shot down another plane as well.

"The first one went down in flames," he said. "The straggler was simple. I dived on him, saw the tracers falling a little short, pulled up a little, and then watched the chunks fly off the plane."

On one edge of the airfield, we found pieces of the Jap bomber which had disintegrated while we watched. There was quite a large section of the fuselage. The metal seemed much more fragile than the skin of the American bombers I have seen.

The cocoanut grove at one edge of the airfield had been struck by a stick of large bombs. The craters were huge. But the bombs had hit nothing of value. A 100-pound bomb had smashed directly into a shack, killing one man, destroying some radio equipment. That was the only visible damage of the bombing.

When somebody came into our tent, at about nine o'clock, and shouted, "Get up, fellas, we're moving up the ridge," we did not waste any time, but grabbed helmets and shoes and left. Only a few minutes later, from the ridge-top, we saw a pinpoint of bright green light appear in the sky to the north. The light spread into the glow of a flare, and then we heard the mosquito-like "double-hummer" tone of a Jap floatplane. It was "Louie the Louse"—a generic name for any one of the Jap floatplanes which come to annoy us at night.

"Louie" flew leisurely, as he always does, over the island, dropping more flares, and then we saw the distinctive flashes of naval gunfire coming from the direction of Kukum.

Just as we heard the boom of the gun, the shell whizzed over our heads and crashed a few hundred yards around. There was a second's pause, and then more flashes followed, so continuously that the sky seemed to be flickering constantly, and shells whined overhead almost in column. They kept coming for minutes on end, fortunately hitting into the jungle several hundred yards beyond us, skimming over the trees under which we were lying. We simply lay there clutching the side of the ridge and hoping the Japs would continue to fire too high.

The barrage kept up for about twenty minutes, then halted. And we waited in silence—the general and the rest of us lying on the ground, waiting to see if the firing would begin again.

We had just got to our feet when an outburst of rifle and machine-gun fire came from the south, apparently only a few hundred yards away. We wondered then if another big Jap effort to break through our lines had begun.

The firing continued, and the noise was augmented by mortar explosions. Then there came the flash of naval gunfire again, this time from the direction of the Tenaru. We hit the deck pronto, but the shells were not coming in our direction. The sound of the explosions indicated they were falling along shore.

Our observation posts reported that four Jap warships—cruisers and destroyers in the usual force—were swinging along the beach, bombarding the shoreline at their leisure, then turning back and making the run in the opposite direction to repeat their performance.

Then the shelling stopped, and, gradually, the small arms and mortar fire coming from the south dwindled in volume. But we did not go back into the valley to sleep this night. I slipped my poncho over my head, put on my mosquito head-net and my helmet, and lay down on the top of the hard ridge to sleep.

SUNDAY, SEPTEMBER 13

We heard this morning that a Jap patrol nipped off one end of our outpost line, last night, a few hundred yards south of the general's CP, on the ridge. That was the firing we heard. The Raiders, who hold the line, are falling back to a better position today, in case a big Jap push develops today or tonight. Last night's fighting was only a minor sort of engagement.

Miller and I went to Kukum this morning to watch the daily air raid, which came in at about noon, on schedule. Interception was good. The bombers got frightened and jettisoned their loads. And Zeros and our Grummans had a terrific dogfight. From Kukum, we could see them dodging in and out of the towering cumulus clouds, occasionally diving down over the water. We saw one Wildcat (Grumman) come diving down like a comet from the clouds, with two Zeros on his tail. He was moving faster than they, and as he pulled out of his dive and streaked across the water, he left them behind. They gave up the chase and pulled sharply back up into the sky. We had a good view of their long, square-tipped wings, and the round red ball of the rising sun insignia, as they turned. They appeared, as the pilots had told me, to be very maneuverable planes.

Many planes were dogfighting in and about the masses of cumulus clouds. I watched two planes, one chasing the other, pop out of the tower of cloud, describe a small, precise semi-circle, and go back in again.

A few moments later they made another circle, like two beads on the same wire. Other planes popped in and out of their levels in the cloud structure, and the whole area of the sky resounded with the rattling of machine guns. With so many guns firing at once, there was a cumulative effect as loud and magnificent as thunder.

Back at air headquarters, we waited for the tally of today's score. It was four bombers, four Zeros.

We went to bed in our tents tonight, but were shortly told to move out and up to the ridge-top. This time I had enough foresight to take along a blanket, and my satchel full of notes.

We could hear rifle fire coming from our front lines a few hundred yards to the south. Then machine guns. Flares went up occasionally and shed a glow over the sky.

I spread out my poncho and blanket and tried to sleep. I was awakened by the blasting of our own artillery batteries, to the north of us. The shells were whirring just over our position in the ridge-top, skimming over the trees, then hitting and exploding a few hundred yards to the south, apparently in the area where the fighting was going on.

MONDAY, SEPTEMBER 14

Shortly after midnight this morning the din of firing grew so tremendous that there was no longer any hope of sleeping. Our batteries were banging incessantly, the rifle and machine-gun fire from the direction of the Raider lines had swelled into a cascade of sound, Louie the Louse was flying about, and flares were dropping north, south, east and west.

We were drawing up a strong skirmish line on the ridge-top. Re-inforcements were on their way up. We knew that the Raiders, Col. Edson's people, out on the ridge, had their hands full. We knew then that a major Japanese effort to break through our lines and seize the airport had begun.

Another storm of rifle, machine-gun and mortar fire came now from the direction of the Tenaru. Was this another attempt to break through? For the present there was no way to find out.

Naval gunfire began to boom from the north. But it was not coming near us.

The general said to Col. Thomas: "Say, Jerry, ask air headquarters is it feasible to send a plane to see if there are any transports—just to see." The general was as calm and cheery as usual.

Some "shorts" from our own artillery fell in the valley where our tents are located. The flashes were as bright as day. One man standing near where I sprawled on the ground was knocked down by the concussion. We thought at first that the shells were Jap projectiles from their ships, ranging on the CP.

The sounds of firing had now become a din. A gray mist began to drift in among the trees on the ridge. It was thicker in the valley. Was it smoke from our artillery? It might be gas. (It was smoke, released by the Japs to create a gas scare.)

An artillery observer came into our communication dugout and reported to Col. Thomas, who was busy with phone calls, checking on the latest information from all outposts, giving orders. The observer said his telephone line, reaching farther toward the front, had been blown out. He had come back to relay firing instructions to our artillery batteries. He said the Japs were trying to advance down the ridge, but that our artillery fire, coupled with determined resistance from the Raiders on one of the knolls of the ridge, was holding up the enemy.

The observer found a line open from this point back to our batteries. "Drop it five zero and walk it back and forth across the ridge," he said. Then we heard the loud voice of the officer directing the battery: "Load…fire!" Then the bang of the cannon, the shells whizzing overhead.

The barrage continued. And after a few minutes, a runner came back from Col. Edson's lines. "Col. Edson says the range is perfect in there," he said, breathlessly. "It's right on. It's knocking the hell out of 'em."

Snipers were moving in on us. They had filtered along the flanks of the ridge, and taken up positions all around our CP. Now they began to fire. It was easy to distinguish the sound of their rifles. There were light machine guns, too, of the same caliber. Ricocheting bullets skidded amongst the trees. We plastered ourselves flat on the ground.

I went to the communication dugout to see if there might be any room inside. But the shack was filled. I picked a spot amidst some sparse bushes at the foot of a tree. A bullet whirred over my head. I moved to another tree.

A stream of tracer bullets arched through the trees from behind us. We heard Jap .25's opening up from several new directions. It seemed now that they were all around.

The whispered word went round that the Japs were landing parachute troops (later proved false). More reinforcements came through our position on the ridge, while the Japs were firing. But we wondered if we could hold our place. If the Japs drove down the ridge in force, and broke through Col. Edson's lines, they would be able to take the CP. If they had already cut in behind our position, as we suspected they had, they would box us in, and perhaps capture the general and his staff.

But the general remained calm. He sat on the ground beside the operations tent. "Well," he said cheerfully, "it's only a few more hours till dawn. Then we'll see where we stand."

Occasionally, he passed along a short, cogent suggestion to Col. Thomas. He was amused at my efforts to take notes in the dark.

The telephone line to Col. Edson's front had been connected again. The colonel called Col. Thomas to say that the Raiders' ammunition was running low; he needed a certain number of rounds of belted machine-gun bullets—and some hand grenades. Col. Thomas located some of the desired items by phone after a quick canvass. They would be sent over soon, he told Col. Edson.

But at about three o'clock Col. Edson called again to say that he was "almost out." The ammunition had not arrived.

We were wondering if the Raider line was going to cave in when more Jap planes came over. There were probably two of them. They dropped more flares.

The sounds of heavy firing to our left rear had broken out again. Col. Thomas checked by phone. "It's in McKelvy's area," he said. "The Japs got into his wire."

Snipers were still popping at us from all sides. We had our hands full. But then Col. Edson called back to say that ammunition and grenades had arrived, and the news had a good effect on morale.

At about four o'clock the snipers were still shooting into our camp, but they had not attacked our skirmish lines on the ridge. Our artillery fire had slackened a little. And the sounds of firing in the Raider area were sporadic. I rolled myself in blanket and poncho (for the early mornings on Guadalcanal are always chill) and lay down in some underbrush on the slope of the ridge. I was able to sleep for about an hour.

As the first light of dawn came, the general was sitting on the side of the ridge, talking to some of his aides. A Jap machine gun opened up, and they high-tailed for the top of the ridge, with me right behind. We were heading for a tent, where we would at least have psychological shelter. Just as we reached the tent, a bullet clanged against a steel plate only two or three feet from us. It was amusing to see the rear ends of the dignified gentlemen disappearing under the edge of the tent. I made an equally undignified entrance.

It was not safe to walk about the camp this morning. Snipers had worked their way into camouflaged positions in trees through the area, and there were some machine gunners, with small, light .25 caliber guns. One had to watch one's cover everywhere he moved.

There were large groups of Japs on the left or east side of the ridge, in the jungles. There was a lot of firing in that area. We had a firing line of men extending south from the CP, out along the ridge, facing those groups of Japs. The men lay along the edge of a road that ran down the exposed top of the ridge, protected only by grass. The Japs were firing at them from the cover of the jungle.

Beyond that firing line, the ridge curved and dipped. It rose like the back of a hog into a knoll, beyond the dip. It was on this knoll that the Raiders had been doing their fiercest fighting.

I worked my way out along the ridge to the firing line, to get a look at the knoll where the Raiders had been fighting. I lay flat next to a machine gunner while the Japs fired at us with a .25 light gun. A man to our right, farther out on the ridge, was wounded. We saw him crawling back toward us, a pitiful sight, like a dog with only three serviceable legs. He had been shot in the thigh.

Beyond the bend in the ridge, the machine gunner told me, there were several more wounded. A group of six or seven of our men had been hit by machine-gun fire. Two of them were dead.

In the jungle at the foot of the ridge we heard our own guns firing as well as the Japs'. Some of our troops were pushing through there, mopping up the groups of Japs.

It was evident that the main Jap attempt, down the top of the ridge, had failed. I moved out a little farther along the ridge, nearly to the bend in the road where the wounded lay, and I could see the knoll where the fighting had been going on. It was peopled with marines, but they were not fighting, now.

We heard the characteristic whine of pursuit planes coming. Then we saw them diving on the knoll, and heard their machine guns pop and rattle as they dived. "They've got a bunch of Japs on the other side of the hill," said a haggard marine next to me. "That's the best way to get at 'em."

I worked my way back to the CP and got some coffee. I was cleaning my mess cup when I heard a loud blubbering shout, like a turkey gobbler's cry, followed by a burst of shooting. I hit the deck immediately, for the sound was close by. When the excitement of the moment had stopped, and there was no more shooting, I walked to the spot, at the entrance to the CP on top of the ridge, and found two bodies of Japs there—and one dead marine. Gunner Banta told me that three Japs had made a suicide charge with bayonets. One of them had spitted the marine, and had been shot. A second had been tackled and shot, and the third had run away. These three had been hiding in a bush at the edge of the ridge road, evidently for some time. I had passed within a few feet of that bush on my way out to the firing line and back. The animal-like cry I had heard had been the Jap "Banzai" shout.

Col. Edson and Col. Griffith, the guiding powers of the Raiders, came into our CP this morning to make a report to Gen. Vandegrift and shape further plans. The mere fact that they had come in was a good sign. It meant that the fighting was at least slackening and perhaps ending, for they would not have left their front lines if there had been any considerable activity.

Maj. Ken Bailey, one of the Raider officers and a hero of the Tulagi campaign, also appeared, dirty and rumpled but beaming like a kid on the night before Christmas. Bailey loved a fight. He showed us his helmet, which had been pierced front and back by a Jap bullet. The slug had grazed his scalp without injuring him.

The Raider officers' conversations with the general and Col. Thomas were held in the general's secret sanctum. But I talked to Col. Edson as he left the shack. He said that the large main body of the Japs, who had been trying to drive down the ridge, had fallen back.

He said that a force of between 1,000 and 2,000 Japs had tried to storm the ridge, with lesser forces infiltrating along the base. His estimate of the Jap casualties, at that time, was between 600 and 700 in the ridge area alone. Our artillery fire, he said, had smacked into the midst of a large group of Japs and wiped out probably 200 of them. Our own casualties had been heavy, for the fighting was furious.

The colonel gave the impression that the big battle of the ridge had ended; that the only fighting in the area now was the mopping up of small, isolated Japanese groups by our patrols.

But snipers were scattered through the trees of the area. I had a brush with one of them during today's first air raid.

I was sitting on the side of the ridge that looks over the valley where our tents are located. A throng of Zeros were dogfighting with our Grummans in the clouds and I was trying to spot the planes.

Suddenly I saw the foliage move in a tree across the valley. I looked again and was astonished to see the figure of a man in the crotch of the tree. He seemed to be moving his arms and upper body. I was so amazed at seeing him so clearly that I might have sat there and reflected on the matter if my reflexes had not been functioning—which they fortunately were. I flopped flat on the ground just as I heard the sniper's gun go off and the bullet whirred over my head. I then knew that his movement had been the raising of his gun.

But there was no time to reflect on that fact either. I retreated behind a tent. And then anger caught up with me. Again the war had suddenly become a personal matter. I wanted to get a rifle and fire at the sniper. Correspondents, in theory at least, are non-combatants. Several of our men, however, fired into the crotch of the tree where the sniper was located.

Miller had come in from Kukum, where he spent last night. He and I went out on the ridge, later in the day, to have a look at the battleground. We climbed the steep knoll where our troops had made their stand and turned back the main Jap drive.

The hill was quiet now. Small fires smoldered in the grass. There were black, burned patches where Jap grenades had burst. Everywhere on the hill were strewn hand-grenade cartons, empty rifle shells, ammunition boxes with ragged, hasty rips in their metal tops.

The marines along the slope of the hill sat and watched us quietly as we passed. They looked dirty and worn. Along the flank of the hill, where a path led, we passed strewn bodies of marines and Japs, sometimes tangled as they had fallen in a death struggle. At the top of the knoll, the dead marines lay close together. Here they had been most exposed to Jap rifle and machine-gun fire, and grenades.

At the crest of the knoll we looked down the steep south slope where the ridge descended into a low saddle. On this steep slope there were about 200 Jap bodies, many of them torn and shattered by grenades or artillery bursts, some ripped, a marine told us, by the strafing planes which we had seen this morning. It was up this slope that the Japs had sent their heaviest assaults many times during the night, and each time they tried they had been repulsed.

Beyond the saddle of the ridge rose another knoll, and there we could see more bodies, and the pockmarks of shelling. The whole top of this knoll had been burned off and wisps of smoke still rose from the smoldering grass.

Miller and I still stood on the open crest of the knoll. "Better watch it," a marine said. "There's a sniper in the jungle over there."

We moved away from the hill crest and had walked about fifty feet when we heard a shout behind us. A man had been hit, at the spot where we had been standing. He had a bad wound in the leg. Our luck was holding.

We went to Kukum to watch for further air raids. But no more planes appeared until late in the afternoon. In the meantime, we heard heavy artillery pounding into the jungle near Matanikau, and saw smoke rising in great clouds above the trees. We heard that a large body of Japs were trying to make a breakthrough in that area. The first reports had it that casualties were heavy, but later we found that the fighting here had been only a protracted skirmish and our casualties were few.

It was dusk when Jap seaplanes made a low-altitude attack. Three of them, monoplane float aircraft, passed back and forth over Kukum, drawing streams of anti-aircraft fire. Others swung over the beach farther to the east, and the island became alive with ack-ack; the sky was trellised with the bright lines of tracer.

Again the Japs dropped many flares, and once we saw an extremely bright white light flaming over the Tenaru, which we thought was a flare—and found out later that it was caused by two Jap planes burning simultaneously.

The Jap planes, we learned at air operations headquarters, had tried to make a bombing attack on the airport. A group of fifteen to twenty Jap seaplanes, slow, ancient biplanes, had sneaked over the mountains in southern Guadalcanal, and tried to make a low-altitude attack. But they had been caught by our Grummans, and nine of them shot down. Four Zero floatplanes had also been shot down. And in the earlier raid of the day, two Zeros and one bomber had been downed—and the bombers had been turned back long before they reached Guadalcanal. The Jap air attacks of the day, like their land effort of last night, had been a failure.

Tonight the general and his staff had moved from the old CP on the ridge to a slightly safer spot, and of course there had been no time during the day to erect tents, cots or the other elementary comforts of Guadalcanal living. So for the third successive night I slept on the bare ground. The senior surgeon of all Gen. Vandegrift's medical troops lay down nearby; he, too, had only a poncho for a mattress, and took the discomfort without complaint. "I'm afraid I'm going to have my joints oiled up a bit if this keeps on," he said. And that was his only comment.

TUESDAY, SEPTEMBER 15

Yarbrough and Kent have shoved off. They sailed aboard a small ship which came in today and made for a rendezvous with a larger craft. Durdin seems to be somewhat pessimistic about the general situation. Miller and I, being somewhat punch-drunk, are more inclined to view the future cheerfully.

This morning we corraled Col. Thomas and asked him to give us a quick outline of the big battle which has been going on for the last two days. He gave us a lucid summary.

The Japs had assembled three large units of troops, by a process of slow accumulation, said the colonel. Two of these large units, totaling 3,000 to 4,000 and possibly more (the figures were estimates based on the observations of our patrols), were massed to the east of the airport; the third, a smaller group, to the west.

"We couldn't get at them because of the terrain," said the colonel, "although we did raid the landing area of the two eastern detachments." (That was the raid which Col. Edson's troops had made on Tasimboko.)

The three groups made three separate attacks, said the colonel. The principal of these was a drive toward the airfield from the south along the top of Lunga Ridge. It was here that the Raiders had had their tough fight.

Two other, much lighter, attacks were made: one from the west, from the Matanikau area; and the second from the east, which was apparently intended to flank our positions along the Tenaru.

Our patrols discovered several days ago that the two eastern groups were moving in, one on our flank, one swinging around to make an attack from the south, our rear.

"On the night of the 12th and 13th," said the colonel, "the Japs came up from the rear [the south] and infiltrated our lines, but did no damage.

"Then, our outpost line being too long, it was withdrawn several hundred yards. One hour after dark on the night of the 13th–14th, groups of 50 to 100 men each broke through the line and attacked the ridge. Col. Edson moved his men 300 to 400 yards to the rear and took up a position on a rugged hill [the steep knoll we had visited on the ridge]. At about eleven o'clock in the evening, the Japs charged in large numbers. Edson had a few hundred men, the Japs about 2,000. Our artillery fire was laid down, causing many casualties. From then on until 6:00 A.M. the Japs made many assaults on the hill, including bayonet charges. They lost 500 men."

On the same night the Japs attacked our eastern flank, but ran into barbed-wire entanglements and retired, leaving about thirty dead Japs in the wire, said the colonel. The attack from the west did not come until yesterday, and, thanks to our artillery and stubborn resistance by our troops, that attempt was also pushed back.

Miller, Durdin and I made another swift survey of the high knoll where Edson's men had fought, and decided that since it had no other name, it should be called "Edson Hill" in our stories.

Later in the day we went to Col. Edson's headquarters to get his story of the battle. He told us about the individual exploits of his men and their collective bravery, but did not mention the fact that he himself had spent the night on the very front line of the knoll, under the heaviest fire.

He did not mention it, but the fact was that two bullets had actually ripped through his blouse, without touching him. Another Raider officer whispered that information to me and I nodded absently, then was startled to see that the colonel was still wearing the garment. Bullet holes marred the collar and waist.

The Raiders told us some good stories of valor; about a sergeant named John R. Morrill (of Greenville, Tenn.), who with two buddies had been cut off from the rest of the marines by a Jap advance. And how Sgt. Morrill had walked with impunity through the Jap positions during the darkness.

Then there was a private, first class, named Ray Herndon (of Walterboro, S.C.), whose squad occupied a very exposed position on the south side of Edson Hill at the time the Japs made their heaviest attacks. The Jap firing hit right into the squad and left only four of them alive, three unwounded, and Ray, hit mortally through the stomach. And then Ray, knowing he was hit badly, had asked one of his buddies to give him a .45 automatic, and said: "You guys better move out. I'm done for anyhow. With that automatic, I can get three or four of the bastards before I kick off."

Then there was a young, round-faced lad from Greensburg, Pa., named Corp. Walter J. Burak, the colonel's runner, who had twice during the night traversed the exposed crest of the ridge the whole distance from the knoll to the general's CP, under the heaviest fire. He had made the first trip with a telephone wire, when the line had been blown out. And the second trip, toting a forty-pound case of hand grenades, when in the early hours of the morning, the shortage of that item became pressing.

But the outstanding story was Lewis E. Johnson's of De Beque, Colorado. Lewis was wounded three times in the leg by fragments of a grenade, and at daybreak placed in the rear of a truck with about a dozen other wounded, for evacuation. But as the truck moved down the ridge road, a Jap machine gunner opened up and wounded the driver severely. The truck stopped. Then Johnson painfully crawled from the rear of the vehicle, dragged himself to the cab, got into the driver's seat and tried to start the motor. When it would not start, he put the car in gear, and, using the starter for traction, pulled the truck a distance of about 300 yards over the crest of the ridge. Then he got the engine going and drove to the hospital. By that time, he was feeling so refreshed that he drove the truck back to the front and got another load of wounded.

To get the story of the attacks on the other two fronts, we went first to Col. Cates' headquarters, to cover the attack that had come from the east, and then to Col. Hunt's for news on the attack which had come from the west, the direction of Matanikau.

Col. Cates referred us to Lieut. Col. McKelvy (William N. McKelvy of Washington, D.C.), the immediate commander of the troops who had held back the Japs attacking from the east.

"The entire attack was delivered against a road called the Overland Trail," he began.

"On the night of the 13th–14th, at about 10:15, I heard shooting. At 10:30 Capt. Putnam [Robert J. Putnam of Denver, Col.] called to say that one of his listening posts had been jumped. He said that a man came in to his CP, and as he arrived he said, 'They got 'em all,' and fainted.

"At about eleven o'clock, Capt. Putnam called and said the Japs had put out a few bands of fire—a few rifle shots, but that there was nothing serious yet.

"Then everything opened up. There was a terrific outburst of firing, and Capt. Putnam said, 'They're inside the wire. They're being bayoneted.' We found twenty-seven bodies on the wire in the morning.

"We were putting down our big mortars and all the rest. All the activity was on that one flank. The Japs were trying hard to take the road."

The colonel stopped to get a large map and point out the road, a trail which led from the east into our lines, toward the airport.

"At 5:30 the attack stopped and the Japs withdrew. They didn't want to be caught in daylight.

"That morning—that was the 14th—we were given a reserve of six tanks. There was high grass across from our positions and we were afraid the Japs were lying doggo in there. While the tanks were in, one of our own lieutenants jumped on one of the tanks. He was a Lieut. Turzai [Joseph A. Turzai of Great Neck, L.I.], who had been wounded by shrapnel, and stayed surrounded by Japs all night.

"Lieut. Turzai told us there were Jap machine guns in a shack in the high grass. Later in the day we sent the tanks after them. They accomplished their mission, with some losses. [We lost three tanks when the Japs opened fire at point-blank range with anti-tank guns.]

"At eleven o'clock last night, the Japs hit us again. It was a minor attack. They shelled us with light mortars.

"Just at daybreak this morning we spotted about 300 Japs in a group. We had our artillery batteries laid for a concentration in that area; the fire fell right on them. They undoubtedly lost a lot of people there."

At Col. Hunt's CP, Lieut. Wilson gave us an outline of the fighting in the Matanikau vicinity. That, too, had been of a minor character compared to the finish fight that had raged along the ridge.

"Yesterday morning, just at daybreak, there was mortar and machine-gun fire into our left flank positions," he said. Col. Biebush (Lieut. Col. Fred C. Biebush of Detroit, Mich.) was commanding our troops.

"At about 8:30 A.M. there came a bayonet charge. But it was repelled with heavy losses for the Japs. The Japs tried it again at 10:30.

"The Japs tried a breakthrough between two groups of troops on our left flank. They were trying to see how far our wire extended. They were beaten back.

"At about noontime, a patrol went out to reconnoiter the enemy position. Maj. Hardy [former Capt. Bert W. Hardy], who led the patrol, sent back a message, saying, 'The woods are infested with snipers and automatic riflemen. I am pushing forward.'

"Information gathered by our reconnaissance enabled us to put down a heavy concentration of mortar and artillery fire which stopped the attack."

I slept in a shack at Kukum tonight, on the bare board floor. I came awake, once in the night, to hear people shouting. I asked a man next to me what was happening. He grunted. "Those silly sailors don't secure their boats," he said, "so when Oscar goes by, they all bust loose when his wake hits 'em." But he was wrong. It was not Oscar who had gone by, but a couple of Jap destroyer-type warships, apparently paying us a visit after landing troops at Cape Esperance, to the east.

WEDNESDAY, SEPTEMBER 16

We had some copy to get to Gen. Vandegrift's headquarters for censorship this morning, and were about to start out for the CP, when an air alert came in. But there was no raid, and we reached our destination with our stories and got them off. Till Durdin feared they would be our last.

Today our dive-bombers and torpedo planes from Henderson Field went north on an attack mission. We checked at the airport later in the day and found that they had been after some Jap cruisers and destroyers located between Bougainville and Choiseul. It was believed they got one torpedo hit on a cruiser and got a bomb hit on a second.

THURSDAY, SEPTEMBER 17

Till Durdin's worry that our story on the Jap attack might be our last, fortunately is not being substantiated. Things seem to be calming down on Guadalcanal. Our patrols on all our fronts contacted no Japs today, and to the east and south, it seems, they have withdrawn a goodly distance. Along Col. McKelvy's front, we heard, our troops have found abandoned mortars and machine guns, some of them in brand-new condition, indicating the Japs fled in some haste.

Nor was there any air raid today, although our fighters, Pursuits and Grummans, went down to Cape Esperance on a strafing mission. Again they had found Jap landing boats on the shore there but no Japs visible. Evidently they had landed at night on the regular schedule and had time to take good cover.

The dust is getting thick on Guadalcanal. If you move on the roads now, you stir up a cloud of the dirty gray stuff. Planes and trucks moving across the airport trail huge triangular black clouds.

You put on clean clothes at nine o'clock and walk down the road and at 9:30 you look like a chimney sweep. When you ride in a car the dust of passing vehicles chokes your lungs and blots out your vision. We now ride about with our helmets held over our faces in an attempt to keep them relatively clean. Schultz has dug up a pair of fancy polaroid goggles somewhere. Also, incidentally, a cowboy-effect belt set with large paste-stones, ruby- and emerald-colored. Where he collects such items on Guadalcanal is a mystery. He has also adopted the glamorous sun-helmet which Yarbrough left behind. Schultz's ambition is to be a state cop in Illinois (he's from Chicago) or a border patrol trooper, after the war.

At air headquarters today we saw a complete tabulation of the number of planes shot down by our fighters to date. The total is 131; of these, our marine fighters (Grummans) have knocked down 109; the Army Pursuiters, four; our Navy fighters (also Grummans), who have been here only a short time, seventeen; and one of our dive-bombers got a Zero. Our anti-aircraft batteries, in addition, are credited with five.

Of the 131 enemy planes destroyed, about half were fighters or other single-engine planes, and about half the fast, two-motored Mitsubishi 97's.

Today I talked to a Coast Guard seaman named Thomas J. Canavan (of Chicago, Ill.), who had just got back after recuperating from a terrible adventure. That adventure happened about a month ago, when Canavan was out on anti-submarine patrol; there were three small boats in the patrol, and they were surprised by three Jap cruisers and sunk. Canavan was the only survivor. He saved his life by floating in the water, playing dead while one of the cruisers came close by and looked over his "body." Then he swam for seventeen hours, trying to get to Florida Island. He finally made the shore.

Canavan, who still looked and talked as if he could feel a ghost looking over his shoulder, said he had only a cocoanut for nourishment during two days on Florida. This he promptly upchucked. He saw fierce-looking natives with spines of bone stuck through their noses and ran from them, but he found later they had been cordially inclined. For when he woke up after falling asleep exhausted on the beach, he found someone had covered him with palm fronds to protect him from the rain and nightly cold. He tried twice to swim to Tulagi Island, and the first time was thwarted by tides. The second time he succeeded.

Our dive-bombers and torpedo planes laden with bombs went out today to target the buildings of the Cape Esperance area where the Japs have been landing. They reported they set the buildings afire.

There are two persistent reports on the "scuttlebutt" circuit today: one is that reinforcements are coming to Guadalcanal—and, on that count, estimates of numbers vary; and the other is that our aircraft carrier *Wasp* has been sunk.

FRIDAY, SEPTEMBER 18

The rumor that reinforcements were en route to Guadalcanal was substantiated today, when they arrived. Early this morning, a certain colonel told me: "I can't say anything more about it, but I'd recommend that you go for a walk on the beach." I went to the beach and saw cargo- and warships and transports steaming into sight.

Miller and I went to the landing point to watch the ships unload. All along the beach our weary veterans stood and watched the process, passively. We had been talking about reinforcements, and waiting for a long time.

They were marines, these new troops, thousands of them, boatload after boatload; they wore clean utility suits and new helmets, and talked tough and loud as they came ashore.

One of our veterans told me he had been talking to some of the new arrivals. "Chees," he said, "these guys want to tell *us* about the war." And we knew then that it would take some time with these men, as it had with us, to get rid of that loud surface toughness and develop the cool, quiet fortitude that comes with battle experience.

Two correspondents came in with the shiploads of reinforcements. They are Jack Dowling and Frank McCarthy, who is relieving Miller. Miller was delighted and made much noise about the fact that when he hit the deck of the ship that would take him out of here, he was going to shave off his beard. We all cheered, for Miller's beard is one of the true horrors of Guadalcanal. It is almost as raggedy as my mustache.

A very reputable source told me today that the report of the *Wasp*'s having been sunk is true. He said she took two torpedoes in an isolated attack by a submarine (actually she took three), and was abandoned by her personnel.

Another persistent rumor these days is that our naval forces and the bulk of the Jap Navy in this area have fought a great battle somewhere to the north. But there is no confirmation from any official, or even informed, direction. The truth seems to be that there has been no major naval action by surface forces since the battle of Savo Island.

Durdin and I sat on the beach most of the afternoon, waiting for the Jap air raid which we thought was inevitable. Our fleet of cargo and transport ships would make excellent targets. But the Japs, fortunately, did not come this afternoon.

They did come tonight, a force of ships estimated to range from two to six. They were too late, for our ships had gone. But Louie the Louse flew over for some time, dropping flares, looking for our ships, and the Jap ships, probably cruisers, lay well offshore and lobbed shells into our coastline.

SATURDAY, SEPTEMBER 19

At the airport operations building this morning, we watched our dive-bombers taking off for some mission to the north. Probably bombing Gizo, or Rekata Bay, or one of the other Jap bases in the Solomons. Our people have been attacking some such objective frequently during the last few days, but have not had much luck in catching the Japanese ships, although they have damaged shore installations.

I checked over my records in an attempt to find out just how many ships our dive-bombers are credited with sinking since the first group of planes arrived here nearly a month ago. The total of ships sunk, I found, is three destroyers, one cruiser, and two transports. Probably a dozen other ships, mostly cruisers and destroyers, have been damaged by hits or near misses; altogether, a good score, considering the fact that poor weather conditions and night operations generally make the location of the enemy difficult.

Still the enemy landings at Guadalcanal go on. Bit by bit, they are building up their forces—even now, so soon after their second big attack to break through our lines and take the airport has failed. Last night the group of ships which came in and shelled us probably also landed their daily load of troops.

This afternoon we talked with some of the Raiders about the Battle of the Ridge, and heard some interesting stories about the Japs, how, for instance, they often ask to be killed when they are captured, but seem relieved when we do not oblige. Then they feel they have complied with their part of the death-before-dishonor formula, and make no further attempt to deprive themselves of life.

Several of the Jap prisoners captured on the ridge, it seems, said "Knife" when they were captured, and made hara-kiri motions in the region of the belly. But when no knife was forthcoming, they seemed relieved, and after that made no attempt to kill themselves.

Later this afternoon we heard that a large body of our troops is going out tomorrow to conduct a reconnaissance in force to the south of the airport, to try to find out how far the Japs have fallen back. Durdin, McCarthy, Dowling and I decided to go along.

SUNDAY, SEPTEMBER 20

Our reconnaissance started at about five o'clock this morning, and after that, for thirteen solid hours, we plowed through jungle and slipped and slid up and down the steepest ridges I have ever climbed. It was a lesson in the geography of Guadalcanal which I will not forget.

Much of the time we were hiking was spent in traversing the sides of ridges. The trails were muddy and slippery from rain which fell early this morning, and I found that a tripod posture, the three supports being formed by two legs and one arm, was the best way to stay on your feet.

We also spent considerable time in the thickest and most unpleasant jungles I have seen. We followed trails most of the time, but even these were covered with tangles of brambly vines, prickly leaves and tree branches protected by long spines.

But our group of troops, led by Col. Edson, at least did not run into any Japs. Other groups which joined in our reconnaissance found a few snipers. A group of our new reinforcements fired continuously, as we had done when we first came to Guadalcanal; they were as chary of shadows and as "trigger-happy" as we had been.

We found evidences that the Japs had moved away in a great hurry and in great disorganization. We found bivouac areas where they had left packs, shoes, flags behind. And I spotted a pile of canvas cases by the side of one trail and found they were filled with the parts of a serviceable 75 mm. pack howitzer. And others found rifles and ammunition. We found the shattered remains of a few Japs who had been hit by our artillery, and others who had evidently died of their wounds.

Today our dive-bombers and torpedo planes had gone out to bomb Rekata Bay, we found on getting back to camp. They had bombed and strafed the base, and uncovered a cruiser nearby and got a hit which damaged, but did not sink, it.

MONDAY, SEPTEMBER 21

The ships which brought us reinforcements, also brought supplies, including clothes. I went to the quartermaster depot this morning, got some clothes that smelled delightfully like the dry-goods department in a store, and went up to the Lunga and had a good bath before putting on the new things. Then to Juan Morrera's mess, which the marines call the Book-Cadillac, and afterward felt like a new man.

We sat about at Col. Hunt's CP and talked about the reason for the slackening in the Jap air raids. The optimists said the Japs had taken such a drubbing from our fighters that they had no planes left. The pessimists said the foe were simply consolidating their forces for another and bigger effort; perhaps they would send over more planes less frequently, instead of twenty-five or twenty-seven every day.

TUESDAY, SEPTEMBER 22

At Kukum this afternoon, I saw Dick Mangrum (now a lieutenant colonel) and Lieut. Turner Caldwell, who led, respectively, the original marine and naval dive-bomber groups which came to this island to work out of Henderson Field. Both Turner's and Dick's original squadrons have been largely supplanted by new, fresh groups, but the two leaders continued to fly until recently.

They had both grown thin as scarecrows, since I last saw them, and their faces were haggard. They told me they were exhausted from the night-and-day stint of work they had been doing.

"When the medicos used to tell us about pilot fatigue," said Turner, "I used to think they were old fuds. But now I know what they meant. There's a point where you just get to be no good; you're shot to the devil—and there's nothing you can do about it."

I heard tonight that both Turner and Dick are going to be sent out of Guadal soon for a rest in some peaceful region.

WEDNESDAY, SEPTEMBER 23

"Signs of civilization are coming to Guadalcanal," said Gen. Vandegrift this morning. He told me how an engineer had come into his quarters and asked where he wanted the light. The general said he was surprised to find that the engineer was actually towing an electric wire behind him. The Jap power house which we had captured was in working order, and they had extended a line to the general's camp.

The general said that he felt our situation on Guadalcanal was brightening a bit. The reinforcements had been a great help, he said, and he seemed assured that the naval protection of our shores would improve. I found out later in the day that a group of motor torpedo boats are on their way to help protect our coastline from the continued Japanese landings.

There is much "scuttlebutt" about more reinforcements coming into Guadalcanal. But the general feeling seems to be that if Army troops are brought in, they will only reinforce, not supplant, the marines, at least for the time being. The old dream of being home for Christmas is fading.

Many of our officers, however, are being sent home, to rest, and to train new groups of troops. That is another sign that we have reached at least a "breather." And the Japs have confirmed the impression by abstaining from air-raiding us for another day, and failing even to send in the usual landing force of troop-carrying warships this evening.

THURSDAY, SEPTEMBER 24

We went to the Raiders' CP for breakfast this morning, and had a good time yarning over pancakes. We talked about some of the close escapes we have had during this campaign, and Maj. Ken Bailey, one of the heroes of Tulagi and the battle on the ridge, said something touching about taking chances.

"You get to know these kids so well when you're working with 'em," he said, "and they're such swell kids that when it comes to a job that's pretty rugged, you'd rather go yourself than send them."

(Maj. Bailey was killed three days later during a patrol action.)

VIII

BOMBER TO BOUGAINVILLE

FRIDAY, SEPTEMBER 25

We went to air operations this morning to get the results of last night's attack on the Jap ships. The story was that they had been discovered yesterday afternoon, at a distance of about 100 miles from Cape Esperance. Our attack groups had gone out and dropped bombs, but the Japs had kept coming. Again, weather conditions and probably bad luck had hindered our marksmanship, and we had scored no hits. But after we had attacked four times, and the Japs had reached a point eight miles from the cape, they finally turned and retreated. Our pilots noticed that they were towing groups of landing boats.

I asked the general for permission to leave the island, and he told me with a chuckle that I had picked a good time. "They're putting in a shower for me in a few days," he said. "And when such luxuries come, the correspondent should go."

One reason for my leaving Guadalcanal is that I have worn out my last pair of serviceable shoes—and unfortunately there are no replacements available for outsizes. I am wearing rubber-soled tennis shoes now—and they are hardly the thing for hiking through the jungle. I went to the quartermaster camp today to try to get a pair my size—which is fourteen—and the good quartermaster held up his hands in horror.

A B-17 came in today, and I asked the pilot, a very calm, very steady man named Capt. Paul Payne (of Des Moines, Iowa), if he would give me transportation from Guadalcanal to a certain point to the south, whence I could make my way back to Honolulu.

Payne said, "Certainly, if you don't mind going by way of Bougainville."

That sounded dangerous. Bougainville is the northernmost island of the Solomons, and the largest. It is within easy striking distance of Rabaul, a great Jap air and naval base. And there is a Jap airfield, well protected by Zeros, on Buka Island at Bougainville's northern tip.

The B-17, said Capt. Payne, will be on a reconnaissance mission. Would I want to go? I said I certainly would.

SATURDAY, SEPTEMBER 26

It was dawn when we climbed into the plane. The captain offered me a chocolate bar. "Our usual breakfast," he said. Then they wound the props, and the starters squealed, and our motors were warming up.

We bounced along the runway, lifted and swung up and over Tulagi Bay. My post was in the cramped nose of the plane; I squatted next to the little desk where the navigator worked. Through the transparent plexiglas we watched the marvelous vista of blue water and sky rolling by. I was given a pair of headphones so that I could listen to the conversations on the communication circuit.

The sun came in the overhead window and was warm. The navigator, a slim young lieutenant named Clint Benjamin (Clinton W.

Benjamin of Noxan, Pa.), took off his shirt. He had already acquired quite a tan, apparently from just such trips as this.

"There's plenty of times when you do nothing but sit for hours," he shouted above the drone of the engines. And that was what we did, until we hit Bougainville.

We passed "up the slot" (along the passages of water between the island rows of the Solomons), looking down at the myriad rugged, jungly islands that slipped under our wings. Time dragged.

We worked our way up amidst the towering banks of cumulus clouds. And finally Capt. Payne's voice cracked into my earphones: "Navigator, bearing on Bougainville."

The navigator replied with the bearing. The plane swung in a gentle turn. And ahead of us we saw a black, irregular island mass lying under the clouds.

Then we saw our first enemy plane. "Plane bearing 25," a voice sang out into the earphones.

Payne's calm voice said: "Two five or three five?"

"Two five," came the answer. And then we saw the plane, moving in a direction directly opposite to ours, and about 2,000 overhead and to the right. He was well out of range. I got a glimpse of him; then he was gone to the rear, out of our vision.

"He'll probably come over in a dive," said Capt. Payne. But the plane did not come back. The gunners, however, stayed at their stations. We were apt to run into a horde of Japs any time now.

The navigator said: "Pilot, there should be ships in the harbor at the southern tip of Bougainville."

"Is that Bougainville ahead?" asked Capt. Payne.

"Yes."

Then a strange voice shouted on the communication system: "There's two Zeros coming up behind us!" It was the voice of the tail gunner.

From then on we had action.

"They're coming in," said the tail gunner. And after a few seconds, "They've turned off." Zeros are chary of the formidable B-17, but in such a moment as this, one thought swiftly of our aloneness over enemy territory and the swarms of enemy planes which must be around.

Ahead of us we saw a ship moving, as small as a toy in the distance.

"What kind of a vessel is it?" asked the pilot.

"I'd say it was a cargo vessel," said the navigator.

"Gunners, stand by your guns," said Capt. Payne.

We were moving over the enemy vessel now, and she was putting on knots. We could see the streamers of white foam at her flanks as she plowed at top speed. She was swinging in a circle, trying to dodge the bombs she thought we would rain on her. I imagined the chaos and scurrying on her decks, having myself been on the decks of ships during bombing attacks. But we were only conducting a reconnaissance, not bombing.

A gunner reported: "Two planes coming up from below, fast. They're 2,000 yards away." And then: "They're turning off."

I saw a plane over on our left. It was a seaplane with a single wing—a Zero float. He was flying the same course as we. One of our nose gunners began to fire. The zips of the tracer bullets arched around the enemy plane, came closer. The empty shells rattled to the floor of our bomber.

Now the Zero's wing dipped and he swung in a sharp turn toward us. Here he comes! I thought, and I saw the plane sweeping in on us, saw its tracers leaping out. In that instant I thought what I always think in such moments: that I was a damned fool to get myself into such a spot as this.

Our plane shook as our other guns along the flank took up the firing. The streams of tracers crossed in front of the Jap, then behind him. He turned away and disappeared to the rear. (We hit him.

The rear gunner said the Jap had gone down with a dead stick, made a forced landing on the water.)

Other ships were appearing one by one on the water below us. The navigator was trying to count them. I saw the long, bristling shape of a cruiser to the right. And there were other ships.

"Anti-aircraft fire to the right!" somebody shouted. And we heard the fragments thwack against the bottom of the fuselage.

"It looks as if our right aileron's hit," somebody said.

Then the anti-aircraft halted, and another Zero appeared ahead of us, flying close in. He turned toward us, and came sweeping in with his tracers reaching out toward our fuselage. For long seconds he seemed to be heading directly toward our nose, and the bow gunner fired long bursts. The nose filled with smoke.

"You're leading him too much," said Capt. Payne, calmly.

Then the Zero was gone astern.

"Anybody hit?" asked the captain. Nobody answered. The Zeros were poor gunners, and cautious. They did not come back again.

By this time we were well past the ships which had appeared below us off the southern tip of Bougainville.

"How many ships were there?" asked the pilot.

"There were twenty-seven," said the navigator.

He had been the only one not occupied with shooting at Zeros; he had taken time to look. The rest had been too busy.

"Was that a boat or shore installation shooting anti-aircraft?" asked the pilot.

"Boat," said the bombardier, laconically.

We conducted the rest of our reconnaissance peacefully and ran into no more enemy aircraft or ships. The overcast weather was on our side.

It was hours later that we landed at an American base which is removed from the Solomon Islands zone and a goodly step toward more peaceful regions.

I had kicked myself, when the Zeros attacked us today, for exposing myself to the danger. Now I was glad I had done it. To have left Guadalcanal on a B-17, by way of Bougainville, seemed highly appropriate, when, as the marines would say, you considered how *rugged* our life had been on that f— — — — — island.

POSTSCRIPT

by the Editors of International News Service

When Dick Tregaskis left that Unmentionable Island—anyone who has ever known a United States marine will recognize the prohibited expletive instantly—the battle for Guadalcanal had not ended.

But the tide already had turned. The first reinforcements had come and others were on the way. The friendly roar of Grumman Wildcats and PBY's was no longer a rare occasion for wild rejoicing. In the making were at least two major naval battles. In the second one, the Japanese in the three days between November 13 and 16, 1942, lost at least thirty warships and transports sunk or damaged.

The moment that battle began Tregaskis closed up his portable at Pearl Harbor and finished translating into trenchant English his "satchelful of notes." He returned at once by plane to the Southwestern Pacific to rejoin the heroes whose story he has told here.

His weeks, the weeks he describes from July 26th to September 26th, were the worst weeks, the almost hopeless weeks. They were—the comparison is inescapable—the Gethsemane of Guadalcanal. But from then on the picture changed. American ships streamed toward the island and American Army troops landed. American fighting and bombing planes made of Henderson Airport an offensive base, destined to play a major role in pushing the Japs right back where they came from.

For a period, at least, the waters around Guadalcanal were cleared of Japanese fighting ships. In the words of Admiral Chester W. Nimitz, the enemy soon would be left "without beans and bullets" and those sorely tried marines who fought so valiantly in the difficult early days were able, with numerical superiority and control of the air, to proceed with the grim but obviously pleasant business of mopping up the enemy one by one.

NEW YORK, AFTER SEPTEMBER 26

This is what happened to Tregaskis after the last entry in his *Diary,* dated September 26th.

"I had no word from anybody while I was on Guadalcanal," he wrote, in a letter home, "even though I had sent out two radio messages from there, saying that I was planning to leave and asking that relief be sent. But no answer came. I had been on Guadalcanal for seven weeks by that time; so I took the chance to get away."

As a matter of fact, relief and money were on their way to Tregaskis, but he didn't know it. Communications in the Pacific war area, to use Dick's own words, are frequently by turtleback express.

"I went to a place," he wrote, "which I may identify only by the name of Amadvu." (This was Dick's trip on the Fortress, B-17.) "I waited for a couple of weeks at Amadvu. No mail, no radios came, and soon my funds were approaching rock bottom and I saw myself becoming a beachcomber and being devoured by cannibals."

Tregaskis is the last man you would want to see in such circumstances. He is six feet, seven inches tall and big in proportion—a lot of man. And a man like that requires a lot of food. When he drew the Pacific assignment, he was kidded—"You'll be some target for the Japs, Dick"—"They'll capture you for an observation post if they don't pot you first"—and so on. Tregaskis took it good-naturedly, though he is sensitive about his size. The day before he left he went to the cashier. "I want a small part of my salary sent to me every week." But why, the cashier wanted to know. It was his experience with war correspondents that they never spend their own. They bank their salaries and live strictly off expense money. "Well," said Dick, "I'm kind of big and I eat more than some people. I would honestly hate to charge the office for two steaks instead of one and, between you and me, I always eat two steaks." That was Tregaskis for you—a lot of man any way you take him.

He decided, on Amadvu, to return to Pearl Harbor. "It then took me four days," he wrote, "to get my orders from the painstaking Mister Ghormley and three more days to make the arrangements with the Army, which did the actual work of hauling me in a plane. By that time I was flat. I had four bucks in cash and a money order for ten bucks which I had borrowed and which nobody would cash without written authorization from Mr. Stimson or Mr. Knox. I arrived in Honolulu with exactly fifty cents."

Poor Dick! He must have felt, as his letter said, like the orphan of INS. But Haller, our Honolulu bureau man, promptly fixed that, and in his next letter Dick was cheerier. He had filled in (with steaks, no doubt) at the Pacific Club, he said, and—he was finishing a book.

"I began it on the Liberator that brought me here. Just set up an office in part of the bomber and typed. The only distraction was a low circle which the pilot described over a certain untouched Polynesian Island. He wanted to see the dusky maidens swimming in the surf and, after looking at nothing but marines, Japs and betel-chewing Melanesian men, I confess I did, too. Shall I send the book?"

We cabled him to send the book. We did not ask about the maidens.

That was November first. The manuscript arrived in New York, by clipper and airmail on November 10th and three days later was accepted by Random House. A few days after that it was chosen by the Book-of-the-Month Club. Even a Tregaskis who had seen action couldn't ask for more action than that!

Of course we wanted Dick to know that his luck still held. It isn't every day that a youngster—Tregaskis is twenty-six—on the greatest and toughest assignment of his life gets the news in the middle of it that his first book has been taken by the Book-of-the-Month Club. We radioed him at once.

Here is the answer from our Honolulu bureau: "Tregaskis away indefinitely. Forwarding him copy of your radiogram fastest but delivery indefinite. Haller."

We knew what that meant. Uncle Sam doesn't tell you, even though you are a big press association, when he taps one of your boys for the great adventure.

Tregaskis had written when he sent the book, "Now that I have had a chance to stretch my legs and feed my gullet, I am set to go joy-riding again." He has gone.

We don't know, as this is written, exactly where Tregaskis is. But we have a pretty good idea—somewhere around that Unmentionable Island again. The American fleet met the Japanese armada and sank or damaged thirty of their warships. We know, because the Navy says so, that the waters are clear where once the Japs sent in their subs and transports. We know our fliers rule the skies. We know the marines are still holding and pushing farther on Guadalcanal. And we suspect that somewhere in the thick of it Dick Tregaskis is telling another story of American valor as he told this one.

A cable or a radio will come soon, please God, and you bet we will answer back, "Okay, Dick Tregaskis, good luck to you!"

NOVEMBER 21

It came.

AFTERWORD

by Moana Tregaskis

The first edition of *Guadalcanal Diary* was published early in 1943. In the nearly sixty years since that original Random House edition, this classic account of Americans in the Pacific during World War II has been translated throughout the world.

There are legions of books about war and few that merit the term "history." This happens because most are written either by historians who did not share the experience, or by those who shared and were not historians. In either case, something is missing. Richard Tregaskis was exceptional. He was a historian who consistently experienced the wars he documented. This is why his writings have the taste and touch of battle combined with the skill of the literary writer.

A scrupulous taker of notes, meticulous researcher, and diligent questioner, Tregaskis shared in the ordeals of the men he chronicled. While participating, he was uncommonly brave, and two generations of American fighting men accepted him as a member of their team. They talked about him, angular and tall, a bit over six foot six, softspoken and very thin, always writing, watching, questioning, and taking photographs at the height of battle.

In addition to these traits crucial to the military historian, Richard Tregaskis brought another quality to the battle lines—it distinguishes the great in both soldiers and civilians—he cared deeply about the affairs of the little man. Readers of *Guadalcanal Diary* and subsequent chronicles quickly realize that the author knows well who the critical personalities are in any war.

Guadalcanal today may have become a minor speck in the world's broad sweep; to men who battled there, it is a shrine. Why was this battle important? Its military significance is enormous because its tactics held many firsts: *Guadalcanal Diary* chronicled the world's first use of combined air, land, and sea operations, a mission that now is taken for granted. Today, historians are still writing about the battle for Guadalcanal; it will be written about forever.

Describing the battle that stood as the turning point of the war in the Pacific, *Guadalcanal Diary* occupies a large place in the annals of war reportage. Americans in moments of courage and fear, discipline and valor, and in vivid times of pain, were recounted by the historian-writer who was with them.

Guadalcanal Diary was Richard Tregaskis' first book. In a newspaper reporting career that began in prep school and continued throughout his university years as a history and literature student, Dick paid his dues, covered the Boston police beat, and mastered his craft. When America entered World War II after the attack on Pearl Harbor in Hawaii on December 7, 1941, Dick knew he had to participate, to write about Americans in war. Accredited as a war correspondent for INS, International News Service, he was sent to the Pacific—no one knew an insulin kit lay deep in a pocket, or that tins of sardines crammed his backpack. If anyone asked about his copy of a manual authored by the founder of Boston's famed Joslin Diabetes clinic, Dick could say it was autographed by a special friend.

After Guadalcanal, Dick returned to Pearl Harbor to write. Daytime, the Navy locked him up to work with his notebooks and locked up the notebooks at night. The bloody experience of Guadalcanal changed Tregaskis. He was still stunned to be alive, and glad for it. On a smudge of Pacific jungle, he had been with men when their best traits took precedence in the most harrowing conditions. Now the desire to share and to write well about Americans in war grew more intense. The battle on that feverish island changed all those who survived it, yet these men couldn't bring themselves to talk about their experiences. Richard Tregaskis, who had been with them, told their stories. He saw, felt, and brought readers into the pangs of homesickness, the tales of scrounging, or the moments of humor.

Leaving the Pacific, Dick chose the European theatre of war. The size fourteen boots Marines called his PTs, for "Patrol Tregaskis," went along. Eventually, luck deserted him. In the battle for Sicily, on a hill called Mount Corno near Cassino, Dick was hit by German shrapnel. A piece went through his helmet, a part of his brain, and out the other side of the helmet, leaving a gaping jagged hole. Somehow, he staggered to the lines of the American 38th Evacuation Hospital, dragging along the helmet. There, managing to convey the word "diabetic" to a doctor, Major William Pitts of Charlotte, N.C., performed tedious, massive surgery. Within a few months, Dick had learned again to speak, again to use his right hand, and was back to duty; Random House published *Invasion Diary* in 1944, followed by the novel *Stronger Than Fear*, centered on an American Army sergeant in Germany.

Somehow, Dick hung on to that helmet. Today, under the care of the Marine Corps Historical Foundation, it is frequently loaned for museum exhibitions.

The goal to write well about Americans enduring life-threatening struggles never ceased. Watching, questioning, and sharing in the vicissitudes of Guadalcanal would lead Dick Tregaskis to devote his life and career to documenting Americans in the course of formidable events. From World War II into the 1970s, articles and books sprouted from his pen. In Korea, Dick joined Americans to document the world's first deployment of helicopter warfare. Armed with an ever-present ledger-notebook, in 1960 he began research on the story of America's first spaceship. Spending long weeks at Edwards Air Force Base, Tregaskis came to know and appreciate the fabled men who flew the big black rocket called the X-15. While this was not war, Dick knew he was documenting Americans with "the right stuff"; their successes and foibles soared through the words of *X-15 Diary*.

With the grievous months on Guadalcanal etched on his soul, Dick reflected on the passage of time. As "after the war" had become a lasting phrase, he was interested in the varied career circuits and stratagems of survivors. Although their paths did not cross in the Solomons, a man he knew in college days was at sea in Guadalcanal waters at the same time Dick was on the island. Now the man was President. While President Kennedy was in office, Dick wrote *John F. Kennedy and PT-109*. At Harvard, Dick Tregaskis and Jack Kennedy were swimmers, and close friend Torbert MacDonald captained the Harvard football team. At competitions for the varsity swim team backstrokers, Dick trounced Kennedy for a slot on the team; it was a special year—they beat Yale. Years later, the President loaned Dick his personal logs and notes to research the book. As press secretary Pierre Salinger took Dick into the Oval Office, the first thing the President said was, "Pierre, Dick beat me out for the Harvard Varsity Swim Team." Tregaskis replied, "Sir, if I'd known you would be President, I would have let you win." Amidst the laughter, one could note that neither President Kennedy nor Congressman MacDonald ever forgot that competition.

A generation after Guadalcanal and Korea, the regular soldier again welcomed Richard Tregaskis—in Vietnam, once again he chronicled Americans in war. Tours in-country spanned several years; newspapers and magazines documented the course of exigencies he shared with the ordinary fighting man. *Vietnam Diary* was a definitive eyewitness account of that combat.

During our life together—despite bouts with diabetes-related complications—Dick kept writing. We returned to Guadalcanal in 1967 where Dick would research an article on the twenty-fifth anniversary of the August 7, 1942, landing. Back on that hallowed soil, nightmares overtook sleep on the island of steaming jungle and mud-ravaged mountain ridges where Tregaskis was with Marine Raiders and parachutists at the battle on Edson's Bloody Ridge. We trekked on that lonely ridge. Razor-sharp kunai grass overgrew the depressions of American and Japanese foxholes, which still held old pieces of shrapnel and spent bullets. Children collected them to sell as souvenirs.

I went again to Guadalcanal in 1992—on August 7, monuments were dedicated to commemorate the fiftieth anniversary. Amidst those who survived the brutal fighting to secure the crucial airfield "at all cost," there is a bond of camaraderie reserved unto themselves. They came—native scouts and veterans—to attend the solemn ceremonies; five wore the Medal of Honor. On lined faces one could see that memories were vivid; perhaps some almost heard again "Red Mike" Edson's call: "Raiders, Raiders, Raiders rally 'round me." And still, children collected shrapnel and bullets.

Dick's last book is a tribute to a warrior. With his well-earned credentials writing of men at war, Tregaskis was precisely the correct author to research and describe the illustrious, war-stormed life of Hawaii's Kamehameha the Great. *Warrior King* remains in print.

In 1973, Marquis' "Who's Who in America" asked for a quote; Dick Tregaskis sent these words: "Reverence for truth, thank God, continues to be a great American ideal. Beauty makes life most pleasant, and humor cushions the worst moments. But courage remains the most valuable of all. My life in many wars has shown me that America has ample stores of all of these values in the face of the most severe mortal dangers."

Nearly sixty years after the battle for Guadalcanal, some now may ask: Why did Richard Tregaskis choose to apply his literary talents to chronicle Americans in war? The reason is plain—he was devoted to his country and to its vigor. In this new century of harried techno-society, that simple answer may strike a troubled chord. Think again. Richard Tregaskis understood sacrifice in the country's behalf; he willingly experienced and chronicled its trials.

ABOUT THE AUTHOR

RICHARD TREGASKIS was a writer and reporter. He received the Overseas Press Club's George Polk Award in 1964 for first-person reporting under hazardous circumstances. He died in 1973.

A NOTE ON THE TYPE

The principal text of this Modern Library edition
was set in a digitized version of Janson,
a typeface that dates from about 1690 and was cut by Nicholas Kis,
a Hungarian working in Amsterdam. The original matrices have
survived and are held by the Stempel foundry in Germany.
Hermann Zapf redesigned some of the weights and sizes for Stempel,
basing his revisions on the original design.